HIMOFF!

The memoirs of a TV Matinée Idle...

Richard Whiteley, famous for his groaning puns and dubious taste in jackets, takes us on an hilarious ramble through his career, from paper boy to schoolboy at Giggleswick (where he sat at the feet of teacher Russell Harty), to Cambridge, ITN, Yorkshire Television and of course *Countdown*. He tells how he escaped the Brighton Bomb, the terrors of interviewing Mrs Thatcher, and how he became the most famous ferret tamer in the world. Richard writes frankly about the many disasters which have befallen him on his way to becoming a true TV matinée 'idle'!

HIMOFF!

HIMOFF!

by

Richard Whiteley

Magna Large Print Books
Long Preston, North Yorkshire,
BD23 4ND, England.

British Library Cataloguing in Publication Data.

Whiteley, Richard
 Himoff!

 A catalogue record of this book is
 available from the British Library

 ISBN   0-7505-1799-9

First published in Great Britain in 2000 by Orion Media
An imprint of Orion Books Ltd.

β WHI
1268583

Published in Large Print 2001 by arrangement with
Orion Publishing Group

Magna Large Print is an imprint of Library Magna Books Ltd.

Printed and bound in Great Britain by
T.J. (International) Ltd., Cornwall, PL28 8RW

The definition of 'Himoff' is entirely the creation of Gill Evans and in no way reflects or represents the work of the *Oxford English Dictionary*.

To the memory of my sister Helen
who made us all laugh, and left the party
far too early.

Himoff /'imof/ *n.* and *v.* Chiefly *Northern English.* [<phr. *'imoff telly,* first attested c. 1968]

1. *n.* a. The act of recognising a (usu. minor) celebrity in a public place.
   b. A celebrity thus recognised, e.g. *'Ooh look, it's himoff telly!'*
2. *v. trans. To* recognise a (usu. minor) celebrity in a public place, esp. whilst announcing one's find in the manner described in sense 1a. above, e.g. *'I was himoffed three times last night in the Ivy'.*

CONTENTS

HOW TO USE THIS BOOK

'Of course, I've never done a day's work in my life' growled a gruff yet benign J.B. Priestley.

'Oh, but how can you say that?' retorted the obsequious interviewer. 'I mean you've written over fifty plays, goodness knows how many novels, all the articles, and broadcasts, you've never stopped working for nearly seventy years.'

'Not what I call work. See these hands. They've never done any what I would call proper work.'

And neither, I suppose, have mine, the hands of Richard Whiteley the obsequious interviewer.

I have been fortunate that in my middle years, I have become well known, in that many people in this country have heard of me, and indeed might well recognise the face - hence the high Himoff quotient I get down any street, in any shop, in any queue.

And I suppose in the celebrity C list, there's only one Richard Whiteley as the old song goes. In a pompous-sounding ad lib on *Countdown*, I once mused that if anyone wanted to write to me, just try marking the envelope 'Dick, England', and it might reach me. Incredibly, several did ... some even adding 'First Class Dick, England', or even 'Dick Head, England'. All very flattering.

But, yes, I am lucky to be Himoffed, and I enjoy all the benefits that such a status can bestow.

Fame hasn't happened overnight, and like J.B. Priestley, I have never done a proper day's work. Even as a census enumerator in 1961, I went home for my lunch and tea. However, over the years, I did actually think that what I was doing was actual work. I've certainly put in long hours. But work? Well, I've agonised, worried, tossed and turned, bent over keyboards, boned up on research notes, sat in front of editing machines, driven at high speed with precious film cans, endured periods of extreme nervousness and mental anguish, all in the call of the great god of telly ... but is that work? Hence the matinee idle bit ... famous for afternoon telly, but not for doing a proper day's work.

Actually, it was possible for me to do even less than Mr Priestley had to do to win his spurs of fame. After all, in television, they do it all for you. All you have to do is to turn up, hopefully sober, and remember your lines. And now autocue means you don't even have to do that. Just be able to read –

and electronics does the rest.

So I have been lucky. But I've also been around a long time. Met a lot of people. Been to a lot of events. Seen a lot happening. Been involved in all sorts of situations. So, if everybody has got a book in them, I suppose I ought to have. But what follows is definitely not an autobiography. I have plenty of material for that, from school exercise books and theatre programmes, to cuttings, letters and old electricity bills. That's for another time perhaps.

The following rambling chapters are mere musings on some significant and enjoyable periods of my life which I hope will interest you and hopefully amuse you. They are set out in a sort of chronology, but please feel free to dip in wherever you want. I think that after writing and re-reading it, my achievement is well summed up by one simple fact ... I now live just three miles from where I grew up ... so I haven't gone terribly far in life.

The mechanics of this memoir writing exercise are simple once you put your mind to it. For years, Jeni Cropper urged me to do it. But I held back, like Hermione Baddeley who, when interviewed by Russell Harty, said she never spoke until she was eleven.

'Why not?' asked Russell incredulously.

'Because I could never think of anything interesting to say.'

Same for me, I thought it wasn't interesting. You, the reader, must now decide.

Vivienne Clore my agent did a dastardly deal with publisher Trevor Dolby behind my back, which condemned me to the keyboard for six months.

Paul Jones, Managing Director of the San Geran Hotel in Mauritius, not only managed to procure a working portable electric typewriter to enable me to get cracking, but also laid on not only a superb environment and cuisine, but also a six day cyclone which kept me indoors at my desk.

Jo Eaves, who had looked after me so well at Yorkshire Television, took a break from the joys of motherhood and childcare to interpret the two fingered typescript. No mean achievement, as will be attested by Kathryn Apanowicz, who on peering over my shoulder on one of her many tea runs, wondered why I was typing the whole thing in Polish. Thanks too, to Kathryn for her cheerful support.

Iain Johnstone, my friend of over thirty years, cast his experienced eye over Jo's fair copies. Time was, I was envious of Iain, an ITN newscaster at only nine months older than I. I once returned from a joyous holiday in Marbella to find him reading the main Sunday lunchtime news. It ruined my holiday, but, Iain, now a distinguished author and film critic, quit while he was out front at the age of twenty-three, and I have benefitted from his friendship and wisdom ever since.

Thanks especially to my PR man, Mr Terry Wogan who has kept my name in front of the breakfasting British public for some time, and still refuses to believe that 'Twice Nightly' is not the case these days. 'Once yearly nearly' being far more appropriate. But, if this is what the Togmeister wants to believe, and isn't too envious, then it's fine by me.

And finally, my mother has taken a great interest in the book from the start, and has often asked if they will be able to buy it in London.

Well, yes, but only if there are any left over from the white elephant stall at Wetwang Gala.

Enjoy!

WHEN I WERE A LAD

I was introduced to the sharp edge of daily journalism at the age of seven and a half. The sharpest of edges, in fact, at the point of delivery. Yes, I was a paper boy. I didn't actually have my own round. That required a big two wheeled bicycle, an earlier start than I was prepared to contemplate, and the sheer strength to drag round a heavy canvas bag.

I was more of a paper boy's assistant, a sort of best boy in film circles. In paper round circles, I was probably the best boy they could get at the time.

My duties were to wait until the paper boy came to our house, a semi-detached in Ferncliffe Drive, Baildon – we had the *Daily Express* delivered you know – and trot alongside him as he would pull out, and neatly fold the papers for me to push through various letter boxes in the rest of Ferncliffe. And then on to the two neighbouring avenues, Greencliffe and Salisbury. After that I ran home for my breakfast and put my tie on ready for school.

The paper boy in question treated me with a great deal of tolerance – wheezy nights, runny noses, spotty rashes and general apathy meant that I was hardly the most regular of assistants. So, when the sun shone and the rain held off, and the day bode well, he did seem to be genuinely and forgivingly glad to see me when I duly reported for duty on such days.

I remember he wore a three-quarter length grey gabardine done up with a belt, National Health horn rimmed glasses, and a perpetual cigarette in his mouth. He struck out down Ferncliffe Drive at a rate of knots, with the big canvas bag over his shoulder.

Did I say paper boy? Well, he must have been fifty if he was a day. He was the cheeriest chap I ever met and his name was Stubbs. Just Stubbs, Reg, Bert, Jack, Sam ... they all could well have been his first name, but to me, he was just Stubbs. He liked being called Stubbs. Mind you, the times were like that. We had a gardener for years who came round to our house, and I just knew him by the name my father always called him, Thornton – just Thornton.

Now this must not suggest to you that the Whiteleys led an *Upstairs Downstairs* existence, complete with Hudson and Mrs Bridges. These in fact were frugal times, those years after the war, although we did have a cleaning lady called Mabel – and there, I know her Christian name and don't even know her surname.

Mabel used to travel up the three miles to Baildon from Shipley, carrying a very interesting bag, as cleaners always do. I never knew what was in this bag, but it always came with her on her arrival and was put down with relief on the kitchen table, as she prepared to blacklead the fire grate.

When the bus journey from Shipley became too much, Mrs Haythwaite from the village of Baildon replaced her, coming for three hours every Wednesday.

Milk was delivered daily, direct from the village dairy in clanking containers and ladled out on the doorstep into kitchen jugs. The cheerful milk lady was called Frances, and I remember giving her stale bread for her hens. By night she was a projectionist at the Bradford Civic Theatre.

Jack, from Albert Hanson's, the grocers in Bradford, would deliver the weekly food order. He would bring it in a wicker hamper and week after week he would unload the same goods onto the scrubbed wooden kitchen table – raisins, sultanas, suet, flour, sugar, all in stiff blue bags. Occasionally, as a treat, there would be biscuits, say half a dozen Kit Kats. My mother would write out the order in her neat writing on a lined Silvine red-jacketed exercise book. Jack would take it away and deliver accordingly. It was a perfect method. We had on-line home shopping fifty years ago! What's new?

Our house, which was one of several traditionally designed semis down Ferncliffe, did have the benefit of a long garden which backed onto a cornfield. I looked forward to harvest time every year which smelt of the newly mown corn and, to me like any small boy, the more exciting smell of the oily tractor. The farmer made stooks out of the cut corn and we hid in them like Indians in wigwams.

I went to the Methodist chapel every Sunday morning with my friend from next door, John Whitaker, who was a month older than me, and his father Arthur and mother Annie. Arthur, a deputy headmaster, always had on his best Sunday suit and shiny shoes as he strode down to the village, leading his flock to the chapel. I took delight in jangling my collection money as we walked down the village because Arthur would always say predictably, 'Very rich today, aren't we?' And he was very thoughtful, as he used to provide crayons and a pad for John and me to play with during the sermon. On the way back we always visited Jock's sweet shop where we bought Spangles and aniseed balls and penny lollies, until sweets came off the ration. After that joyous day, it was chocolate Flakes and Crunchie bars. Later on, I joined the Methodist Wesleyan Cub Pack and passed my knots and became a sixer.

From the age of four, I went to a sort of kindergarten where the fees were six pounds a term. It was situated on the other side of the village, on the upstairs floor of an outbuilding of a big house and attracted about twenty children. I particularly remember the toilet facilities which amounted to an Elsan chemical system for the use of one and all. I made local headlines in class when, in order to amuse and placate a weeping six year old called Sheila Briggs, I snatched a favourite doll from Felicity Norris and threw it down the Elsan. It came up not exactly smelling of roses, and neither did I, because, while Sheila was amused, Felicity wasn't. I learnt at an early age that you can't be popular with all the girls all the time. We listened to *Music and Movement* on the school wireless with Marjorie Eeele, and *Singing Together* with William Appleby. We went on nature walks and played French cricket. It was a most pleasant few years.

I loved the *Daily Express,* but could never understand how the news got there. We also had *Rainbow, Playbox* and *Children's Newspaper* delivered every week, later graduating to the *Eagle* and the *Beano.* My favourite day was Friday when the *Radio Times* arrived because I listened to the wireless endlessly, especially on Sundays. I loved *Chapel in the Valley* with Sandy McPherson, and I thought that young Marion was a real person rehearsing her hymns for our Baildon chapel service later that morning. I used to scan the sparse fittings of the Wesleyan chapel looking for the microphones. I never missed a record on two-way *Family Favourites*, but the best of all was the *Billy Cotton Band Show* at 1.30. This, of course, was at the time when thousands of families sat down for their Sunday lunch and sang and laughed along to Billy and his gang. My hero was Alan Breeze and years later I had a great thrill when someone pointed out to me the pub in a village in Suffolk that he eventually owned.

I first had the little single bedroom at the front, which you can picture if you are familiar with the regular configuration of a standard semi. When my new born sister Helen came back from the Duke of York's hospital in Bradford, as I had done five years earlier, I graduated to the double bedroom at the front. Sometimes, when I was poorly, which was often, my mother lit a fire. I had a black and white Bakelite radio which I wish I still had. *Workers' Playtime* was my favourite programme but I never missed *Children's Hour* with *Jennings at School* and *Wandering with Nomad*. I also liked George Elrick on *Housewives' Choice* and all the comedy shows at the time, especially *Ray's a Laugh* and *Educating*

Archie. This programme had a special magic with its procession of soon to be famous tutors like Max Bygraves, Tony Hancock and, of course, Julie Andrews. Like Archie, I was in love with Julie who seemed to be a girl of my own age.

My father went off to work at the mill every day. First in a Standard 10, and then from 1950 in a black Daimler which had been restored by Thornton Engineering of Bradford, dating as it did, from 1939. It had the ultimate luxury of a car radio and I remember big running boards. The Daimler was bought purely for practical reasons. My father had had a Standard Vanguard on order for at least two years and, while waiting for it to arrive, the Daimler became available.

My father came back from work every day at exactly twenty to six and I used to go to the top of the road to wait for him to come. He never went to the pub for early doors, like lots of people's fathers. In fact I never saw him go into a pub at all. There was never any substantial amount of drink in the house, although my parents occasionally had what they called Cocktail Parties for at least half a dozen people, where I heard the phrase 'Gin and It' being casually tossed around.

Every year though, there was a dance which lasted over three nights in nearby

Saltaire. It was called the Conversazione ... the Conversaz for short. This was the high point of the social scene in this part of West Yorkshire. My parents never managed all three nights, but generally did the two.

I had a Granny and Grandfather, my father's parents, who lived in Ilkley. We would go there for tea on Sundays and also visit Auntie May, my father's auntie who lived nearby, and whose phone number for years was Ilkley 12.

It was a big day for me when the van from Jefferson's, the village electrician, arrived, but to my disappointment he delivered a beautiful Ecko radiogram. Disappointment because I really wanted a television, but I reconciled myself to the radiogram because we had a few records and I was the proud possessor of what I regarded as a winning double sided disc – 'The Teddy Bears' Picnic', coupled with 'Rudolph the Red Nosed Reindeer', sung by Bing Crosby.

My parents' records dated back to their courting days and tended to be by people called Ambrose, and Flotsam and Jetsam.

Generally I was happy and content, wanting just two things. One was a TV, of course, and the next rather grander.

On my newspaper round I loved to deliver to a detached house in Greencliffe Avenue, the next door street. This had a lily pond in the front garden which I took great delight in jumping over, having made my delivery. This was now a doctor's house but they said that Ronnie Burnet, Captain of the Yorkshire Seconds, and Captain of Baildon in the Bradford cricket league, grew up there. Now I loved Yorkshire cricket and I had a bat signed personally by Len Hutton. To live in that house would indeed be a dream come true.

To celebrate the arrival of the radiogram however, my father brought home two new records, 'September Song' and 'Bali Hai' from *South Pacific. My* mother used to say one tune she couldn't bear was 'Donkey Serenade' and it was a source of great amusement whenever this was played on the *Light Programme.* The radiogram was regarded as a piece of furniture, rather than the box of tricks it was meant to be, and I was told off on a regular basis if I left the lid up.

Much as I appreciated the thrill of the autochange, and a far clearer reception of Radio Luxembourg, I desperately wanted a television set. I used to go round to Anthony Naylor's after school and watch his. His father was a surgeon in Bradford and therefore rather richer than us; he drove an Austin Princess, and then a Bentley. They had a TV with a purple screen and a magnifying glass. We watched *Billy Bunter* on Tuesdays, which was a great treat, a wonderful performance by Gerald Campion as Bunter. On Saturdays, my parents were asked round to watch *Café Continental* – the epitome of television variety.

In November 1952, Jefferson's van again appeared outside the house and this time my dream had come true. Mr Jefferson himself delivered a Ferguson television in a walnut cabinet with doors. It had a purple screen, but being fourteen inches, the very latest, we didn't need a magnifying glass. I watched a programme that first evening about the American Presidential election which was imminent, and straightway decided one thing. No, I was not going to be President of the United States... I was going to be a television cameraman.

The next year Britain, that is a New Zealander and a Sherpa, conquered Everest and we watched the Coronation on our own television and asked the neighbours in. My father kept saying he thought the Bishop of Bath and Wells was wonderful. My mother thought the Queen Mother was wonderful. My sister, aged five, kept waving back at Queen Salote, and I, aged nine and a half spent the whole nine-hour broadcast working out camera positions and trying to spot cameras and television equipment in shot.

That same year, 1953, England won the Ashes, and in early September I went to the

Scarborough Cricket Festival to see T. N. Pearce's Eleven, which was almost the English team with even more Yorkshire players squeezed in, play the Australians. As kids scrambled round the pavilion that day for autographs, I stayed cool and stood back. The reason was that Eric Abbott, the London agent for Whiteley's Mill, had procured a sheet earlier in the season with the autographs of all the Australian team. I have it still, and it would have been a noteworthy collectors' item were it not for the fact for some reason I traced the illustrious names with carbon paper into my autograph book, thus getting an autograph book of not very good blue signatures and a totally vandalised original sheet.

However, as far as our family was concerned, the big news for 1953 was that my father bought that house in the next door road for just over four thousand pounds: 6 Greencliffe Avenue, the house with the lily pond. The house was called Greenhill and those Greenhill years were my real childhood. We weren't rich in any way. My father was the third generation of Whiteleys in Thomas Whiteley and Co, worsted manufacturers of Eccleshill in Bradford.

Thomas Whiteley himself had been the founder, a man of his times – a leading figure in the textile industry, the worldwide base of which was Bradford in the late nineteenth century. When the wool barons of Bradford did their buying, it was in the Wool Exchange in Market Street and the repercussions of the deals done there were felt Empire-wide, in South Africa, in Australia and in New Zealand.

The big Bradford banks grew in their imposing buildings and the money flowed in and out as the city prospered. The woolmen themselves had big houses in Manningham and Heaton, and when they retired they went to live in Morecambe or Grange over Sands. They were non-conformist folk and ran Bradford in a paternalistic, charitable and, indeed, pioneering way, far better chronicled by J.B. Priestley than by me.

The Whiteleys of Eccleshill were well known, but no more or no less than the hundreds of family businesses which made up the various processes involved in the massive textile trade. Whiteley's came at the end of the process, weaving the yarn into fine quality cloth. This was exclusive in its way and sold well, but because of its very exclusivity, in demand for high fashion, high quality garments, it meant only short runs could be manufactured. This, of course, was expensive in the design and production process, and while when times were good, the business prospered, in leaner times, longer production runs were the only economic answer and these were not easily found.

The turn of the new century were good years for Thomas Whiteley. He had a brother Frank who moved out to wave the flag in South Africa. Frank became Lord Mayor of Mafeking at a rather inauspicious time for the city ... it was laid siege to in the Boer War for six and a half months from October 1899. Sir Frank was Lord Mayor when Mafeking was relieved, and returned to Bradford in triumph, to be fêted by a nine course civic dinner in the Midland Hotel in Bradford. I still have the menu. Thomas himself had six children, four boys and two girls Agnes and May. The sons – Percy, Frank, Lewis and Sam – went straight into the mill. The daughters of course did not, but Thomas named the new steam engine after them in 1900 – Agnes May. Only one of the sons, Sam, my grandfather (full name Samuel Johnson Whiteley, hence my love affair with dictionaries!), had any sons and only one at that – my father, Kenneth.

My father lived and grew up in quiet comfort in Shipley. The family had a full time maid and enjoyed supporting the Congregational chapel and its cricket club. My father himself, like many of his age, was sent away to prep school at eight, to Scarborough College and then to Giggleswick at thirteen. His letters home were rather fuller, and frankly, nicer than mine. 'Dearest Mother and Father', they always opened and were always signed 'your loving son, K', compared to mine, 'Dear M and D, will you *please* send the tinned mandarin oranges I asked you for two letters ago.'

My father wasn't particularly a star at school, in fact, on Giggleswick's greatest star gazing day, the total eclipse of 1929, which attracted the Astronomer Royal and Ramsay MacDonald, he managed to be ill in the school sanatorium and missed all the excitement.

One of his pastimes, I gathered from his letters, was to stand outside the school gates on the A65 main road to the Lake District and spot cars with Bradford registration numbers. Well, what else was a boy to do on a Sunday afternoon? There was no soccer to watch on television!

After Giggleswick, Father did a course in textile design at the Bradford Technical College and after brief sojourns in other local textile organisations (work experience), ended up very junior indeed in the family business. Thomas Whiteley and Co of Eccleshill. The war, of course, intervened and he was called up, served with the Durham Light Infantry, was badly wounded in the legs in the North African desert, and after being shipped two thousand miles to hospital in South Africa and then back again to Wakefield, he was finally invalided out in 1942. He had met my mother at Heaton Tennis Club which was the place in Bradford to see and be seen in those days – she being a draper's daughter from Farsley which is between Bradford and Leeds. She had had a sad childhood, both her parents had died while she was under ten, and she was brought up by two maiden aunts in Bradford, Auntie Bessie and Auntie Nanny. And so it was in December 1943 that I came along.

As a boy I used to enjoy visiting the mill, overawed by the noise and energy of the huge steam engine pounding away, driving all the machinery in the mill by a network of leather straps, wound round steely silver shafts. The clanking of the looms in the weaving shed where long serving and loyal weavers toiled in noisy conditions, making the cloth. The warehouse with the huge yarn baskets called skips. The huge plate glass window, beside which cloth was hung up and perched to find any faults visible to the naked eye. In particular, I liked the office, and loved playing with the typewriters and the carbon paper. I can remember the weavers talking to 'Mr Kenneth' about me and saying, 'Isn't he shy?', and I suppose I was and still am. I had no desire to go into the businesses, or, as contemporaries of mine who were born into family businesses would say 'to go in wi mi Dad'.

To be fair, my father never wanted me to follow him into the firm. I think he sensed that the good days were over and there is, of course, the old maxim, 'clogs to clogs in three generations'. The other two generations had had it fairly good and there wasn't really much left. The writing was on the wall for family businesses in the late Fifties and early Sixties. I remember once my father coming home and sitting rather white faced at the kitchen table. When asked why, he said he had just seen a Mr X (I can't remember the name), and Mr X had been the head of a prominent family business in a part of Bradford. My father had just seen him cutting someone's hedge in the village, doing jobbing gardening. Obviously times were bad for him, and it really shook my father that he was reduced to this. The textile trade was being assailed by competition from overseas, and survival meant investment in the latest equipment, big bulk orders which only the likes of Marks and Spencers could provide, and indeed, a strong and gifted management. None of these essential props were available to my father, who was really running a business single handed. He was designer, sales manager, personnel manager, office manager, creative consultant, financial director, all rolled into one. He was amazingly knowledgeable about Bradford and its history, and in particular the history of the textile trade and the people involved, and while there was little he could or wanted to do to interest me in joining the firm, it was directly due to him that I had my first encounter with the BBC.

It was while on the school run on a Saturday morning, coming back at lunchtime from Bingley across the moor to Baildon, that I saw it. It was there standing proud and magnificent and impressive. To most people who were passing, it was just a large van with big wheels painted a dull shade of bottle green with a crest on the side. To me it was a very temple, dedicated to the new culture which I was determined to follow.

It was a BBC television outside broadcast van.

I was so excited I could hardly control myself as I demanded the car was brought to a halt. We got out and walked round the van. There was no one there. Eventually, the door of the van opened and a man emerged. This was the first person I had ever met in my life who worked for the BBC. To me he was royalty.

My father had to do all the talking. 'My son's very keen on television and anything to do with the BBC. It gets him very excited. Can he have a look?'

'Well if it interests him, by all means look,' said the bored BBC god, drawing on a cigarette, and purposely not issuing an invitation to enter the holy of holies.

He himself went inside and shut the door behind him. The van was what I now know to be the most mundane, yet the most essential of all parts of television paraphernalia, namely a links van receiving the signal from the outside broadcast, and beaming it from there to the transmitter, in this case Holme Moss. No cameras, no lights, no microphones and no stars. Just a van full of electric cables and boxes of tricks. However, it was from the BBC.

In the mid Sixties the end came for Thomas Whiteley and Co, and the business was sold mainly for the site value of the property which indeed was impressive. The first thing the new owners did was to demolish the chimney which they reckoned was too expensive to maintain. Had they left it up, it being the highest point for miles around, they would have made a fortune out of it now, hanging aerials off it. My father stayed on – albeit in a lowly grade, but he toughed it out until retirement, whereupon a morning job with a young and ambitious quantity surveyor in Bradford, kept him in enjoyable part-time employment until only weeks before he died at the age of eighty-two.

It was a struggle and a sacrifice for my parents to keep me at Giggleswick School. Even though I had a scholarship of one hundred and five pounds a year, there was still another two hundred and fifteen pounds plus extras to find. Helen was sent to Bradford Girls Grammar School but quickly took over from me as the star turn in the family. At Heather Bank, my prep school, I was bright and vied for top place in class with Barrie Burnet, the nephew of the charismatic Yorkshire cricket captain Ronnie Burnet. He was a glorious all rounder both in work and in sport, while I had to content myself with being travelling linesman in the winter with the soccer team, and cricket scorer in the summer (numbers game beckons!). These positions, offered more out of sympathy rather than my own deserving, at least got me away with the team in taxis to other schools for away matches, and I at least felt one of the lads. At the cricket match at Wood Hall, a school near Wetherby, Sir Len and Lady Hutton used to come and watch their sons, Richard and John, who were boys there. They sat together in a grey Ford Anglia, only emerging for parental duties at the end of the game. But at least at Heather Bank I did distinguish myself off the field. I co-wrote a play performed in front of the parents at Christmas, and swum a mile at Bingley baths – as my schoolfriend Peter Colman told the world on my *This is Your Life*, it was quite a day. I started with the others at two o'clock in the afternoon, and ploughed up and down, up and down, up and down. Meanwhile the other boys finished, got dressed, walked the mile up to the school, had afternoon lessons and early prep, walked a mile down the hill to the bus stop, only to meet me emerging from the town baths having done the required seventy-two lengths. If I had known the meaning of the word knackered that's what I would have said I was. It was positively and certainly my last sporting achievement.

I went on to edit the school magazine, I was head boy, and I cried on Wednesdays when we had blancmange for lunch. I caused the headmaster Mr Griffith to interrupt the two minutes silence for King George the Sixth, because he thought I was giggling with a boy called Roper. I founded a gang of three which had the best den in the grounds. The gang was called Sops, and we were flattered by the fact that some of the biggest boys in the school wanted to join in. I did brilliantly at Common Entrance and hence was put straight into the fourth form at Giggleswick, but with my birthday being in December, I missed the start of the school year, and joined in January. When term began that January of 1957, being a sickly child, I was indeed sickly, and missed the first week. I therefore had the disadvantage of not only not joining in September, but not even joining at the beginning of term like the other new boys.

So there we have it ... a childhood in a chapter. Psychologists will make of it what they will. But it was what it is. I enjoyed it, I loved my mother and father and sister. We were happy, but never spectacular. It was fairly ordinary, and indeed, for someone who went through his early life merrily telling everyone that I wanted to be a television cameraman when I grew up, I think I did rather well.

GOOD FOOD GIG

In February 1962, at the age of eighteen years and two months, I had a letter from the senior tutor at Christ's College, Cambridge saying that the college would be pleased to admit me to read English at the beginning of the Michaelmas term that year.

Now most undergraduates win their places at university by virtue of academic achievement or exceptional ability in a particular field. I have to say that I owe my place at Cambridge entirely to food, and school food at that. Burnt sausages and stodge. They were the staples of the Giggleswick diet, not to mention porridge every morning except Sundays, milk puddings and quarters of fried bread with a curly bit of bacon balanced on the top. These dishes weren't always to my taste. But I benefited from a tip remembered from my father who had been a pupil at Giggleswick in the late Twenties.

I had purloined an empty bandage tin at the san, small enough to conceal in the jacket pocket, but big enough to contain a whole portion of tapioca or suet pudding. I was a rather delicate child, and required little sustenance. So, discreetly, most lunch-times, the contents of my plate would end up spooned into the tin, to be emptied into the dustbins shortly after. We sat in the dining room in house tables, the house-master at the top serving out. Every week we moved two places round, the two at the far end acting as clearers for that week.

The first courses, to be fair, I could normally deal with. But it was the seconds which worried me. The classic dish was the steamed pudding, cooked in tubular moulds about eighteen inches long. These puddings came in various guises: plain, ginger, chocolate, with currants, or without currants – but still basically the same stodge. These would be brought steaming from the serving hatch by the clearers and placed like some triumphant haggis before the housemaster to serve. Mr Dean, my housemaster, was a product of the old school. He'd seen them starving in India. What would they give for a slice of pudding like this? He was, however, a humane and caring man, receptive to the whims and idiosyncrasies of the more pathetic boys in his charge.

When the stodge appeared, the message was duly passed down the table from boy to boy until it reached Mr Dean. 'Can Whiteley have a small please?' – that was polite and tactful enough. Inevitably, the message arrived ten boys later as a gruff commandment. 'Small for Whiteley.' I used to scan Mr Dean's face for signs of sympathy. Sometimes there was a raised eyebrow, as if to say 'tut, tut, what a wet'. Sometimes, if he was in jovial mood, a smile. Sometimes he was distracted, talking, but always the action was the same. A small, if say, a prefect happened to be in charge one day, was a slice as normal, but cut in half. Mr Dean was consistent. He'd cut a slice, but he'd make it twice as thick, and *then* cut it in half. Some small! Inevitably, it ended up in the tin.

Only when it was my week to sit next to Mr Dean at the head of the table, did my plan flounder as he would surely notice the tin. But salvation was at hand. Often, having served, he would thankfully be engaged by Mr Dutton, master in charge of rugby, on the topic of that afternoon's Colts Fifteen, and with him duly preoccupied, out came the tin. Otherwise, it was a case of chew and bear it.

It's that kind of public school discipline that makes a man of you. Actually, it didn't make much of a man of me in the physical sense. I was a regular visitor to the san, and almost had a regular appointment with the school doctor, Dr David Hyslop from Settle. He was a tall, physical, hearty, Humber driving, country doctor. He was more interested in rugby injuries or pot-holing accidents than in the whimsies of a pale, thin boy with a sore throat. But to me, he would deliver that which I most desired – an off games slip – this document was as precious to me as share options in a dot com company are to many people today.

As a result of nature, genes and a carefully controlled diet, for years I was the thinnest boy in the school. This fact was confirmed by the dreaded thrice termly ritual of weights and measures, and if you find it hard to believe as you contemplate my present jolly and cuddly proportions, I am afraid it's true.

After lunch on these occasions (getting weighed straight after a meal seems illogical to me – I certainly never do it now, always pre-breakfast, post-morning constitutional for optimum results) we would troop off to the gym, strip naked and stand on scales set up by the officer in charge of the Cadet Force, and PT instructor, Major Wardle. Every boy would step on the scales, then the Major would slide the measure along, and bark out the weights to a prefect with a clipboard, who would duly note it down. This information was later transferred to the termly reports, but unlike those reports, this information was hardly confidential.

'Williamson – eight stone, four pounds. Watson – nine stone, six pounds.' He would shout these out in his typical parade ground style for all to hear. 'Walker A.P. – ten stone, three pounds.' And so on to the general disinterest of boys getting their kit on again, and preparing for the afternoon activities. Until 'Whiteley J.R. – five stone, eleven pounds.' There seemed to me to be a great silence descending over the gymnasium as boys young and old, great and small, but ne'er so small as I, stopped in mid buttoning as if shell shocked by this astounding information. 'Whiteley J.R. –

five stone, eleven pounds!' Was it only I, or could everyone hear this proclamation echoing and re-echoing round the beamed rafters of the ancient gym? Did this moment last forever, frozen in time, or did it only last a couple of seconds? Was every boy in the school looking at me, Whiteley J.R., the smallest and lightest boy in the five hundred year history of Giggleswick? Me, Whiteley J.R., the centre of attention of all the boys, with not even a couple of tries at rugby in the junior house matches to my credit. How I hated being the centre of attention. Still do, of course. Note to readers – the proclamation is now a source of equal embarrassment, but this time the other way! 'Whiteley J.R. – fourteen stone, seven pounds' he would say now. Everybody would still stop and stare!

This torment went on term after term, until one blessed day, a new boy arrived who looked smaller than me. Certainly Major Wardle thought so, because he issued him with a carbine rifle, rather than those full, heavy, beastly, constantly needing cleaning rifles, that the rest of us in the CCF used to have to shoulder. At the first weigh-in of term, it was confirmed. 'Atkinson T.D. – five stone, eight pounds.' Two hundred pairs of eyes zoomed towards the poor lad. I felt for him, but not too much yet! I was the next lamb for the slaughter. I, desperate that lunchtime, had eaten a full portion of stodge and three Jaffa cakes from my tuckbox for good measure. I waited for my thrice termly humiliation. Then it was the turn of the W's. 'Whiteley.' At last. I stepped on the scales, hardly daring to look as the Major deftly slid the chrome balance along. Five twelve, five thirteen and no tilt. And then, joy of joys, he moved the stone indicator to six and slid the ounce one along and there it was. 'Whiteley J.R. – six stone, two pounds.' And do you know, while two hundred boys were getting dressed, not a single eye was cast in my direction. Over six stone at last. What an achievement. Who can ask for anything more. Mind you, I was fourteen and a half years of age, but it was to date, the happiest day of my life.

I did eat, of course. We had our tuckboxes containing crisps, Cadbury's, sometimes cakes, biscuits, of course, and best of all, tinned fruit. I always saved myself a tin of Prince's mandarin oranges and treated myself to one after chapel on Sunday evenings, savouring each segment as I spooned it out, managing to make it last the full *Sunday Half Hour*, as we joined in with the hymns on the Light Programme.

Then there was the tuckshop. This was situated in the chapel gatehouse, which was up a one in four gradient. This was most inconvenient in winter – battling against wind, rain, and gradient. It also used to shut at an inconvenient time for me. It could well be that the other boys could make the five o'clock closing time after the afternoon's sporting activities, but then, they did the High Rigg and Station cross country in forty-five minutes or thereabouts. For me, coming in after an hour and a half, the deadline was a hard one to beat. The redoubtable Mrs Creswell served the ice cream and her own brand of homemade biscuits. Her husband Charlie, also the groundsman and chapel caretaker, would do the sweets. 'Charlie, tell the boys to be quiet,' was her mantra, as she peered out under her headscarf.

In the summer, though, the tuckshop was transformed. Standing as it did in the gatehouse, looking on to the cricket pitch, the chapel, on its prominent knoll, and the tennis courts, it was a delightful place to consume a Walls wafer and watch the games. So at least I didn't starve. The school cook was called Frank, and I can remember seeing him as I looked out of my dorm window, waiting for the seven o'clock getting up bell, stirring the huge vat of porridge in the kitchens, three storeys below. I never had reason to go into the kitchens or indeed any desire to, but it was the state of those kitchens that I have to thank for my further education at Christ's College, Cambridge.

There's a huge gastronomic divide between burnt sausages and stodge, and *terrine de canarde* à *la Maitre,* stuffed pheasant Lady Margaret style, and *crème brûlée façon de* John Milton, just as there was an environmental divide between the back kitchen at Giggleswick overlooking the dustbins, and the senior combination room at Christ's overlooking the first court and the master's garden. But uniquely, in the histories of these institutions, both of which span over five hundred years, they were brought together, united by a common cause that February by one Whiteley J.R.

The spring term of 1960 had seen the arrival of Mr O.J.T. Rowe as headmaster. Thirty-seven years old, former head of classics at Charterhouse. There would be changes and assuredly there were, as the eager young head tried to turn round some of the post war austerity and traditional attitudes still reigning at the school. But money was needed for capital improvements, and an appeal was launched. The first project to be tackled was an update of the kitchens. At the same time, a hundred and fifty miles away, the fellows of Christ's College were also looking at their catering arrangements and were embarking on a radical refurbishment programme, including a pioneering self-service area.

The association between Christ's and

46

Giggleswick went back to the seventeen hundreds, when William Paley, an old boy of the school, became a distinguished fellow of the college (even now he is commemorated in one of just four portraits adorning the high table). Christ's had provided a member of the governing body for many years, and while just as selective in their recruitment as other colleges, they were generally friendly to Giggleswick. So when the then master heard of Giggleswick's kitchen expansion plans, Mr Rowe was invited down to inspect the work in progress and to garner ideas. I like to think that after the tour sherry was taken in the combination room before dinner at high table and then, after dinner, as the easterly wind whistled across the fens and swirled round the first court in the best C.P. Snow fashion, the dons would retire for port to the combination room, and the conversation would go something like this.

Master – 'Well, Headmaster, you've picked our brains. Now you know as much as we do about deep fat fryers. Let's pick yours. Do you have anyone for us? We're always looking for new talent here.'

Headmaster – 'As a matter of fact, Master, we do. Bright chap. O levels at fourteen, A levels at sixteen, distinction in English at S level last summer. Our first for some time. Just failed Oxford by a whisker, terribly disappointed ... Oxbridge material if ever I saw it. Very good school chap, you know, debating society, editor of school magazine, very respected, energetic, a real contributor. At the moment it looks as if he'll have to make do with King's College, London or perhaps even Bristol. I'd be very disappointed. Just can't think why Brasenose let him slip through the net.'

Master – 'Sounds a fine chap, Headmaster. Of course, it being February, we've been through our usual entry process here for Michaelmas. Mind you, we might be able to squeeze another one aboard in English. What do you think Senior Tutor?'

Senior Tutor – 'Oh, he sounds splendid. Always thought entrance exams per se were hopeless. Only prove who can remember what on the day. We like well-rounded characters at Christ's. Contributors. We do, of course, have seven of the University Fifteen rugby from here. Is he a games player? Well, perhaps not. Never mind. Look, just send him down for a chat. We'll have a look at him, and I'm sure if he's our kind of chap, well, who knows.'

Headmaster – 'He won't let you down. I assure you. Now, another thing, about the plate warmers...'

Whatever was said, I duly journeyed to Cambridge. For some reason I was spared the usual pre-entry ritual at Christ's College whereby the senior tutor chucked a rugby ball at you on entering his study. Legend has it that if you caught it neatly, you were in with a place. If you returned it to him in a deft movement, you got a bursary, and if you drop kicked it straight into his wastepaper basket, then you had a good chance of an open scholarship. Anyway, I remember Dr Pratt, the senior tutor, as being the first person I ever heard who on answering a knock on his study door would say 'come', instead of 'come in'. The subsequent interview was chatty enough, with little reference to English or, thankfully, rugby. He did ask me what I would do between school and university. 'Travel,' I replied, thinking it the right thing to say. 'Oh, where?' he naturally asked. I was then rather flustered. My only foreign trip to date having been a week in the South of France, with my parents. But I had seen the *Guns of Navarone* at a cinema in Cambridge the night before. 'Greece,' I stammered. He seemed impressed. Probably thought I was a bit of a classicist on the side. Anyway, the upshot was, I was in. And so by virtue of S level English, the *Guns of Navarone* and a shared interest in vegetable steamers, I had secured my place at Cambridge University.

The stodge at Gig had worked its wonders and no one in the next three years could ever understand why I always enthused about the food at Christ's.

'Are you coming to the Indian for a curry?'

'No, I'm going to college self-service dinner at Christ's.' They all thought I was mad. But I knew who I had to thank.

Many people in life get opportunities through the back door. Here was I, at the threshold of the biggest opportunity life could offer at the time – and I was stepping in through the kitchen door.

In the summer of 2000, thirty five years on, the *Independent* published a story about the top Cambridge Colleges, compiled over a twenty year period of League Tables. Christ's College came first in excellence.

The headline ran – 'College which produced John Milton, Charles Darwin and Richard Whiteley' ... the question is, how did those other two scrape in?

RUSSELL

A lot has been written and said about Russell Harty. His television career brought him into many people's lives and his untimely death saddened millions – friends that he never, ever, dared to think he had. Famous friends, in whose company he revelled, have also had their say, but I have an advantage: I knew Russell years before they did.

I can actually remember the very first time I set eyes on Russell Harty. It was January of 1958 – the beginning of the spring term at Giggleswick.

Now, I loved Giggleswick School, then as a whey faced thirteen year old, and love it now as a well fed Governor. It is an old, established place founded in 1512, built out of grey Yorkshire stone, overlooking a pretty and historic village. It is sometimes bleak, it is often breathtakingly beautiful.

At thirteen, entry into boarding school life wasn't easy, especially for a weakly asthmatic such as I. But it wasn't then, and certainly isn't now, a replica of Tom Brown's schooldays. Nevertheless, arriving mid-year, and in a class of boys generally two years older, there was some catching up to do. I had an excellent and sympathetic house-master, Mr Dean, but in those first terms found most masters indifferent to me except one who taught me French.

I was the youngest boy in the school – just thirteen – and he was the youngest master prior to Russell, about twenty-four I would guess. He made learning French as cheerful as he could, he put me in a non-speaking part in a one act play, and he hated games as much as I did. Therefore I was greeted with bad news when I returned to school that cold Monday evening to begin my second year. The French master had suddenly left in the Christmas holidays. 'Who would take his place?' I thought, rather mournfully.

We didn't have long to wait. After three or four days or so of French lessons given in emergency session by the fearsome and respected second master, a classicist of the old school called Mr Dutton, we heard of the arrival of a replacement. He was a master who joined the prep school – Catteral Hall. It was usual for boys to start there at seven or eight, and at thirteen transfer to the senior school. In the senior school, of course, you didn't give two hoots about the sprogs in Catteral, or their teachers, so a prep schoolmaster coming up to teach us was something of a novelty.

The new master was one Mr Harty, and he had a study in Catteral next door to another new master, Mr Brookes who had arrived when new staff were meant to come, at the beginning of the school year in September. So we duly trooped in to our first French lesson with this Mr Harty. Funny name, most of us thought, blessed as we were with solid northern surnames like Brooke, Ackroyd, Whitehead, Hartley, Waddington and Heseltine. Not to mention Whiteley. And then someone found out his

Christian name was Russell, so it was not long before the new French master was known throughout the school as 'Sprout'.

Later he became 'Fredarty' as his first name, Frederic, was detected. He was, at first acquaintance, a clone of the departed French master. Twenty-four. Dark hair. Slim. Hated sport. Keen on drama. Laughed a lot. Seemed to be more on our side than the other teaching staff. As that spring term wore on, we began to realise what a very special teacher had come to Giggleswick.

So what are my earliest memories of Russell? He wore a blue shirt with a white collar with his suit for Sunday morning chapel, thus pre-dating David Steel by a good twenty years. He had one of the earliest so-called portable television sets – the Murphy, with a fourteen inch screen and a purple carrying handle. His study at Catteral Hall always seemed to me to be wonderfully cosy. Lamplit, with a plate of cakes supplied daily by the housekeeper, a fire going in the grate, and a beguiling selection of books, photos, pictures and pottery figures on the shelves. It was always a pleasant experience to wander down there on a dark evening to hand in your prep. Other masters had functional and rather austere rooms – Russell's was distinctly homely. He even had a car – a black Morris

Minor which he bought from his Oxford friend Alan Shallcross. Alan, who was now a BBC trainee in Manchester, was a frequent visitor, often coming to school to give talks about the BBC. This was a great thrill for me. It was the closest I had come to a real live BBC person since the disinterested outside broadcast man on Baildon Moor, and with my broadcasting career already planned in my mind, he was an icon as far as I was concerned.

Another of Russell's friends used to visit the school – you would see him skulking around the master's porch waiting for Russell to finish teaching. He wore a sandy coloured duffle coat, a college scarf and what looked like the National Health glasses of the time.

'Who's that chap?' we all used to ask, with only mild interest, although visitors were rare in those days.

'Some friend of Sprout's from Oxford,' others volunteered. 'A sort of Don.'

It was, in fact, Alan Bennett – the third member of an exclusive gang of three at Exeter College – Alan S, Alan B and Russell H.

We knew that Russell came from Blackburn. We Yorkshire boys were in fact, frankly, rather disturbed by his Lancashire burr, especially the 'rr' sound. Imagine, our dads paying four hundred quid a year for us to be taught by someone with a Lancashire accent. He used to say 'Shall you' instead of 'Will you', a lorry became a 'lurry', and even then the phrase 'You are – are you not' was in common usage. But he had style, and what today we would certainly call charisma. Those boys who came from Blackburn, said his dad had a fruit and vegetable stall in the market. We, not that we were snobs (Giggleswick was not that kind of school) found it difficult to believe. One day, though, a big Jaguar Mark Ten appeared outside the main hostel building, and Jaguar Mk 10s were big! 'Whose parents have one of those?' we all asked with great excitement. Mine had a Volkswagen Beetle, of which, quite honestly, I was rather ashamed. Others boasted Austin Westminsters and Rovers and the car I would have liked most at the time, the Ford Zodiac Convertible. We craned out of our study windows, and Russell's mum and dad got out and greeted him. I think, on reflection, he was hugely embarrassed by their appearance, and the trappings of wealth occasioned by the joys of the market economy in Blackburn were never mentioned.

Above all, Russell was worldly. He was the breath of fresh air so powerfully portrayed in the American film *Dead Poets' Society*. I saw the film in Brighton once without knowing what it was about. As it developed

I had this weird sense of déjà vu. A young and energetic English master arrives at a small private school in the country. The other staff are generally grey haired time-servers. The master builds a coterie around him, of pupils inspired by his exciting teaching and his modern approach. They would do anything for him as his inspiration triggers their imagination and their enthusiasm. As the film wore on I recognised a plot which seemed to echo the arrival of Russell at Giggleswick – without deaths or shootings, for those of you who know the film.

His teaching was, quite frankly, inspirational. He made *Sir Gawain and the Green Knight* as exciting as *Robin Hood*, with Richard Greene at the time dominating teatime viewing on Sundays. Shakespeare he loved, often playing every part in class and bringing the four hundred year old text right up to date with his heroic performances. His didactic yet conversational manner of teaching in class endowed him with great authority and ensured total attention – a genuine willingness to listen, join in and learn. Boredom was an unknown seven letter word in the English room.

Years later, I used to listen to Russell's television interviews with my eyes closed. I heard exactly the same voice, detected the same manner and intonation that we had all witnessed as pupils twenty years earlier in Room 9 at Giggleswick. He brought with him a vision of the world outside school which few of us had experienced. His tutor at Exeter College had been Nevill Coghill. Show me an English student of the Fifties for whom Nevill Coghill was not only a hero, but a trusty friend. His translations of Chaucer's *Canterbury Tales* were the most well thumbed and useful Penguin in anyone's desk. And to think, our English teacher actually knew him!

Furthermore, Russell knew people in the BBC. He once came back after the holidays, and told us he had been to London and visited Television Centre at White City. This, as it happened, was my own personal Mecca. Just as Harold Wilson stood outside Number 10, my total ambition was to go and poke my head through the railings of Television Centre. Anyway, Russell told us in his offhand and seemingly bored way, for that was always his trademark style, that he had been in the bar there and had had a drink with Eric Sykes. We were transfixed, and indeed proud that our master had hobnobbed with the likes of Eric Sykes. Later in 1960, his friend Alan Bennett became a huge star in *Beyond the Fringe* and Alan's success rubbed off very definitely onto Russell, who basked in reflected glory.

Albeit Russell had replaced the French

master, he was primarily a teacher of English. He had, like many others, drifted accidentally into teaching. His generation at Oxford was the first to consider a career in journalism, theatre or the media, as reasonably respectable. Teaching, of course was, as was the Civil Service, traineeships in banking, industry and commerce, or even the Church. Russell had flirted with the media, mainly thanks to an appearance on *Criss Cross Quiz* – but even his limited success there did not secure him a job with Granada, which was after all his local TV company. He was interviewed, but not chosen. Their loss, it seems to me, especially for a company who rarely put a foot wrong in those days, was Giggleswick's gain. Thank you Sidney Bernstein!

So while Russell's Oxford friends went off to pursue glamorous ventures and to seek glittering prizes, he found himself doing a bit of primary school teaching, and ended up back home with mum and dad. So, it was a surprise to get a phone call that Christmas holiday from his old headmaster, Trevor Benson, formerly headmaster of Queen Elizabeth's Grammar School, Blackburn.

Mr Benson, Benny to his cowed underlings, was a tough, powerful voiced orator, with a chin like Desperate Dan's. The sight of him begowned and hooded, swaggering purposefully down the aisle at chapel to read the lesson or give the blessing, still fills me with awe. Benny had been a housemaster at Giggleswick, and had moved on to become head at Blackburn before returning as headmaster of Giggleswick.

With the sudden departure of the French master over Christmas, he was in a dilemma, until he remembered the young F.R. Harty, a former star pupil of his. Indeed, hadn't he met his dad recently who had said something about his lad not having a proper job yet? Only Russell could tell the tale of his interview with Mr Benson, for only he knows what went on. I have heard it, it involves much stroking of a stubbly chin, a voice like gravel, a distinct disinterest in his third class degree in English, more an interest in when he was available to start, and how good his French was, and half an hour of total trepidation from young Russell himself.

So it was that two or three days after the beginning of term, young Mr Harty found himself being engaged as a master at Catteral Hall, prep school for Giggleswick. As befits a newly qualified graduate with an English degree, he was allocated twenty periods a week of French, and ten of Maths. Things were like that in those days. It all seemed perfectly normal to us and remember it was long before the days of OFSTED.

Russell was always amused by the method

of his arrival at Giggleswick, but his story was never as good as that of Philip Curtis, who was the school chaplain.

When Mr Curtis arrived at Giggleswick station, he was obliged to walk the mile and a half to the school buildings. On entering the village he passed an institutional looking establishment, grey and forbidding. Indeed, to call it austere would be flattering.

Justifiably assuming it was Giggleswick School, he rang the bell by an imposing front door. It was opened by a uniformed lady.

'Is the headmaster in?' he enquired.

'Not yet,' was the simple reply.

He had, in fact, arrived at Castleberg Hospital, a former workhouse, then used as a mental hospital.

Russell's career at Giggleswick was just as spectacular as was his subsequent showbiz one. The year of his arrival coincided with the appointment of other young masters who were not against partying late into the night. I can well remember on several occasions being safely tucked up in bed in my cubicle, perhaps reading the obligatory book with the obligatory torch and eating the obligatory bag of Smith's crisps, and hearing the church clock chime 10.30, and then hearing the sound of stifled laughter and a Morris Minor being revved up outside the hostel block. The end of another riotous evening for Russell and the other masters, Warwick Brookes, Richard Taylor and certainly Hugh Stalker, the school organist.

It was a novel experience for us that our teachers actually had lives that didn't involve us. I was sometimes quite envious.

What did Russell think of me? He wouldn't have noticed me much at first, but when I eventually entered the sixth form at the dreadfully early age of fourteen to study English A level, then he had to take notice. There were, after all, only six of us in the class. I expect he thought I was quite bright, and looking back at his comments on my report, he was reasonably generous and keen to teach me. He sensed that I was impressed with his circle of friends, indeed, as I grew older I became more and more envious of him. A sentiment shared, incidentally, by Alan Bennett who has observed with great frankness how this envy lasted even until the day of Russell's funeral.

So Russell and I sort of jelled. At school he threw himself into drama, first appearing in a staff production of *The Winslow Boy*. He played Johnny Watherstone. The head, Mr Benson, played Sir Robert Morton. I venture to suggest that the scene when he reduces the boy Winslow to tears to the anguish and annoyance of his father, and then says 'The boy is clearly innocent,' has never been bettered.

The next year Russell embarked on his own production of *The Merchant of Venice*. This was, in fact, the first full length play put on by the pupils for many years and heralded the birth of the dramatic society which is now one of the most highly respected in any school in the country. I had been front of house assistant on *The Winslow Boy*, so was an obvious choice to be assistant producer on *Merchant*. I don't think he thought of auditioning me, and I can't blame him. I can't really think of a part in the *Merchant* for a thin, weakly, quickly spoken and spotty individual with glasses, but Russell did let me assist him. He would conduct rehearsals in a hands on way, consulting with me and listening to my observations. But mainly I was prop master, and he was thrilled when I produced three caskets which I had borrowed from the Bradford Civic Theatre.

There was one vivid memory of Russell. At the dress rehearsal he announced that everyone should wear jock straps under their tights or whatever. An earnest voice piped up from the back, 'Sir, does that include people with small parts?'

We also met on the sports field. As sports was compulsory for boys, so it was for the staff. Three times a week we played rugby: Tuesdays, Thursdays and Saturdays. Never really understanding the rules, I graduated from beginners to the legendary fourth set. This was reserved for older boys who were never going to make anything of their rugby, and Russell was the master in charge. I hated playing. He hated taking the game. I used to play left wing and the afternoon was spent gently shambling up and down the touchline, never running fast enough to get the ball if it went loose, and there was never a chance of anyone being so foolish as to pass me the ball.

And so after thirty tortuous minutes each half (Russell would conveniently play short time so we all got in the baths first), he would blow the final whistle. Always, with a defiant gesture, but one which I think was tinged with sympathy, he would toss the ball directly at me. I seldom caught it cleanly. 'Whiteley – take the ball back.' It was the only time I ever touched it. I proudly hold an unlikely record at Giggleswick, never likely to be broken: the most number of games played without ever touching the ball while it was in play. My rugger shorts, attests my mother, were as clean when they came home in December as they were when they went away in September.

My academic career, however, blossomed under Russell, but also under the head of English, John Dean. John Dean was also from Oxford. He was in his late thirties, a

Brasenose man, and of the old school. His father was a distinguished and ennobled Civil Servant. John himself did a stint in the Indian police before arriving at Oxford.

His teaching was immaculate and punctilious. A contrast to Russell who wallowed in flights of fancy. I suppose we would now say that Russell adlibbed a lot in lessons while John Dean stuck to the text. John Dean taught from his own notes taken at Oxford. He instilled in us a love of and respect for books, always leaping up to his own shelves to consult or display a particular volume. He had a love of poetry and spoke it well. He taught us grammar, pronunciation, and made us learn the important passages of Shakespeare and Milton, Donne and Pope. It was a winning combination and looking back, unlikely to be equalled in quality by even the great schools of the time.

It certainly worked for me. I got three A levels at sixteen, two years early, and a distinction at S level in English a year later. I owe it all to messrs Dean and Harty, and looked a cert for Oxford to read, naturally, English. Actually, I ended up at Cambridge, having failed to impress Oxford.

I think Russell enjoyed his days in Catteral, the prep school, the most. Certainly those days were the source of most of his more hilarious anecdotes. Apart from the teaching, there were the pastoral duties such as supervising writing letters home on Sunday afternoons, running excursions to the treacle mines of Rathmell (this involved previously burying tins of Tate & Lyle in a farmer's field) and doing what he could to make boarding conditions seem as homely as possible. Once, a boy ran away after lights out, but was quickly picked up. In the subsequent interrogation he told Russell of the daring escape route, which involved several windowsills, and drainpipes.

'Why,' said Russell sternly, 'did you not just walk down the main stairs?'

'Oh Sir, we're not allowed to use the main stairs after lights out.'

Russell loved this story.

With the arrival of a new headmaster in 1960, Russell moved up into the senior school. The new head introduced a system of house tutors to supplement house-masters. Everybody wanted Mr Harty to come to their house. In the event he went to Style house, presided over by Mr L.P. Dutton, who was the much respected second master who had served the school at that time for over thirty years. His home, Beck house, was by far the finest staff accommodation, and the Duttons had furnished it with great taste. Mr Dutton – Dutt, to those few who dared call him that, had Mr Chips like, been passed over for two headships at Giggleswick, but was fiercely loyal to the school. Again, Chips like, he and Joan had no children, but like Mr Chipping 'he had hundreds of children'. To this day, old boys of the school who were in Style house, still think themselves very privileged to have been under his tutelage.

He and Joan took Russell to their bosoms. He became the son they never had. He was always in their house, and Russell's young set of worldly friends became the Dutton's friends. He inherited much of their wisdom and love of the Dales and of Scotland, and they assimilated his wit, and his younger generation's approach to a changing world. It was a friendship which was to last over twenty years.

Russell soon became a housemaster himself and seemed set for a lifetime at Giggleswick. But really he was restless, and his friends Warwick Brookes and Hugh Stalker knew that Giggleswick School would be just too small a stage – although he returned to live in the village in the last, happiest five years of his life. I, meanwhile, left Giggleswick having wormed my way into Cambridge by virtue of my good S level English results. Now that I was a fully fledged Old Giggleswickian and an adult of eighteen years and three months, Russell arranged for me to meet him in London and took me to a performance of the then hottest ticket in town *Beyond the Fringe* at the Fortune Theatre. It was a lot smaller than I expected and I was thrilled to see Alan Bennett, the man whom I had encountered many times skulking around Giggleswick, on such wonderful form. Afterwards Russell had said he would take me out for supper. I had naïvely expected an Angus Steak House at the very least. However, supper turned out to be a plate of pâté and some crusty bread at the Oxford Street flat of Alan Shallcross. So, this is swinging London, I thought. But then Alan Bennett himself turned up straight from the theatre, bringing with him no less than Peter Cook and Dudley Moore. Well, who could ask for anything more? It was an evening I will never forget and I was always grateful to Russell for treating me in such a grown up and, frankly, such a privileged way.

And so I duly went off to Cambridge to read English. I was a poor student, mainly because there were no John Deans or Russell Hartys to stand over me. Skip a lecture – sure it's the done thing. Miss a supervision – why not, they won't mind. No time for an essay this week – don't worry. My butterfly brain rose to the challenge of finding any single excuse to avoid work, however flimsy.

After graduating, I lost touch with Russell for several years. He finally left Giggleswick after nine years and went off to lecture at a college in New York in the early Sixties, and to a teaching training college in Derby. All those boys who encountered him during those years will have a similar admiration for a man who taught them so inspirationally. He himself was proud of them all. And, for the record, in the light of Russell's known homosexual tendencies in midlife, there was never any evidence of any inappropriate behaviour at school.

One night, by now I was employed deep in the newsroom at ITN, returning home to Campden Hill Towers in Notting Hill Gate, I bumped into him in the car park. He was on his way to his flat in Campden Hill Road, three hundred yards away. What a small world! He was working for the BBC, he told me, as an assistant producer on Radio Four's *The World of Books*.

I went round to his flat a few times, but he had a very definite set, rather camp I suppose, always ringing each other up with a lot of giggling and making arrangements for further meetings. It was all a bit beyond me, and anyway, I felt I was not particularly welcome in that set. We kept in touch, though, and later arranged lunch at Broadcasting House the week before I was to leave ITN to join Yorkshire Television.

As we sipped coffee in the fifth floor canteen, he puffed on the inevitable cigarette and deliberately looking out over the roof tops of W1 murmured, 'So how much are you getting at YTV?'

'Two thousand six hundred,' I said, almost without moving my lips.

'Bloody hell,' he inhaled. 'Two thousand six hundred. Do you know what I'm on here? Fifteen hundred and fifty. Two thousand six hundred. Bloody hell.'

I was deeply embarrassed. Salaries aren't normally discussed, especially by Yorkshiremen, but the man I still regarded as my teacher asked me, so I told him. And I, aged twenty-four, was getting a thousand a year more than he was. We parted, and I didn't really see him again to speak to for another few years, although I followed his rise to fame with a special interest and a great pride.

It was in 1978. I had a phone call. 'Russell Harty for you,' shouted someone across the *Calendar* newsroom (I was presenter of Yorkshire TV's evening news programme by this time). People looked up from their typewriters. I had often said I knew him, of course, but no one really believed me. Now he was actually on the phone. Was I free that night? Could we have dinner? Was Mario and Franco's the best place to go? Let's meet at 8.00. There was, of course, a reason. Alan Bennett and Thora Hird were doing a night shoot for one of Alan's plays in Leeds

Town Hall. Russell had a couple of hours to kill. During the coffee, he lit up the inevitable and interminable cigarette and scanned the clientele.

'So how much do you get at YTV these days?' he murmured. As he was still, of course, my teacher, I told him. 'Fourteen thousand five hundred.'

'Happy with that?'

'Yes, it's fine. In fact, I'm probably one of the best paid people there, apart from the VTR men and the sparks.'

'Know what I got last year from London Weekend?' he inhaled. He paused. He exhaled. He averted his gaze from me, suddenly finding the poster advertising the delights of Portofino challengingly interesting. 'Fifty-three thousand,' he said, with the conviction of someone telling me how many miles it was between Leeds and Blackburn.

Russell eventually divided his time between a flat in Lexham Gardens in London and the Yorkshire Dales. First he bought a barn next door to another barn purchased by his childhood friend, Madge Hindle. When she was still Madge Railton, I had been taken by Russell to see her act in a performance in Blackburn as part of a sixth-form trip. Now married to Michael Hindle, an accountant, and after a stint in *Coronation Street*, she was a well-known and accomplished northern actress. Together they converted their barns at Keasden, a remote hamlet near Clapham. These were the beginnings of a Harty coterie. Alan Bennett bought a cottage in Clapham. Thelma Barlow, Mavis from *Coronation Street* moved in nearby. Hugh and Joan Stalker, Russell's great friends from Giggleswick days, returned from the South to a nearby old farmhouse. Alan Shallcross bought a place in Settle.

Meanwhile, Russell scaled new heights of popularity with the nation's viewers. He returned to the school on visits and was often quoted as saying that he would like to be headmaster, or at least a governor. It was at about that time that I became a governor. He was generally OK about it, but I think at first he was genuinely miffed. He would, I suspect, have been unsuitable. He could never have been headmaster. Such a position is no longer the preserve of cloistered Oxbridge classicists. Now it is the job of a chief executive with the attendant peripheral skills, such as personnel management, marketing, financial control, a deep knowledge of education, and the ability to take on the occasional period of third form teaching. That process was beginning in the Seventies. Had he applied, it would have been one interview at which Russell would not have been successful.

Russell as a governor would have been

splendid PR for the school, but the school benefitted hugely anyway from his frequent allusions to it, and the many interviews he did in which the name Giggleswick was mentioned. But Russell would have been bored by the long meetings, the minutiae, the Board papers, and so on. What he would have liked though was to have sat on the platform at Speech Day. He loved Giggleswick, the school, the village and especially the chapel, an exotic Byzantine building topped by its unique green copper dome. This provided a setting and an acoustic for an enduring tradition of church music at Giggleswick. He loved the theatrical quality, the purity of the trebles, the mighty anthems, the simple carols at Christmas and the resounding voluntaries from the Willis organ. So it was no surprise when he bought one of the nicest houses right in the centre of the village of Giggleswick. There was seldom a weekend without exciting guests from Russell's wider life – Edna O'Brien, Michael and Mary Parkinson, John and Jane Birt.

When I visited the house for the first time, memories of that little room he had at Catteral Hall all those years ago, flooded back. The cosiness. The exquisite taste. The porcelain, the pictures, the books, the roaring fire, the welcoming kitchen. Everywhere you looked there was something interesting. The piano, the cards and the notes stuck up randomly around the kitchen. I noticed once he had my phone number on a sticky note! And he loved his garden.

One idyllic summer's evening he gave a drinks party in honour of Gyles Brandreth who was opening some classrooms at Catteral Hall the next day. We sat on the terrace in that walled garden watching the June sunset. As we looked out we saw the grey slate roofs of the village and the chimneys, some with smoke wisping into the evening sky. We saw the stone church tower and heard the clock chiming each quarter as it did all those years ago when I lay awake at school, worrying about tomorrow's exams or whatever. On the skyline, and dramatically silhouetted against the setting sun, we saw the chapel with its impressive dome. Russell uncorked several bottles of white wine, and explained his plans for the garden. Work was going on apace. He had two full-time gardeners, a fact which amazed Alan Bennett.

'Russell has two gardeners,' he would exclaim to friends.

Russell, sadly, was never to see his garden completed.

Russell played a big part in my life. I don't know what he thought of me, and he certainly never told me. He may well have spoken to other people but, frankly, it doesn't matter. I have a memory of him which is full of snapshots. Interviewing him on an afternoon chat show I did for YTV, we started with a sepia sequence pretending to be in the classroom with Mr Harty admonishing Whiteley J.R. And what followed was for me one of the best interviews I have ever done.

Afterwards I can remember him standing at the front door of YTV debating whether to go shopping in Leeds or to go home to Giggleswick. 'I can't decide whether to go impulse shopping or not.' One of his typical epigrams.

I remember getting furious with my father on an exeat day at school because he didn't offer Mr Harty a cigarette. I remember holding a drinks party at home in Ilkley for Barbara Taylor Bradford who had just published *A Woman of Substance*. I tried to invite as many well known people as possible to make Barbara feel at home, if she could ever feel equally at home in a cottage on the edge of Ilkley Moor, as she could be in her exclusive New York East Side apartment. Russell, obviously, was on the list. In fact, he would have been the star guest. I really hoped he'd come. Instead, a handwritten reply came in his stylish writing. 'I can't come for drinks with Barbara Taylor. I would of if I could of, but

I can't, so I won't.' To this day, Carol Vorderman and I say 'would of', and 'could of', deeply ungrammatical, of course and hugely written in about by our meticulous audience on *Countdown*. But, it's a sort of in-group tribute to Russell Harty.

Russell did appear in Dictionary Corner, on *Countdown*. Quite a novelty. I was the boss this time, and I had to keep my old teacher in check. He was, of course, excellent at the job, although, if I am frank, rather lazy, choosing to read funny bits out of *Private Eye* for his contributions into the break. If I had been giving him marks, I would have given him beta minus for effort, although alpha plus for performance. And I remember him appearing on *Countdown* just the week after the devastating allegations in the *News of the World*. It was his first public appearance – before a studio audience of one hundred and fifty. Had he been a woman, I suppose I would have squeezed his hand and led him sympathetically onto the set. Obviously, I could not do that. But I could only imagine what he was feeling, having to face that middle class crowd. He needn't have worried. The warmth and the affection that the British public had for Russell was present in abundance in the studio that day. I took him home for supper. Ironically, after a triumphant day in the studio, in the car he confided his thoughts that his career would be in ruins, his reputation shattered. Naturally, I reassured him, quoting the events of the afternoon, and then I stopped for petrol. As I filled up I heard, as I am sure he heard sitting inside the car, two youths who had been buying sweets. 'That's that poof on TV in that car,' one observed. I got back in the car and we never mentioned the subject.

On the morning of the *News of the World* story, I spoke with Susan Brookes. Susan was then making her way into the media world as a TV cook with Granada. She was deeply shocked by the story. She said how for years she had wanted to be famous and get her name into the papers a lot. Looking at what had happened to Russell that morning she said she was so very glad that she hadn't. Many people who knew him personally, and many who didn't, wrote to him with comfort and support. I, too, wrote straightaway, never expecting a reply. I have that card today – again the stylish writing and the message 'For one whose business is words, I am now totally lost for any to say thank you enough.'

He could, though, be a beast. Was it just me, or was he seemingly bored with everyone's conversation at an early stage! We hung on his every word as he was a hypnotic raconteur; he seemed to seek every opportunity to look over your shoulder as

76

quickly as possible as if seeking someone more interesting. He was a wonderful deliverer of reported speech and ever one for the witty response. For example, one day at a governors' meeting, we sat all day in an increasingly cold and increasingly draughty library in early December, interviewing candidates for the vacant headmaster's post. Eventually at five o'clock we came to our decision, informed the winning candidate of his luck and finally the meeting broke up. Weary and wanting a drink, I knew I would be welcome at Russell's house. There he was in his cottage, as cosy as ever with the fire glowing and lamps lit. A pleasant atmosphere. He affected total disinterest in the fact that Giggleswick was to have a new headmaster (he had never applied of course!).

'What's his name?' he asked languidly, the very least he could possibly ask.

'Hobson,' I said.

'Oh,' he said. 'Is his wife called Joyce?'

'No, as a matter of fact,' I said, 'she's called Amanda. Why should she have been called Joyce?'

'Well, then,' he said, 'Giggleswick would have had Hobson's Joyce.'

He always seemed about to get bored with whatever you were telling him. His eyes would dart round the room, he was looking eagerly to change the subject, or to talk about somebody else. I thought it was just me, perhaps it wasn't. But I remember in 1982 when I had become the first face on Channel Four, there was quite a bit of publicity, although *Countdown* was hardly a critical or a ratings success. My name was hardly on everybody's lips and indeed I could have walked down many a street of the United Kingdom without anyone batting an eyelid. But Russell, surely, being in the business, would have known that his ex pupil had achieved that signal honour. At the school carol service, an essential date in our mutual calendars at the end of the December term, I found myself shuffling out of chapel beside Russell. In 1982 he was a very big star indeed.

I greeted him as we both admitted we'd shed a tear over David Fox's perfect performance of 'Three Kings from Persian Lands Afar' and as we reached the chapel doors – 'So what are you doing these days?' he asked with an air of casual innocence. You beast Mr Harty, you beast. You jolly well know.

Memories of Russell end with an evening at the home of Warwick and Susan Brookes. Russell was godfather to Sophie, one of their two daughters, a lifelong visitor to their house and highly regarded 'Uncle'. That night he was on great form and was playing the piano, performing with great gusto a school song for Giggleswick. There was no official school song at the time, and Russell invented a tune and ridiculous words which were sung with great hilarity by all present. 'Come back to Giggleswick,' was the inspirational first line. Warwick was, by then, second master, deeply committed and greatly respected. He had watched his old friend Russell move on to the realms of extreme celebrity, and like the whole Giggleswick family, was proud of his former colleague. Both the Brookes girls, Gilly and Sophie, were then pupils at the school, as co-education had dawned! As I sang along, I thought how fantastic it was for this family and the girls to have this talented and unique man as part of them, and I thought, that even though I had met many famous people in my line of work, how privileged I was to be included that night in that family group, watching Russell let his hair down and be at his most relaxed and happiest. Jeni, my girlfriend, and I were staying the night at Russell's and were to be off early in the morning. We walked back through the dark village to his house and then retiring to our room, we said our goodnights. As I closed the door I could hear Russell talking with Jamie, his partner, with whom he was to find the greatest content, although Jamie had the 'charming' habit in Russell's later years of running him down in company, calling him to his face, 'an ex chat show host'. But he was the best for Russell, and very popular both in the village, and indeed with the sixth form girls, some of whom had a boarding house directly opposite Russell's bedroom. As I went to close the door, he shouted up in his mischievous way, 'Don't look in the third drawer down'. Naturally I did. There was nothing in it. I could hear them on the stairs outside their separate rooms. 'Do you want me tonight?' said Russell. I never heard the reply. They were the last words I ever heard Russell Harty speak.

Later that morning I got home to find *The Sunday Times* lying on the mat. There, on the back page blinking at me, was me. Quickly grabbing the paper, wondering in panic why my picture should be all over the back page, I realised it was adorning Russell's regular column.

The rigours of filling a weekly column are not unknown to me, and poor old Russell must have been desperate that week. I read about myself as a young boy in an anecdote of a happening at Catteral Hall while Russell was a master. Wittily written, as you'd expect, but, bless him, he'd substituted my name, as someone who even he then had to admit was quite well known, for the actual eleven year old it was. Anyway, I laughed, and naturally was grateful for the publicity. I had meant to ring him and josh with him about it that morning, but never did.

Two weeks after this, I, as a proud governor of Giggleswick, joined a seventy strong party of pupils and staff touring Australia. There were cricketers, string players, choral singers, actors and dancers. A boy who opened the batting in the afternoon against a school in Brisbane, might very well be a rude mechanical in *A Midsummer Night's Dream* that night. The two plays – the *Dream* and *The Boyfriend*, were spectacularly successful ... and I will never forget a thousand girls in the audience at a school in Toowoomba (and we think Giggleswick is a funny name) chanting 'Giggleswick! ... Giggleswick!' after a wonderful performance of *The Boyfriend*.

Now this was the tangible measure of the success of the school Drama Society (President Alan Bennett Esq) which Russell Harty had founded twenty-five years earlier. Hardly a day went by without his name being mentioned, and somehow, thousands of miles away, we were all aware of his presence. We arrived back in Manchester on a grey Tuesday morning after the long and tiring flight. It had been a terrifically emotional tour, and arriving home was obviously an anticlimax.

As we entered the arrivals hall, I caught sight of a news stand and the headlines in *The Sun*... 'Russell has not got AIDS says sister'. It was the first I, or anyone on the tour, had heard of any illness.

The rest of the story is well enough chronicled, especially the grisly way in which the papers dealt with this. I had a sort of private view, in that YTV were making *Jimmy's*, a fly on the wall about St James's Hospital, at that time. They agreed not to film Russell, obviously aware of the fact that they had a big story on their hands, but choosing to respect the man and his privacy. I did get discreet bulletins from the senior producers, and also managed to send Russell dates for the next *Countdown* recording we needed him for, in the hope it would cheer him up.

He was buried on a beautiful summer's afternoon, in Giggleswick's ancient churchyard, with the sound of leather on willow drifting over from the cricket field next door, as the boys of Catteral Hall played a match. Russell was a star of his time, an unlikely one, but not a reluctant one. Although his chosen medium of television is as transient as light, he deserves to be remembered and I do my best to keep his name alive.

The celebrities who flocked to his memorial service in St James, Piccadilly were evidence of his eminent position in these shifting sands of fame. But in the end, when the London lights were dimming, it was his old friends to whom he returned, those lesser lights who had never gone away, with whom he had always anchored his life when he was swirled into the nonsense of notoriety, and the fickleness of fame. Quietly solid Warwick Brookes and his noisy and effervescent wife Susan. There was never a more hospitable or welcoming home in Yorkshire. Hugh and Joan Stalker. Hugh, the school organist, who had been known to keep the whole school waiting for hymns at assembly after a late night with Russell. Their moorland farmhouse was always the safe haven where Russell fled, at moments of stress, and where he went for laughing dinners and wicked weekends. The two Alans, and his friend Thelma Barlow. Madge Hindle, his lifelong friend from Blackburn, and her dependable husband Michael.

Everyone who came into contact with Russell, and there were hundreds, will have their own tales to tell. This is just mine.

THE VARSITY RAG

The gap term between Giggleswick and Christ's College, Cambridge was, in the words of a former Prime Minister, very agreeable indeed. I worked as a teacher at a primary school in Bingley (an eye opener... I had never met children who were on free school dinners before). I joined the Young Liberals in Shipley and threw my weight into the local election campaign that May (an eye opener... I had never met anyone who had ever voted Liberal before. I did stand as a Liberal in the mock election at the school in 1959, but only because the two other parties had been bagged). I also drove a delivery van for the local grocer (an eye opener... I had no idea how long the working day was and just how hard people actually had to work). I also lived at home full time for the first time for five years (an eye opener...). So much for an all round education!

Thus, well equipped in educational, political, and social awareness, off I trotted to Cambridge early in October 1962. Now, I was nothing special at Christ's ... far from it, but I found that unlike most of my first year contemporaries who had got a room in college, I was not allocated the standard bedsit, but a room with a separate bedroom and study, in one of the main buildings. This, of course, was purely based on the alphabet, so with my lowly 'W' normally having condemned me to being among the last of things which were being handed out, I now found I had got lucky.

On arrival I unpacked, scuttled to Woolworth's to buy the regulation social necessities of teapot, kettle, cups and saucers and turned up for dinner, joining the queue at the super duper brand new self-service arrangement in an upstairs hall. I uttered a silent prayer to the Patron Saint of Kitchen Renovations ... St Aga presumably ... for without his divine intervention I would have been ... well ... where would I have been? Perhaps still driving that grocery van.

My aim at Cambridge was clear. Naïve though I may have been about the ways of the undergraduate world, with its agenda of foreign food, disco dancing, gin and orange and pints of mild, French films at the cinema, and late night discussions about God, washed down with cocoa and chocolate digestives, my campaign was intimately planned. I would distinguish myself in some prominent way at Cambridge, probably as a drama director, and would end up as

President of the ADC. In that role I would be a natural for selection as a BBC general trainee, the producer training scheme that Alan Shallcross enthused me about, all those years ago. End of story. Oh, and I might hopefully collect a degree as well. Certainly a special, they didn't like people to fail in those days, so they were awarded a special. I was bound to get one of those at the very least.

So that was the plan. Yes, pretty bold but I didn't see any obstacles in the way. Drama Director? What qualifications did I have for that? Well, I did assist Russell Harty in *The Merchant of Venice* and *Twelfth Night*, and I did do front of house for *The Winslow Boy*. I also helped on props in the Bradford Civic Theatre production of *Roots*.

So, to the Societies Fair I went, heading straight for the drama stands. There it was, the ADC. And there too, the Mummers and the Marlowe Society, and a host of college dramatic societies. So much choice. I looked at the sort of people gathering around. Frankly, they didn't look my type. No one had a tie on for a start. Their hair was long, and some even had beards. Fancy having a beard at eighteen. How could they do that? They all seemed to know each other and conversed in an easy and languidly cool way. Nobody seemed in the least interested in even handing out a leaflet to me. As I

86

hovered, I wondered who all these self-confident people could be. Later, I found out that they had names like Richard Eyre, Trevor Nunn, John Shrapnel, Michael Apted, Stephen Frears and Miriam Margolyes.

On the next door stand was the Footlights which said it was a cabaret club which put on 'Smokers' on Sunday nights. Not for me, I thought. I was brought up to stay in on a Sunday night. Lounging round there were people called John Cleese, Bill Oddie, Graeme Garden and Tim Brooke-Taylor. They were all doing a lot of laughing amongst themselves and didn't seem particularly interested in hearing my impression of Frankie Howerd. Well, I hadn't heard of any of these people, and they certainly didn't look as if they knew that a future Director General of the BBC was mooching around their stand.

Eventually, I decided I would take my time before answering the call of drama. For some reason I joined the Cambridge University United Nations Association, the Union Society and the Yorkshire Society. I resisted the temptation to join the ballroom dancing class even though the leaflet pointed out that with the male/female ratio of nine to one, you would get absolutely nowhere in the mating game if you couldn't foxtrot and waltz at the Dorothy Ballroom on Wednesday nights.

So, my game plan was knocked back a bit by not being immediately accepted into the drama circle. Meanwhile, people of my own year were getting ahead. I heard that someone called Eric Idle was already wowing them at the Sunday night Smokers. Well, I thought, there's plenty of time. Perhaps I might become a big deal in the United Nations Association. The BBC might like that. My plan took a further setback as the early days went on. Casual conversations with fellow freshmen revealed their career ambitions. People reading architecture wanted to be architects. Some wanted to be farmers and landowners – they were reading land economy. Some wanted to be Civil Servants – they were reading classics. Some wanted to be engineers – they were reading engineering. I was relieved that they were out of the running because I was conscious that the BBC would only recruit a maximum five from my year. Of the rest of the students I spoke to, those reading history, economics, modern languages, and English, especially English ... those that didn't want to join ICI, GKN, Barclays Bank or Boots, all of them said they'd like to join the BBC.

I was furious. What did they know about radio and television? They didn't know who had produced *Hancock's Half Hour* on the radio in the Fifties. They didn't buy the BBC yearbook and read and memorise all the lists of various hierarchies. Who was the assistant head of the current affairs group? They wouldn't know that. Who played Mr Grove in the *Grove Family?* Who could hum the original theme tune of *Panorama?* – and I bet they didn't sit in the school chapel working out camera shots in case the service was ever televised. They didn't take the *Radio Times* every week and look at the production credits. Bloody cheek. They should go off and get a job somewhere, and not try for mine.

Meanwhile, there were lessons to cope with, or as they were called lectures. My very first one on the Monday morning was in the Mill Lane lecture room addressed by Professor C.S. Lewis. Now I had heard of him, although I hadn't read any of his books. I sat through his opening salvo reasonably mystified. I cannot for the life of me remember what the lecture was about. Indeed at the time, I kept wondering what on earth it had to do with English Literature, and thought perhaps I had come to the wrong lecture room. It sounded more like philosophy to me. It was certainly very deep and certainly not as entertaining or as easy to understand as Mr Harty's classes. I can remember that, as the eleven o'clock bell rang, he ended the lecture and lit up a cigarette and inhaled furiously. Well really, what an example.

I also remember sliding into a spare seat next to a girl wearing a powder blue PVC coat. She had the most beautiful, wistful, dreamy and gorgeous face I had ever seen. She haunted me for three years and eventually became the only reason I turned up for lectures, although I never dared sit next to her again. Her name was Helen. She apparently came from Sheffield and had two sisters who were then famous authors, and are still more famous now. I never did speak to her during the whole of the three years. She will know who she is. Her second name began with a D. So if she reads this I would be grateful if she would give me a ring, so that we could talk about old times, and the times that might have been.

After that first term, I did actually dip my toe into thespianism, and directed a one-act play for the Mummers. It was, in fact, the first three scenes of Arnold Wesker's *Roots*, which I had remembered from Bradford. It seemed to go quite well, and even had two girls in the cast whom I did dare to speak to. But I did feel that this Giggleswick boy was a little out of his depth with the drama set. I should, perhaps, replan my strategy and approach the BBC by a different route.

It was Jonathan Sale who told me he was doing a bit for *Varsity*. Jonathan had the end room along my corridor, and he was in my year in English. He knew his way round the place very well, his father Arthur having taught English at Magdalene College for many years. Jonathan had been to school at The Leys, the independent school on the edge of town, and his family lived in Girton village. He also basked in the reflected glory that not only did he look like, but he actually knew Bamber Gascoine, because his father had been his tutor a couple of years before. Jonathan Sale was good news. Jonathan, or Jonty, as he was quaintly known to his family, offered to take me along to *Varsity* and introduce me to the team.

Like every undergraduate, I read *Varsity* avidly. It was a very professionally produced newspaper, indeed essential reading for gown, and some of the town as well. So, the spring term of 1963, not only saw the Cam frozen over in the coldest winter Cambridge had experienced since the latest C.P. Snow book, but also saw me make an exit from the sublime world of the theatre and enter the more immediate world of journalism. Who knows what could have been had I stayed to develop a theatrical career? My generation at Cambridge produced two directors of the National Theatre ... there could have been a third. My generation produced Pythons a Plenty and Goodies a Gogo ... who knows to what heights comedy could have risen had I soldiered on and starred at the Smokers. I did sell programmes for the Footlights at the rag week review so I had made a start. But it was not to be. The power of the written word beckoned, and a new strategy was hatching. Let someone else do the ADC, let someone else take charge of the Footlights. Let someone else become President of the blessed United Nations Association. My plan was clear. I will become editor of *Varsity* and surely walk straight from there into the BBC's current affairs unit and be Director General by the end of the century. (At this time, Greg Dyke was still at primary school, so I had a head start on him.)

I had, mind you, a long way to go. I was only a callow first year when I met the news editor, one Colin Morris, who had the endearing habit of referring to everyone as a little grey grot. Nevertheless, he was an amusing and gentle chap and gave me a couple of stories to get my teeth into. The front page story on my first week in *Varsity* was 'Johnsman Sent Down'. Sending down, or expulsion in crude terms, was the punishment meted out to this unfortunate fellow who was caught by a porter in bed with a lady, in the afternoon, in his room in college. Actually, this shocked the whole university. Most of them being shocked by the punishment, rather than the crime. I actually couldn't work out what the offence was. In bed with a woman... He was a first year as well, the same age as me. Was his offence the fact that she was a woman? Had he been in bed with a man, would that have been OK? Or was his offence being in bed in the afternoon, when he should have been at a chemistry practical? Or was his offence that he hadn't sported his oak (i.e. closed the outside double door, which you did if you didn't want to be disturbed). I often wonder what happened to this man whose name I can still remember. This buccaneer could be head of a city institution by now, but more likely he's a long-serving maths master at a prep school in the West Country. Top reporters were assigned to that delicate story and I was relieved that on my first week my only contribution to that issue was a paragraph on new opening hours for the University library.

I liked the set up at *Varsity*. They had extensive offices, including a private lavatory, there were free telephones, and a big lounge, carpeted and furnished by G Plan, with a TV and sofas, and from where we could enjoy commanding views over Bridge Street and Magdalene Street. When *TW3* came on and the Cambridge streets were emptied on Saturday nights, we had the best view in town from our twenty-one inch television, courtesy of Pye, who were a local firm. I used to like looking back at the bound copies of past years, thus developing my hobby of byline spotting. There was a distinguished list – Nicholas Tomalin, Jonathan Miller, Michael Frayn, Anthony Armstrong Jones, Benedict Nightingale, George Perry, Ron Hall, David Frost. *The Sunday Times* particularly seemed to be staffed with ex *Varsity* chaps. That was a good sign.

Promotion was fairly swift. Every term the board elected a new editor who then chose his team. It wasn't long before I found myself assistant sports editor. Just right for a guy who had never touched a ball in anger, certainly never for pleasure, in his life. However, this was an excuse to write up minor sports and gain experience and good training in thinking up headlines. My favourite, referring to an uncertain future for a cricket team called the Quidnuncs, just said 'Where now for Quidnuncs'. Geddit?

I was a natural choice for full sports editor the following term and this put me on conversational and matey terms with all the university heavies, with the rugby First Fifteen, with the boat race crew, Mike Sweeney and popular cox Robert Stanbury, with Mike Brearley's famous cricket Eleven, and indeed all the sporting stars of the year of 1964, David Rosser, Terry Arthur and

Mike Gibson – all future rugby inter-
nationals. The fact being, of course, that as
the world's worst sportsman, I hadn't a clue
what they were talking about most of the
time. But I employed that well honed
journalistic technique: pretend you know
what you're talking about, if you don't,
invent it. Or if you were lucky enough,
delegate it to someone who does. I used to
scan our rival paper, the Oxford *Cherwell*
and noted how thin and amateur looking it
was compared to *Varsity*. This did have,
though, a better gossip column than we did
called 'John Evelyn' and a very good sports
column by somebody called Jeffrey Archer.

So these were heady days. A *Varsity*
presscard was a passport, not only for free
films at the ABC, but a visiting card to
access the gilded greats of student life. I sat
in the press box for the varsity match at
Twickenham, and got an interview with
David Frost when he came back to Cambridge to put on a charity concert in aid of
a literary magazine called *Granta*. Legend
has it that while David Frost was on the
editorial board, his own excesses had
contributed to the parlous state of its
finances in the first place. Now, at twenty-
three and an incredibly famous old boy, he
returned with a cast of friends to put on this
show one Sunday night at the Arts Theatre
to pay off the debts, and I was in charge of

coverage. I remember seeing Danny Williams backstage, preparing to go on to sing Moon River, wandering round looking lost and coming up to me and saying 'this Granta charity we're here for ... what country is this orphanage in?'. David was obviously as persuasive in his younger days as he was to be in his later years.

As I approached the final year, it looked as though I had a good chance of being editor. There was a certain amount of Buggins' turn, but there still had to be an election by the board and I reckoned I had the qualifications. I had spent my first long vacation working for the Deputy Editor of the *Yorkshire Post* in the splendid old offices at Albion Court in the centre of Leeds. Mr W.T. 'Bill' Oliver was a gentleman journalist of the oldest of old schools and the paper was still influential nationally under the flamboyant and literary editor, Kenneth Young. My summer job there was fixed, just as these things still are, by knowing someone who knew someone. In this case my Aunt Barbara Jones, my mother's sister, worked as secretary for John Braine in Bingley, typing out all his books from his longhand in exercise books. At Auntie Barbara's behest, John wrote to Kenneth and I was in at the *YP*, benefitting greatly from the tolerance, patience and the paternal friendship offered by Bill Oliver. I shall always be grateful to him, and also to Bobbie, as we called my aunt. She was something of a writer herself, and always encouraged me and was heartened by what I eventually achieved. I used her and my mother's maiden name, Bentley, as my nom de plume in certain articles.

Looking back to those days at the *Yorkshire Post*, I would really have done very little of use and certainly nothing that Bill Oliver couldn't have done himself. I used to send new books out to reviewers and collate the reviews on their return. I was allowed by Bill to do a few myself, which he kindly made space for. Returning to Cambridge the next term as features editor, I was able to cash in on my new best friends and managed to impress the board by getting John Braine himself to write for *Varsity*. The paper itself was going through a purple patch. Graduate recruitment advertising was at its height and every issue contained lovely juicy full page ads from national firms, which together with pages of local business ads, all made for a very thick and prosperous paper. To avoid paying income tax, excess profits were squandered unashamedly on summer parties on college lawns and winter parties in oak beamed halls.

As the prospect of editorship hove into view, I pulled off a great coup at Christ's. By being involved with a university wide

organisation like *Varsity* I was not a particularly good college man, although I did
attend the May Balls and support general
college activities. Our second and third
years were meant to be out of the college
and in digs. My first digs in Melbourne
Terrace did not actually have running water
and Mrs Newman would oblige with a jug
of hot water and a bowl left outside your
door at 8 am. Yes, this was student life in
1963. In fact, it was in those very digs, while
dressing in black tie for the annual dinner of
the Yorkshire Society, that I heard Leonard
Parkin bring the news of the shooting of
President Kennedy. Nothing against Mrs
Newman but I did fancy a hot bath at least
a couple of times a term, whether I needed
it or not, so I vowed to get my third year
back in college. *Varsity* did the trick. The
next editor at the start of the third year was
to be Graham Lord. Now Graham was
married and lived, therefore, in a family
house with his wife and child. My argument
was that the editor of a University organ
needs college space to entertain, hold
meetings, and generally be available to
persons of distinction in the town at large.
Because Graham was domiciled in the
suburbs, I, as deputy, would have to assume
these painful duties. The college fell for this
and I got a fine old room in the third court.
This afforded me views of all parts of

college life, especially the procession of Christ's men, I cannot call them Christians, escorting young ladies out of college on Sunday mornings. I found it remarkable that so many such ladies wanted to come to the college for Sunday breakfast. No one that I'd ever invited seemed the least bit interested. Perhaps I should have pointed out that early communion was not compulsory.

So, in the final year, a room in college, and in that spring term of '65, the editor's chair and my very own office, two paid secretaries to work for me, and a great power of patronage handing out the jobs on the editorial board. It was like a Prime Minister forming his cabinet. And what a talented list I had at my disposal. Celia Haddon became deputy editor. She is now a writer beloved by many pet-loving readers of the *Daily Telegraph*. Suzy Menkes, my fashion editor, later the doyenne of them all, internationally famous, as fashion editor of the *New York Herald Tribune*. If she couldn't get a first year undergrad to pose for the fashion photo of the week, she'd think nothing of donning stockings, suspenders and bra and posing herself for a feature about sexy underwear from Etam. Paul Whitehouse, the circulation manager, went on to be a career policeman, becoming Chief Constable of Sussex. Patrick Eagar, the picture editor, became the most successful cricket photographer of the last thirty years. Jonathan Sale was a columnist and since then has written his way through *Queen* magazine, *Punch* magazine and now the *Guardian* and many others, and thirty years later is one of the most delightful and readable columnists around. Matthew Robinson was my news editor who did the unthinkable and became a thespian, ending the century as executive producer of *EastEnders*. A sharp one, this chap. One weekend my sister Helen came down from Yorkshire to visit me, and Matthew took quite a shine to her. On the Monday afternoon seeing I was busy, he asked if he could take her from the *Varsity* office to the station to see her off. Sure, I agreed. On his return, he demanded three and sixpence for the taxi fare. James Wilkinson, who out-trended the other students by wearing a pink shirt, and asking Cilla Black to a May Ball, sailed straight into the *Daily Express* as assistant to the legendary Chapman Pincher. Graham Lord, my predecessor, sailed straight into the *Sunday Express* as assistant to Robert Pitman, the literary editor. Martin Adeney, another ex editor, got one of the two top jobs on the *Guardian,* which were offered every year. It was a one way procession. No one, admittedly, getting a BBC traineeship but, well, there had to be a first. Mind you,

I was getting to be rather bitten by this journalism bug...

When I became editor, it was in my final year and only two terms to the final exams. My English tutor, John Rathmell, a Yorkshireman from Knaresborough, was bemused but sympathetic. Out of seven third year pupils, no less than two, messrs Whiteley and Sale, were constantly pleading this *Varsity* thing as an excuse for the non delivery of essays. And there was to be good news for me. *Varsity* was so awash with money that the Board of Directors had decided they would produce a twenty page colour supplement with the last edition of the term in March. This, in 1965, was a huge venture. *The Sunday Times* was then very much the Sunday papers, and its colour supplement the very leading aspect of contemporary weekly journalism. We were to produce our own version. So, it was an exciting term. Thursdays were the best nights. Working late on the final pages before the trip to Bury St Edmunds to the HQ of the Bury Free Press, where *Varsity* was laid out on the stone and printed on the Friday. Cycling back to college at two or three in the morning, down Trinity Street and then turning left where Market Place adjoins King's Parade, the city was asleep and deserted. But it was also beautifully lit by the street lights and often by the moon. Each time I rode home, I used to think that all this beauty, all the colleges, King's College Chapel, Great St Mary's, everything I could see, all of this was here entirely for my benefit. All of it was built especially for me. Which, of course, it was ... because there was surely nobody else in the entire world looking at these buildings as I was at that time, so they must be there especially for me. On subsequent visits to Cambridge, finding myself subsumed in the mass of humanity that clogs these streets by day, I felt both resentful that these people were getting in the way, but also a bit superior and knowing, remembering that once I'd had all this to myself.

There were several notable events that term. One night, while working late in the newsroom, I, fun-loving, devil-may-care swashbuckler that I am, phoned the BBC Light Programme to ask for Jimmy Young to do a request on his Round Midnight Show, *Light Night Extra*. Having done it, I immediately forgot about it, we finished our work, and I cycled home exhausted and fell into bed. In that half state of consciousness, I heard Mr Young in that chirpy way of his, read out my request and dedication for all the staff of *Varsity* in Cambridge working so hard to put the paper to bed. It was a great thrill, I can tell you and I have always rated

JY from that day to this, commode and all.

I also made my first appearance on television. Stuart McClure was making a film for the BBC religious slot about student apathy. His research had led him to the Mill, a well-frequented drinking point in Cambridge, at lunchtime. He was keen to interview as many students as possible and asked if those who were interested could turn up at the same time the next day when the cameras would be there. I, of course, hearing the magic words 'TV cameras', didn't need asking twice. All I will say is, that the number of students who bothered to turn up for a discussion on student apathy, was precisely three. Thus I made my first television appearance, and watched proudly on the big twenty-one incher in the *Varsity* office. I wouldn't say I was talent spotted because students in those days were always being on TV. Anglia televised some of the debates from the union, starring luminaries such as Norman Lamont, Kenneth Clarke, Michael Howard and John Selwyn Gummer – later to become the Cambridge Mafia in the Tory Cabinets. But one Tuesday afternoon, I got a phone call which was to change my life. It was from Anglia TV. They had heard about our ground-breaking colour magazine plans. Would I come to Norwich to appear live on *About Anglia* to talk about it? Wouldn't I

103

just! So, clean shirt, corduroy jacket and college tie, I was away in the taxi.

I was treated like a star at Anglia House, which I was familiar with, having previously visited for a feature about Anglia for *Varsity*. There was boardroom hospitality, there was a brief meeting with the interviewer, Mr Michael Partington, and there was also an event that I could hardly believe, a meeting with another of the studio guests that night ... none other than Russ Conway. I couldn't believe it. My first pop hero after Max Bygraves. Russ Conway! I had insisted my parents take me to stand outside his house in London on my first visit there when I was fifteen years of age. Russ Conway. I have got all of his records you know. I remember when he had the first three of the top ten on Radio Luxembourg for most of the summer of 1959, 'Sidesaddle', 'Roulette' and 'China Tea', and there we were on the same television show. Michael Partington did what I now know to be an immaculate piece. There was a crisp intro, during which he displayed copies of the existing colour supplements, to the camera. *The Sunday Times*, the *Observer*, the *Sunday Telegraph*. And he said there was to be another one from *Varsity*. It was to be the biggest ever edition of a student newspaper blah blah blah... And here is the editor Richard Whiteley. It was an easy chat, but being

Michael, there was just a hint of confrontation.

'Well, it's easy to make all these elaborate promises, but how can you be sure that this magazine will ever come out?' Good question, Michael.

'I am sure, you'll just have to wait until March the sixth,' I replied confidently. Good answer, Whiteley.

'What a smart arse,' Mr Partington must have thought. 'Hope to get a real person to interview tomorrow. Bloody students.'

Afterwards, far from melting away as interviewers tend to do these days, Michael entertained me to a whisky (manlike thing to have I thought) in the boardroom. He explained that he, like me, was a Yorkshireman, Harrogate raised and editor of the *Pudsey News* at an early age. He had been an ITN journalist before coming as a senior man to Anglia. I was very impressed. He seemed to have some empathy with me (common bond I suppose ... minor public schoolboys from Yorkshire) and asked me about my career plans. I didn't say I intended to edit *Panorama*, produce the next election programme but one, and be DG by the turn of the century. Well, I said I was always very keen on becoming a BBC trainee. But when I saw the appointments board at Cambridge, they seemed strangely reluctant to encourage me (I haven't told

you this, but they were less than en-
thusiastic). Totally unimpressed with my
Varsity career so far. Asked about what I had
done in the Union (nothing apart from eat
lunch), what I had done in the United
Nations Association (nothing apart from go
to occasional dinners), and didn't I consider
doing something in the drama line? The fact
that I was then secretary of the Yorkshire
Society cut no ice at all. So my BBC
prospects were drying up. But anyway, I
went on, 'I'm now totally hooked on
journalism – the print, and the layout and
all the fun of news and newspapers. In fact,
I have had an offer from the *Daily Mail* to
join them in Manchester.' Michael Partington listened and then sniffed, 'Thought of
ITN?' he said crisply.

'No,' I replied. I knew of ITN, of course.
Reginald Bosanquet and the jolly signature
news tune.

'They take two trainees a year. Didn't the
appointments board tell you about that?'

'No, they jolly well didn't,' I said, thinking
that as far as they were concerned, the only
thing they would direct me to was the *Batley
Bugle*, so unimpressed were they with my
two poor thirds so far ... and lack of
progress in drama circles.

'Well,' continued Michael. 'It seems to me
that ITN would be just right for you. It
combines television which is your first love,

and news and journalism, your latest love. I have just left there. It's a wonderful place to work, why not write to Geoffrey Cox.'

And so that was it. Stopping only to swig my whisky and get Russ Conway to sign my autograph book next to Len Hutton, I was away back to Cambridge, and the next day a letter was in the post to Geoffrey Cox.

That week, on the Saturday, Sir Winston Churchill died. The funeral was to be the next Saturday. Now Cambridge's newest college was, of course, Churchill, and there in splendour was a superb bronze bust of the great man ... which gave me an idea for the front page of *Varsity* for the day of the funeral. I got our chief page three girl photographer (yes, we had them in 1965) to photograph this bust bathed in light from a simple spotlight. It was a starkly beautiful photograph, especially in black and white. I ran this over seventy per cent of the front page, with pictures of college flags at half-mast all along the top under the *Varsity* masthead and the text of a tribute from the master of Churchill. It was a stunning front page, and sales that Saturday were well into six thousand, a record at the time. I presumed to send a copy to Lady Churchill, pompously saying it was a tribute to a great man from the undergraduates of Cambridge who were so proud to have such a tangible association with him. She, in turn, graciously replied, which gave me a great thrill.

Meanwhile, work went on on the colour supplement. St John's College were persuaded to display their silver to be photographed en masse and in colour for the first time. Second year English students posed in fashionable attire from the high street shops on King's Parade, and Patrick Eagar went out with exclusive access to the Blue Boat and came back with stunning colour shots of the boat race training sessions. In addition to the magazine, the paper itself was to be a bumper edition with a special section devoted entirely to works and articles by old *Varsity* hands, and there was to be a big celebration dinner at the Garden House Hotel, attended by luminaries such as Michael Winner, Michael Frayn, Katherine Whitehorn, Gavin Lyall, half of *The Sunday Times*, and Charles Wintour, editor of the *Evening Standard*, as chief guest. It was a busy term.

Oh, yes, Geoffrey Cox's office wrote. Would I turn up for an interview? You bet.

I arrived at ITN pre-armed with theories on how I would alter the presentation of the news, and clutching, of course, the famous issues of *Varsity*, and indeed some of the comments from famous people to whom I had unctuously sent copies. Luckily, Geoffrey Cox and David Nicholas, the deputy editor, who sat in on the interview, didn't seem to want to know my production ideas, but were, I think, quite impressed with *Varsity*. Anyway, they'd let me know. A week later, I had a message to ring Mr Cox at three o'clock precisely. Deep in revision, I emerged into the sunshine outside the University library and made a phone call from a phone box on the backs. I notice it is still there ... Sir Gilbert Scott style and all.

The voice came on the phone – 'I'm glad to tell you we can take you on. You can start in the first week of July. Perhaps you could ring the Personnel Office about your pension arrangements. (Talk about forward planning.) By the way, you have a salary of nine hundred and forty-five pounds a year,' and I remember him finishing, 'Now you've got your job sorted out, there's no reason at all why you shouldn't work flat out for a first. I will be expecting it.'

'Yes, sir, thank you sir, I will sir,' I stuttered and hung up. 'Whoopee,' I yelled at the top of my voice as I leapt three feet in the air. 'I've got a top job with a top salary.' Well, I would have done that had this sequence of my life been photographed with a speech bubble. In the event, I was very happy, a bit shaken. I thought bugger the Beeb, and went back into the university library to work flat out for my third – and, of course, raise a coffee cup to Michael Partington.

NEWS AT EIGHT TO TWO

The day work broke out, in my case, was Monday 5 July 1965. My first job. The first day of the rest of my life. An editorial trainee at Independent Television News.

I was certainly very lucky to be chosen as one of the two trainees that ITN took in those days and I was fortunate in that I was to start work only three weeks or so after leaving Cambridge. No gap year – in the money straight away, nine hundred and forty-five pounds a year. Incidentally, a pretty good wage compared to those of my contemporaries who were becoming trainees with Boots, ICI or GKN. Even a couple of people who got plum jobs on the *Guardian* were only getting eight hundred and fifty. It was actually not as good as my friend James Wilkinson, ex *Varsity* reporter, who had landed a job as assistant to Chapman Pincher on the *Daily Express*. He had been there for over a year and was already on twenty-six pounds, ten shillings a week and regular lunch appointments at Rules. However, I could hardly believe I had managed to be offered such an opportunity. Twenty-one years old, thirteen years since setting my heart on a job in television, ever since we got our first set in 1952, and six years since I had pressed my face up against the railings of the BBC Television Centre, imagining how utterly blissful it must be to work there. And now, here I was, walking down Kingsway, about to enter Television House, a huge block adjoining the Aldwych which housed both Associated Rediffusion Television and ITN.

Into the foyer. Wait for the lift. A uniformed commissionaire was there to work it, and a small group got in. 'Six please,' said Desmond Wilcox – then a reporter on Rediffusion's *This Week*.

'Six for me,' said Anthony Howard – then working on a Rediffusion teatime current affairs show, *Three After Six*.

'Five,' said Cathy McGowan – then presenting the cult programme *Ready Steady Go*.

'Seven,' boomed six foot four Andrew Gardner en route for the ITN newsroom.

'Seven for me too,' squeaked Richard Whiteley en route for fame and fortune, glory and glamour.

And so began that search and, like the corridor which greeted me on the seventh floor, between the lift and the newsroom, that search was a mighty long one.

The funny thing about getting the job at ITN, was that as soon as I had got it, I had to constantly reassure myself about it. It's not that I didn't want it. It was just that it was, well, ITV, after all, and ITV was not the BBC. I had set my heart on the BBC, although in the end I never even applied. Sure, ITV was the nation's favourite and led the way in variety and filmed series, as well as many popular programmes. But was it actually OK for me to be in ITV? I read and re-read as much about ITN as I could. There was no doubt that within ITV it was a very respectable organisation. Geoffrey Cox, the editor, was a well-known and distinguished former newspaper correspondent, and a Rhodes scholar from Oxford to boot. In fact it seemed to me that ITN itself was actually quite posh. Take Reginald Bosanquet. Surely far more upper class than anyone that the BBC had, and look at the famous old boys – Chris Chataway, Robin Day, Ludovic Kennedy, the first editor Aidan Crawley, and so on. All very distinguished figures in those years. I even looked at the small print in the *TV Times* – ITN had a director called Diana Edwards Jones. So there we are, a double barrelled name working in ITV. Now there is posh. So, I thought it was going to be all right, especially when one of my sister's girlfriends said that she really fancied Peter Snow.

My date with destiny was two o'clock in the afternoon. It did seem a strange time to report to work – a funny time to board the Ferris wheel of life's career challenge. I didn't then appreciate the necessity of a shift system to cope with the transmission times of the bulletins. But that was when I boarded the capsule at the bottom of the wheel and waited for it to carry me up. I naturally never thought that having reached the top, it would bring me down again.

I was staying a few nights with my old college friend Tony Gable, at his parents' house in Walthamstow, not yet having anywhere to live in London. I had a two-tone grey Ford Anglia at the time and had driven it to Tony's. I couldn't wait to get an ITN sticker to put in the front windscreen. This would identify me to all concerned, not only as a pretty sharp guy working for a pretty trendy outfit, it would surely let me park anywhere, get me in anywhere, and arouse admiring glances from passing women down the King's Road and arouse envious comment from my pals back home in Yorkshire. Later I found out that ITN did not have any stickers, and if they did, only camera cars were allowed them. So, eventually I made my own by cutting up a sheet of ITN stationery and sticking the logo to the window with Sellotape.

Anyway, that Monday morning, besuited and scrubbed, I stood at Walthamstow station waiting for my train. I had no idea what exactly would await me at ITV, but I did expect a totally fulfilling scenario. I imagined I would be whisked straightaway into the hurly burly of the television news business, everyone I met taking account of my distinguished journalistic career at university, not to mention my degree in English. In actual fact no one did ever mention my degree in English, to this day, and no one has ever, for serious purposes, asked me what class of degree I have got. Certainly, as I was to find out, people were even less interested in my distinguished journalistic career at Cambridge.

I would, I thought, be immediately called on to be a reporter and appear on the screen. So I rehearsed a piece to camera on the platform, first standing still, and then walking. In the first I imagined I was Sandy Gall, reporting from a war zone. In the second I was Alan Whicker, walking through some fleshpot of southern Florida. Neither man, if they had heard of the strange antics of a young man on Walthamstow station needed to have worried about his career prospects. I thought I would soon at least be producing the news and then surely the next election results programme. If not, I fully expected to be sitting at one of those desks in vision behind Alastair Burnet on Budget days. I imagined I would be tearing around London and the rest of the country, reporting from hotspots and cool climates, being widely recognised wherever I went and, above all, of course, being the envy of my Cambridge contemporaries, all of whom were now setting out on their various careers.

Celia Haddon was one such. She had been deputy editor of *Varsity* with me, and in fact, we were both offered jobs on the *Daily Mail*. Me, to my chagrin, in Manchester, she in Head Office in London. However, I took the ITN job and we started work on the same day. As I travelled in, I wondered about Celia. Blonde, vivacious, with a habit of rubbing her eyes vigorously when she was excited or amused. She was, indeed, a Zuleika Dobson figure at Cambridge. She always attracted all the top class men. I was personally terrified of her for ages, especially as she became the first person I ever knew who admitted to all and sundry that she was taking the contraceptive pill. The story goes that in her third year at Cambridge, while enjoying some afternoon delight with a particularly luscious student drama critic, there was a knock on the door of her lodgings and in entered a timid first year undergraduate.

'Is there anyone from *Varsity* here?' he murmured as both of them sat up, rather startled.

'Yes,' said Celia. 'Would you like to speak

to the deputy editor or the drama critic?'

She had style. The *Mail* would never have sent her to Manchester!

She was due to start work that day at 10.30 – far more sensible it seemed to me. Like everybody else I suppose, I can remember every intimate detail about my first day at work. I can remember very few days since – they all mass into one, thirty-five year long, blur. But that first day is crystal clear. Reporting at reception. Being shown into the editor's office. Geoffrey Cox, nice enough, well groomed and beautifully mannered. Smallish, bright eyes, black hair immaculately slicked. Friendly, but more business like and awe inspiring than he was when he interviewed me so benignly two months previously. But after all, I was an employee now and lowly at that. Not an eager applicant. After the opening pleasantries, I was handed over to David Nicholas, the deputy editor. Into the newsroom we went, down that long corridor. I immediately knew that my quest for glamour and glory would be tough. Newsroom. What a powerful word. News. What visions did it conjure up? What images did it create in the mind of one like me, a child of these television times? And room. Well, a colloquial word for what I imagined was to be a pulsating palace of excitement, entertainment and experience.

It was a very big room. Lino-floored, with desks, arranged in threes or fours, assorted individuals sitting typing, and people ambling along in apparently random fashion, although seeming very busy. So this was the Newsroom. But where were the cameras, the mikes, the lights, the screens, the whole, wonderful and exciting paraphernalia of television which I had been seeking for all these years?

I was introduced around in a polite but cursory way. The chief sub. He was wearing a black open neck shirt. The output editor. He was tall, benign, a white shirt and a tie, and smoking a pipe. The director – not the one with the double barrelled name – and someone called the shift leader – a gentleman whose name was Cyril. Someone pounding a typewriter with two fingers as though the defence of the realm depended on it. His name was Peter Sissons. And there was Peter Snow, sitting at a desk, shaving with a battery shaver. I noticed with some amazement that he was wearing a sports jacket and separate trousers. Somehow I imagined anyone who appeared on British television would be wearing a suit. I looked for other famous people. And there was Reginald Bosanquet himself, walking into the newsroom from an office up the corridor. He too was wearing a sports jacket. Everywhere there were girls. Girls typing. Girls on the phone. Girls speaking in loud voices. Everybody seemed to know what they were doing.

Now Whiteley's law of the workplace is quite simple. Be nice to people on their first day at work because they always remember and it could do you a lot of good in the future. When I went on to YTV and had been there a year to two, I was the first person in the newsroom to speak to and befriend a tough looking young guy with a moustache, who came from the evening paper in Scarborough. His name was John Meade. He later went on to be the producer of *Countdown,* a programme which did me a bit of good.

A couple of years later, I was the first person to speak to a bespectacled, bewildered looking, shy bloke, who looked worryingly like me. Hoping that he had not been hired to usurp my position as ace news reporter. I had a word with him as he sat alone at an empty desk. I need not have worried. He'd come as a mere researcher, and had no ambition at all to appear on the box and be a star. With almost audible relief I offered to show him where the gents was, and where he could get a cup of coffee from. He later told me how grateful he was for my early display of friendship and sympathy and he said he had never forgotten it. When did he tell me that? Oh, some fifteen years later when he was a big cheese at Channel Four – Director of Programmes no less. His name was John Willis.

So, I'll never forget the first person who befriended me that Monday afternoon. David Nicholas had introduced me to the chief sub and retreated, his job done. The chief sub, of whom more later, indicated a place to sit, and gave me an early edition of the *Evening Standard* to read. Three other subs were working, rather intermittently, I thought. The chief sub would pass them some pieces of paper (sometimes bundled together with a paper clip) which I could see had been ripped off a clattering teleprinter housed in a giant wooden cabinet in adjoining room. 'Do me twenty seconds on that,' he would say.

The sub would read the papers, insert copy paper, carbon and yellow undersheet in the typewriter and type furiously for two or three minutes, before handing it back to the chief sub. Then he would resume his reading of the *Evening Standard* or, in one case, the *Sporting Life*. So this is TV news I said to myself. I said it to myself because there was no one else to say it to – at least no one who seemed slightly interested in who I was, why I was there and what I was meant to do. At least, I thought, I am wearing a suit.

And then, a lady sub, who had been

studiously doing a story that took her rather longer than the normal three minutes, spoke. 'Are you a trainee?'

'Fraid so,' I joshed. And then thought: Why am I apologising? It's terrific to be a trainee. I beat a hell of a lot of competition to be here today.

'Which university are you from?'

'Cambridge,' I said. There was silence. 'You a trainee too?' I said eagerly.

'No.'

'Which university are you from?' biting my tongue as soon as I had said it. Why did I assume that everyone there was from university. There was a big wide world out there.

'Hull,' she said.

And I was relieved. She was a pretty, open-faced girl. Brown curly hair and cheerful eyes and beguiling lips. She could be my friend, I thought, especially as at dinner break after the early bulletin, she took me to the canteen and let me eat with her. Her name was Sue Thomas, and although we were eventually to become working colleagues, we never became great friends. But she was the one who spoke to me first, and I bless her for that. She, too, must have benefited from Whiteley's law of the workplace. She attained dazzling heights at ITN and became exceedingly senior and respected, masterminding ITN's political coverage and relationships with various governments on the highest level. I have seen her around over the years, and often reminded her of our first memorable conversation. She is a Dame of the British Empire now and seems to have no recollection of the event.

I returned to the joys of Walthamstow later that first night. We were not released until after the late bulletin, at that time transmitted at five to nine. I ruminated on the events of the day. I had read all the papers, I had watched the bulletins go out from the control room, I had eaten egg and chips, I had seen Reginald Bosanquet, I had looked in vain for the lady director with the double barrelled name just to ascertain how posh she really was and I watched all the subs go off for a drink at ten past nine without inviting me. I was a trainee, supposedly. No one had offered to train me in anything. I had not been called upon to give my well-rehearsed views on the use of underlay in the title sequence. I had not been called upon to go out reporting and do my piece to camera, in a style so well honed that morning on Walthamstow station. I had not even sat in the background of any newsroom shots. Still, it was only the first day, but I was impatient, I could not wait too long for fame, if not fortune.

I wondered how Celia had got on at the

Daily Mail. I thought it was too late to ring her that night so I'd check with her in the morning. Next day at lunchtime I stood again, like a seasoned veteran, on the platform at Walthamstow. It still seemed a strange time to be going to work. I bought the *Daily Mail* – still then a broadsheet. As I casually flicked through, I saw something which I could hardly believe. There was a story – atop the page on page five. A big headline *and* a byline. It said 'by Celia Haddon'. There it was in twelve point bold caps. I was stunned. While I had been reading the *Standard* and eating egg and chips, she had been out reporting on her first day, and had actually got a byline. How could that happen? I had been editor of *Varsity* – she was only deputy. And now her name was in print. No public evidence at all of my efforts on my first day at work. Something must be done. 'Well done Celia, a byline on your first day,' I hypocritically muttered over the phone. I was deeply depressed, especially when the second day, and the third, and the fourth, turned out identical in under achievement. Indeed nil achievement for me. Just where was my career going? I know ITN didn't give on-screen credits, but I just wanted some tangible evidence for those at home and in the outside world that I had arrived and my career was well on track.

Actually, it was to get a whole lot worse. I wasn't angry with Celia personally, just ever so jealous. So, imagine when, one whole year later, and my ITN career was something less than spectacular (my activities being mainly confined to the football results and stories on Bank Holiday traffic jams, which always contained the words 'the great trek home') I heard that someone who was on my staff at *Varsity,* and therefore, a whole year below me, had also got a job as a television trainee. Not at ITN, I was relieved to hear, but at ATV. He immediately started work on a programme which transmitted on Saturday nights *On the Braden Beat.* I watched the first edition eagerly to see what he'd done or what evidence of his involvement there was. Nothing discernable at least on the programme. So that was a relief. But then, to my horror, on the screen under 'researcher' there was his name, in black and white, in front of millions of viewers. And that horror turned to absolute fury when I myself flicked through the *TV Times.* There I saw he got a printed credit, just below the set designer and above the studio director. So there we had it. A chap junior to me, younger, getting not only an on-screen, but also a printed credit, week after week after week. It was intolerable. The name in question – it was Matthew Robinson.

Matthew who had courted my sister, and who did a roaring trade selling bicycles and gowns at the start of each academic year. Now he was undoubtedly more famous than I.

To be fair, Matthew had some style. He moved into an expensive flat with advertising man Robin Wight and ex Cambridge Union President John Costello. They furnished it entirely from Peter Jones, and threw a huge party, at which Norman Lamont asked me to lend him five pounds so he could take out a young lady he'd met there (this was 1966). Fifteen years later, when he was a junior minister, he eyed me across a crowded room at a Tory party conference, and pressed a five pound note into my none too eager hand. I had expected a bit of interest at least.

So, in those early days, I sat there on the subs table, each day waiting to be given a story of substance to cope with. The chief sub would often pass me – which is a euphemistic word for chuck – a bundle of tape. 'Do me a spare on that,' he barked.

A spare was a story that would only get read in an on-air emergency – if, say, a filmed story failed to arrive. Now, the chief sub did not care for the likes of me. Trainees. *Varsity* types. Just know alls. They think they've got the star quality. Fast track. Having it easy, while chaps like him had come up the hard way. Worked their way up from provincial weeklies.

I don't blame him for not liking me. I wouldn't have taken to me if I had been him. So he was damned if he was going to make life easy for the likes of me. A regular routine developed. He'd chuck the tape at me, saying how much he wanted – ten or even fifteen seconds. I'd write it and gingerly check it over. He would then read it. He'd then make a tutting noise with his tongue against the back gum, raise his eyebrows in apparent frustration and show it to the copy taster sitting alongside. He, actually, was genial enough, but he liked a bit of sport and mischief. He too, tutted in total agreement and they exchanged conspiratorial grins. The chief sub made flourishing annotations and corrections and either passed it back to me or sent it through the process to be typed up.

I was terrified of him. Talk about having it easy. No way. Sleepless nights were plentiful, relief only came when it was the other chief sub on shift the next day. But we boys were there to learn and, looking back now, I reckon his attitude was quite correct. One Thursday afternoon, four weeks into my employment, there was the familiar routine. My perusal of the *Evening Standard* was interrupted.

'Do me twenty seconds on this.' It was

about a horse race. A big one. There had apparently been a steward's inquiry and a controversial result. I wrote up the copy based on the agency tape and duly passed it over. The usual ritual followed. It was flung back at me. 'Put the starting price on.'

Where do I get that? It wasn't on the tape. And, coming from a sheltered childhood, I didn't know what the 'starting price' was.

'The betting,' the sub reading the *Sporting Life* whispered to me, on my discreet enquiry. Why wasn't he doing the story, I wondered. Anyway, I resorted to my trusty friend – the well-thumbed *Evening Standard*. The betting was duly inserted, the story handed in, and unbelievably duly approved by the chief sub. It went through all the processes. I watched as the output editor approved it. I watched as the newscaster, Andrew Gardner, read it and I could see he made no alterations to my words. I saw it checked by the director who needed to decide what visuals should be inserted. It was then typed out by the PA on the grey pieces of paper which made up the master script and then passed to the teleprompt to be typed up on the teleprompt roll. Later on I watched the rehearsal for the bulletin on closed circuit. The story was actually in the running order. I was beside myself with excitement. It might actually go out! And it did. My story.

Words that I had written myself. Broadcast to millions, actually read out by Andrew Gardner. I swelled with joy and pride. Nobody else, by the way, seemed to think it was anything special. They all still went off to the White Horse after the bulletin without inviting me. Going home on the bus, I was living in Battersea by now, I looked in at all the lighted windows of all the houses and flats from my seat on the top deck. I wondered if they had all seen the news, bound to have done. Everyone watched ITV. They would all have heard my words. Fantastic. More viewers than Celia's got readers!

I slept well that night. I was on my way.

On shift again at two the next day. Into the lift I got.

'Good show last night Mr Frost,' said the lift man. 'I really enjoyed your interview.'

'Do you think so?' said David. 'Thank you, thank you so much. Thank you. Super of you to say so. Terrific. Thank you so very much.' Thus making the liftman's year.

My TV hero, who was just four years older than me, got out at the sixth floor. I was alone with the liftman for one floor.

Would he congratulate me on my story on the news. The crisp way in which the controversy over the big race was told? The air of authority which Andrew Gardner gave to the words that I had written, precise, accurate and clear. He must have seen it, if he'd seen David Frost's programme. Not a murmur.

As I turned down the corridor towards the newsroom, there was David Nicholas, the deputy editor, walking towards me from the far end of the corridor. Now corridor encounters are always difficult. You try to pretend you are not really there, or if you are, you really shouldn't be. You pretend that the other person has more right to be there than you do and you don't really know where to look. David Nicholas did know where to look. Straight at me and it was a long, long corridor. We closed on each other. He still fixed his gaze on me. The corridor seemed to go on forever. It was like the scene in *High Noon*, apart from the fact it was two o'clock in the afternoon.

Now David was, and is, a kindly man. Soft spoken, sounding at first a little hesitant and nervous, but it's just his Welshness. A genuinely nice chap, and incidentally, one of the best practitioners ever of television news producing.

'Ah, Richard,' he said. He knows my name, I glowed. 'Did you do that story about the big race at Ascot yesterday?'

Inwardly I swelled further with pride. 'Yes, I did Mr Nicholas.'

'Well done boyo – only been here four weeks and already writing first class bulletin material. Keep it up and you'll be up there with the other trainees. Look how successful they are. Peter Sissons, Sheridan Morley, Brian Wenham. All of them rising fast. Good work. You were obviously the right choice.'

That is what he didn't say.

'What betting did you put?'

'Eight to two,' I said.

'And where did you get that from?'

'The *Evening Standard*.'

'Well, there's a problem,' he said. 'For a start, there is no such price as eight to two. It would be four to one. What you wrote down was the weight of the jockey. Eight stone, two pounds. It was broadcast to millions. We have been inundated with complaints. It's been a hell of a morning. The betting organisations have been in turmoil.'

He was, as I say, a kindly man. But we both knew that things did not augur well for my career as an ace television newsman.

FROM KINGSWAY TO KIRKSTALL

In the early summer of 1967, the Independent Television Authority announced the winners of the new ITV franchises. This marked the biggest shake up of ITV since its original structure which had stood since 1955, was to dictate the shape of the commercial channel and was to last, more or less intact, until the Nineties.

Rediffusion, a company which as Associated Rediffusion was the very first to go on the air, had certainly done nothing wrong, and probably a great deal of things right, especially when you think they were starting from scratch and were run by a bridge full of retired naval officers. *This Week* was as sturdy a current affairs programme as you can get, certainly a serious rival for *Panorama*. Drama under Peter Willes was strong and inventive, game shows flourished under Hughie Greene and Michael Miles and whoever will forget that the weekend started here with *Ready, Steady, Go*. So, they didn't have a local news. Well, that wasn't good, but local news programmes seldom work in the Capital. The family feeling which unites regional viewers to their company doesn't work in London. If you dwell in Mill Hill, then you can be forgiven for being less than interested in what happens in Tulse Hill. So Rediffusion had to merge with ABC, which had energetically provided entertaining weekends in the Midlands and the North. *Armchair Theatre* is still remembered, as is *Tempo* the arts programme to rival *Monitor*. I am sure someone remembers *The Other Man's Farm*

and *Sing along with Joe, Mr Piano Henderson.*
Holiday Town Parade was the greatest and
should be living at this hour. Thames Television was the result of this forced marriage,
and in its turn departed in the Nineties and
is generally sadly missed. ATV got the
Midlands all week, and Granada had to
move out of Yorkshire to make way for the
new Yorkshire company. Their consolation
prize was getting Granadaland to themselves all seven days.

Granada, for all its pioneering efforts in
every genre of television broadcasting, both
then and since, did little for the Yorkshire
area. A single, remote-controlled camera
studio in Leeds was never operational due,
according to Granada, to 'union difficulties', which apparently lasted for nearly
a decade. Occasionally reporters like Brian
Trueman and Michael Parkinson would
cross the Pennines for a couple of days and
enjoy the pleasure of an overnight stay in
Bradford, and were expected to return to
Manchester with half a dozen stories for the
local news magazine. Nevertheless, ITV
viewers in Yorkshire liked what Granada
did, at least because as Northerners they felt
that Sidney Bernstein and Co were doing
their bit for the whole north of England,
indeed the Granada on-air station ident had
the words 'From the North' above the
Granada logo. Anyway, the northern region

of the Beeb was also very much Manchester run in spite of the wonderful efforts of Barney Colehan and Alfred Bradley in Leeds, producing first class entertainment. Programmes like *Sooty* and *The Good Old Days* in Barney's case and gritty northern radio drama from Alfred Bradley, nurturing such talents as Stan Barstow, David Storey, John Braine, Keith Waterhouse and Willis Hall.

I greatly enjoyed the gossip of this time, with the rumours and speculation, but like most people really was unaware of the true extent of the deception and double speak that was going on round restaurant tables and in discreet meeting rooms. Certainly, nobody asked me to lunch, to sound me out, not even anyone contemplating the Yorkshire franchise. The trouble was, nobody had heard of me. The only consolation was that to the best of my knowledge, neither had anyone contacted Matthew Robinson! But one very big name had certainly been approached.

One of the groups bidding for the Yorkshire contract had signed up Paul Fox, then one of the most influential men in the BBC. He was the fearsome Controller of BBC1 and dubbed Paul 'Ratings' Fox by *Private Eye*. He had been with the BBC since joining as a scriptwriter on television newsreel at Alexandra Palace at the end of the Forties and worked his way up to control BBC1 by way of editing *Sportsview* and *Panorama,* and the current affairs group. He was a very big fish indeed, and to land him in your team was a great prize.

But Paul, like some others in the BBC, who had been discreetly approached, had to keep his involvement confidential in the extreme and this meant that meetings had to be particularly secret. Paul himself tells how there was one meeting in Leeds which he just had to attend. It was almost a case of trilby and dark glasses, Paul being an impressive figure who you would certainly notice sitting among the Leeds businessmen on the train. At the end of the day he arrived back at King's Cross with his secret safe from both interested parties, or indeed satisfied that he had given nothing away on any casual encounter on the trip. Imagine his dismay when on stepping out onto platform three at Kings Cross he, and the rush hour crowds, heard an announcement booming out over the tannoy.

'Would Mr Paul Fox of the BBC, passenger from Leeds, report to the Station Master's office.'

'Oh yes,' the interested parties could have asked, 'and just what was Paul Fox doing in Leeds?'

Well, there could have been a dozen legitimate BBC related reasons, of course, like entertaining Barney Colehan to a well-earned lunch. But Wiseacres could doubtless have put two and two together and come to an interesting conclusion. Incidentally, Paul's group did not get the franchise but, of course, he duly arrived at Yorkshire Television in his own right later, and was to ensure that YTV punched above its weight for nearly twenty years.

Meanwhile, at ITN we observed all this restructuring, a worrying time for everybody else, with a certain amount of effortless disdain. It didn't affect us, we thought, ITN will go on. Our franchise isn't up for grabs. Actually, it did affect us because Sir Geoffrey Cox emerged as the Deputy Chairman of the consortium which won the Yorkshire franchise and would therefore be departing. This, almost on the eve of the launching of *News at Ten*, the baby he had struggled for years to conceive, and which was due to greet the world in early July. It was a blow to lose a leader whom everybody respected, and it was a measure of that respect that there emerged a spectacular list of top class editors and personalities who were rumoured to be in the running for his job.

I was quietly flattered to think that the great Sir Geoffrey would be heading up to the land of my fathers or perhaps, more appropriately, 'the land of me dad's'. I didn't know how he would rate the joys of Moortown compared to the salon society of Hampstead but I thought it was a great achievement for Yorkshire TV to attract a man of this calibre. I hadn't heard of share options in those days! Mind you, I'm sure he hadn't either.

So I paused briefly in my busy life to half think the unthinkable ... should I, who had left my native Yorkshire for the greatest honours and glittering career that a Cambridge third class degree could bestow, should I, who so proudly displayed the (home made) ITN sticker on my front windscreen, should I, the man to whom Andrew Gardner once said, 'I'm nice to young people like you because one day you'll be my boss', should I throw up all this and return to Leeds? There was a chance that YTV might have located in Harrogate – a nicer class of place altogether, but Leeds in 1968! It was indeed the original home of Mr Marks and Mr Spencer, but I tell you that Mr Harvey and Mr Nichols would not have been seen dead in the place in those days. Besides, I was getting on nicely at ITN. Rarely being trusted with the racing results or even the Inter Cities Fairs Cup, in which I famously couldn't tell my Arsenal from my Bilbao, I was becoming an expert on Vietnam. This usually meant writing thirty seconds of commentary over

American news agency film. When ITN sent out their own men, notably Sandy Gall and his brave crews, that precious film on arrival at ITN was handled by bright script writers like Peter Sissons or benign journalists of the old school like Cyril Manning. Peter Sissons, by the way, was one of those people who always looked busy. He wasn't one for mooching around the newsroom in quiet periods, picking up the papers and glancing at them for the sixth time like the rest of the script writing team. For him, it seemed, there were never any quiet periods, he was always bashing away on his typewriter, jacket off, tie loosened. I always wondered what he was doing. Funnily enough, thirty years later, I saw him in the BBC newsroom and as I approached he was typically bashing away at his computer and peering earnestly at the screen. I tried to sneak a glance to see what he was working at. I may be mistaken as my eyesight isn't good these days but I think he was rapturously engaged in the newsreaders' roster for the next three weeks.

However, back at ITN, Peter also read the commentary voiceover when film items came on. The thinking at the time was that a second voice, newsreel style, added pace and authority to the bulletin. I think it did. Peter also read the news headlines late at night and at weekends. I swear I can remember him having pens and a comb in the top pocket of his sports jacket but perhaps this is only my imagination. Peter though was a star trainee and he later deservedly went on to win glittering prizes. He almost gave his life for ITN being badly wounded in Biafra. Later he became industrial correspondent and then anchorman of Channel Four news. He too was on the screen on the first day of Channel Four – but not before me – I was two hours earlier!

There was one weekend when I too got a glittering prize. Asked by David Phillips, an energetic and in my view the most talented of all the bulletin editors, to script a piece about some spring event in Hyde Park that Sunday afternoon, I persuaded David to let me have the film cut to piano music, and run like a silent movie, putting captions up in black and white script between the sequences, hence no commentary. David, who anyway was a bit of a risk taker, readily agreed to give it a go. His enthusiasm was not shared either by the film editing department, graphics, who had to make the captions, or the studio director. It also baffled the PA who on asking why there were no out words on the cue sheet as I had put 'Out Cue "Jingle, jingle, jangle"', was less than amused.

Anyway, the piece duly went out on the teatime bulletin to the general mystification or dare I even say cynicism of the rest of the script writing team. For some reason I was not invited to the White Horse at supper break. I felt, frankly, rather foolish and while I respected David for allowing it to go through, I desperately hoped that Sir Geoffrey Cox hadn't been watching at home. The next day I expected a memo or at least an informal meeting with that nice David Nicholas in the corridor. Nothing was said and nothing was heard until the early editions of the *Evening News* arrived. I was aware of a general harrumph from the top desk, as senior figures, of whom I was totally in awe, craned over to read the TV review.

'Whiteley, you're in the papers.' That was Tom Hutchinson, a genial but mischievous copy taker. He liked me, but particularly enjoyed watching me getting into bother with the chief sub. 'Come and take a look.'

The faces of the senior figures were set in stone. My heart sank seven floors, and I wished I could have been swallowed up by the crowds on Kingsway.

What went through my mind was: ITN standards falling, lazy work, slipshod effort, dumbing down ... James Green, the TV critic, had reviewed that Sunday teatime nine-minute bulletin (never heard of before) and had liked the Hyde Park item. Words like 'inventive', 'novel', 'cheeky', swam before my eyes as I peered nervously over the chief sub's shoulder. He was reading it in silence, but there was more. My own name swam before me... The first time I had seen it in print in a proper newspaper since the *Shipley Guardian* reported my promotion to a sixer in the Wesleyan Methodist Cubs. James Green had indeed done his research. 'I gather the script writer was a young trainee Richard Whiteley. Congratulations to him and producer David Phillips.' It was a magic moment. The column was passed round the newsroom and read widely. People shot surreptitious glances at me. I saw Alan Pearce the NUJ union man, pleasant but someone who also made me nervous, making a beeline. Would he be bringing the formal congratulations of the NUJ? Would I now be upped from a probationer to a full member? Anything was possible now. surely. And when did Peter Sissons get his name in the papers?

'I've been going through your things. You haven't paid your subs. And you weren't at the last meeting. You're expected to attend.'

He strode off. Alas, it seemed the influence of James Green in the ITN newsroom was sparse. And, I noticed for the second night running, I was left on my own at supper break.

There are lots of random memories of the ITN years. Reginald Bosanquet, a man with humour, breeding and fun oozing from every pore... Entering the newsroom and putting a sympathetic arm round me one evening after the supper break, scanning the lino-floored, wooden desked, fluorescent tube lit, yellow walled, cramped vista, which was the sum total of the glamour of one of the world's most vibrant and successful newsrooms, he said, 'Richard, I want to share something with you.'

I naturally expected tips on how to succeed without really trying, how to eventually impress the chief sub, or at least, coming from this great man, the secret of eternal life.

'See all the girls here,' he gestured, and I took in the assembled cast, all beavering away – production assistants, news desk assistants, sub editors, teleprompt operators – all of whom I was generally too timid to speak to. 'See them,' he continued, 'how are you getting on with them?'

'Well,' I stammered, thinking, fancy him being even remotely interested in how junior life is making out. 'Well, they are all very nice and they are all very patient with me,' I replied.

'Yes, they're all very nice, I can tell you,' he chortled. 'I've had 'em all, except one.' And with that off his chest, he chuckled his way out of the newsroom and up the corridor to his own office. But which one, Reggie, which one? I still lay awake at nights worrying about this.

And there was Nigel Ryan. Not a household name but an impressive man in the news business who was to become Editor at the young age of thirty-seven after Sir Geoffrey's departure. Nigel worked on a weekly programme *Reporting 66* based up the corridor, but would often stride round the newsroom, tall, thin, dark wavy hair, slightly tanned olive skin, dark double breasted suit, often fiddling with keys in his fingers, speaking in a clear, rather clipped English, Reggieish sort of way. In fact, if you closed your eyes and Reggie, Sandy Gall, an old Etonian producer called Anthony Rouse and Nigel Ryan, paraded in front of you and said 'what are you having dear boy ... would you fancy a large one?' you wouldn't be able to tell them apart. It was the ITN voice.

Nigel had enjoyed great success dashing round Africa for Reuters news agency in the troubles of the Sixties. Multi-lingual, stylish and extremely quick and resourceful, I suspect he was, or could have been, up there with the great foreign correspondents – James Cameron, René Cutforth, Alastair Cooke, William Boot. He was also a master of creativity in the expenses department. This, the journalistic equivalent of the 'knowledge', is a fine art which is passed down jealously from one generation to

141

another. Legend has it, that while encountering transport difficulties in the Congo, he hired a car and drove several thousand miles across the Dark Continent. On his return, he was called into the General Manager to explain a sum spent on car hire.

'This surely can't be right,' said the GM in a patient, yet threatening way. It was ninety pounds.

'Gosh, no, no, of course not, terribly sorry,' said Nigel, looking at the sheets and quietly inserting another nought on the grand total before sweeping out of the office.

With the arrival of *News at Ten*, Nigel headed up a team called Unit Two, a small department making advance features. I was thrilled to be chosen to join this. It would get me out of the office, and by now I had a credit on *Reporting 67* as 'programme editor'. This went universally unobserved, even by James Green, but in my own estimation, at least, I had achieved a notch on the career plan. Nigel had an adjacent office to ours and I was aware of the fact that Ruth, his secretary who sat with us, spent much of her time fending off phone calls and invitations to him from many of London's fashion glitterati of the time.

'Nigel,' she'd call out. 'It's Alexandra. She wants lunch tomorrow.'

'Tell her I'm in Swaziland. Sudden coup. Just got to go.'

Or 'Nigel, it's Millicent. Just in from Paris. Can you do the American Bar at the Savoy at six tonight?' And so on. Nigel was not to be tempted.

One day he really was trapped. The editor of the glossiest of glossies actually appeared in reception unannounced, asking for Nigel. Reception was just opposite his own office, and therefore, there was no escape by the main door. But exhibiting before my very eyes all the pazazz and resourcefulness which was to make him such a spectacular editor of ITN, he opened some French windows which gave out from his office onto a seventh floor balcony, and probably I fancy, more like Inspector Clouseau than James Bond or John Pilger, he edged deftly along this narrow ledge, high above the Kingsway traffic.

On his way he had to pass Sir Geoffrey Cox's office, giving him a cheery wave as he did so. It was all part of a day's work. At the time Sir Geoffrey was briefing the Chairman of the Independent Television Authority on the current state of *News at Ten*. History does not relate the relevant reactions. Then, hopping over barriers like those men of the SAS at the Embassy siege years later, he was seen knocking at the window next to the foreign desk in the newsroom, where an astonished secretary, Jane Taylor, let him in. From there escape was simple. Down the backstairs, and lost in the anonymity of London streets.

Gordon Honeycombe was my first famous pal. Like the other main newscasters, apart from Reginald Bosanquet, he was the regulation six foot three minimum, à la Andrew Gardner and Peter Snow. He was an Oxford man, but an actor by inclination and not a journalist. Sir Geoffrey took him on, doubtless for his excellent diction and his unique appearance. He was balding before the days when Clive James made hair loss sexy. He also had, of course, a lovely name, as indeed did many of ITN's talent ... Snow, Bosanquet, Gardner, Honeycombe, Chataway, Ludovic Kennedy, Ian Trethowan. I don't think I'd have ever made it with a name like Whiteley. Rudyard Whiteley perhaps. Anyway, back to Gordon. On days when he wasn't newscasting, Gordon, eager to learn, did shifts on the subs desk, like we other backroom boys. Although he was by far the most famous TV star I had ever met, he was engagingly modest and unassuming.

We didn't get out much at ITN. Indeed, in my very first year, the only time I left the building in the line of duty was one Budget Day when my job was to sit in a phone box in the reporters' gallery at Westminster to keep the line open for Julian Havilland, as he would rush in from the press benches, grab the phone and report on the latest measures. That was instant news gathering Sixties style. While I was happy to be part of news in the making, with even so humble a position, I was disappointed that my long held ambition of being at a desk in the background of the studio shots was thereby thwarted. Luckily in those days, there were regular Budgets and mini Budgets and so I soon assumed my much longed for role sitting three people behind and one to the right of Alastair Burnet.

So my forays into the wide world as a dashing young newsman were limited, but the late shift at weekends was a bit of a thrill. With the canteen closed, we were forced to make our own feeding arrangements. This meant a trip down the Aldwych and across the Strand to the exotic Lancaster Grill which nestled on the left hand side of Waterloo Bridge. Gordon, as the weekend newscaster, would sportingly come along. I was very impressed that this great man would choose to have chicken and chips with us. Surely as a face so well known to the nation he would have more appropriate arrangements, but apparently not. And so it was with no little excitement that I eagerly plodded along beside him as we made our way to the Grill. Although resplendent in hat, thereby disguising his trademark pate and glasses which he never wore on TV, muffler and green great coat, looking more like Sherlock Holmes than the news icon that he surely was, he could not disguise his height. I experienced vicarious pleasure by walking in the company of a great man who was not recognised so that I was the only person who knew who he was, ... or him being recognised, ... thereby becoming the first of the Himoffs, and me as his friend walking side by side basking in reflected glory.

Every day the newsdesk produced their schedule of what the crews were doing, and I constantly scanned this for news of what if anything was happening at home in Yorkshire. The answer was very little. In fact, in all my three years there I can remember ITN cameras only filming twice in the Ridings. Once when the Queen opened a shopping centre at Seacroft in Leeds, and another occasion when the cooling towers of Ferrybridge Power Station collapsed. So my native county was not a very hot news area, and therefore, had little appeal for an ambitious TV newsman like me. I subsequently learned that most 'news' only happens if there are journalists and cameras handy to report it. Come the arrival of YTV in 1968, and thus a dedicated news team, the place was never out of the headlines, e.g. the Black Panther, the Yorkshire Ripper, the Scarborough Hotel falling into the sea, Hillsborough, Bradford City, Flixborough explosion, Yorkshire Cricket Club rows etc, etc.

So, I was enjoying life at ITN especially with the arrival of *News at Ten*, working on Unit Two, preparing advance features and backgrounders. I worked with Peter Fairley, the unflappable science correspondent of the *Evening Standard* who also doubled as ITN's space expert. He was putting together immaculate yet seemingly fanciful pieces about America's current and projected adventures in space to a generally incredulous production team, and indeed more incredulous TV audience at home. Later, that team with Peter and David Nicholas and Frank Miles, dominated television coverage of the moon landings and subsequent space stories for a decade to come.

I watched footage coming in from Aden and the Six Day War, feeling very important, under the guidance of a very calm, pipe smoking producer called Eric Stevens. Alan Hart was a swashbuckling reporter to outdo them all. He joined ITN at something like twenty years of age, as a syndication scriptwriter. Because he worked throughout the night, he was entitled to a minicab home in the early hours. Living in deepest Kent as he did, these bills mounted up and eventually Geoffrey Cox thought it would be cheaper to put him on the reporters' rota and send him home by tube or train at a reasonable hour. Good journalistic judgment Geoffrey, but bad financial planning. As a reporter, Alan began to realise the benefits of the good life that is to be had on the road. He discovered a taste for oysters, then the epitome of lavish living. In my case at the time, the epitome of lavish living being an avocado pear. Alan's expenses were apparently nearly as legendary as Nigel Ryan's. They are still subject to the fifty-year rule of secrecy at ITN, lest other reporters pick up a few ideas. The one story I do remember concerned his efforts in the Indo-Pakistan war. Alan was reporting from some deserted region in hostile border territory. Montezuma's revenge was rampant. Legend has it that one entry read, 'To arse wiping ... twenty rupee notes'.

ITN had the first and best of the bullet dodgers. Front line reports from the Middle East were setting new standards in war reporting. One day when Eric Stevens and I were watching newly arrived rushes from Aden, we sat open mouthed as our reporter, crouching, big stick microphone in hand, dodged all over the screen as bullets, he told us, were flying in all directions. This was nail biting reporting, seat of the pants stuff, any cliché you want. I remember thinking, if the reporter is dodging the bullets, where is the cameraman standing and how come he's so still? I thought there would be a special technique for this and perhaps there was. At one point Eric ordered the film to be stopped and re-run. As the reporter was dancing about, you could see a white-coated waiter, albeit in negative, and therefore black-coated, walking left to right of frame in the background carrying a tray of drinks. Surely it could not be that the brave ITN hero was delivering his powerful piece from the lush gardens of the Aden Hilton. Perish the thought!

ITN was full of giants in those days, both in front of the camera and significantly behind it ... the producers, editors, technicians, and above all Sir Geoffrey Cox and David Nicholas. Sir Geoffrey with his international background, a political animal of extreme effectiveness, having turned ITN from a low budget and poorly treated member of the ITV family, into a major player in news programming nationwide and worldwide. And his number two David Nicholas, was the best 'sleeves rolled up' TV practitioner of the time. There was nothing he relished more than mounting a 'special' at four hours' notice. But although I was keen as mustard and ambitious, I was never going to shine at ITN. Mike Morris, the trainee who joined with me, and a former *Cherwell* editor from Oxford, stayed on for many years after I left, forging a career which took him from NUJ chief activist in the late Seventies, to Director of Personnel in the Nineties. A poacher well and truly turned gamekeeper.

I often wondered what would have happened to me if I had stayed at ITN. I loved the adrenalin buzz and frantic activity of the control room, the tight deadlines and sheer bravado which set ITN apart from other news broadcasters. It was small, and probably under resourced. But those ITN boys: David Nicholas, Don Horobin, the Home and Foreign News Editors, the brave reporters, Sandy Gall, Alan Hart, Michael Nicholson, Gerald Seymour, Richard Lindley, and especially the camera crews, left the opposition standing on a regular basis. I would never have achieved their status. I expect I would have become a PR man, organising parties.

So Yorkshire TV beckoned. It beckoned beguilingly not particularly because I wanted to leave ITN, far from it. I was beginning to get recognised as a reasonably talented youngster and indeed, had even appeared on the screen, reporting from Leeds, of all places. In fact, it seemed a rather retrograde step to leave London and go to the regions. Most people in the business aspired to do the reverse. But my plan was always to return, say after a year or two, having become rich and famous in Yorkshire and then swanning in to whatever top job there would be in London. How different things turned out. In the event, my little two hundred mile trip from Kingsway to Kirkstall lasted over thirty years.

THE KIRKSTALL ROAD END

I arrived at the Television Centre in Leeds at 9.30 am on 7 April 1968 armed with a guilty secret. It was that Yorkshire Television might have made a terrible mistake when they were recruiting, and a certain Richard Whiteley presented himself. They might have got the wrong man! This is what happened.

I had written to Donald Baverstock, the Director of Programmes, to express an interest ... not actually apply for a job if you see what I mean. As I said, I was very happy at ITN and secondly, I didn't relish the prospect of getting turned down. That is probably why I have only ever had two employers, because I have this terrible fear of rejection. Psychologists please take note. By the same token, I suppose, I refused to have an answering machine at home for years, because I couldn't bear to go home after a day at work, or especially a weekend away, to be told I had got no messages. Even now, with a little to be proud about, I regard the smug, self satisfied and rather patronising tone of the computer generated woman on the mobile message service who says 'You have no messages', as deeply insulting. She seems to relish the fact. Likewise, when she says, 'You have *three* new messages', why does she sound so very surprised?

So, I had no real desire to subject myself to the indignities of the thumbs down, but watching with envy my erstwhile friends and colleagues getting bylines and credits and going to swinging parties in the King's Road, and expense account restaurants in Covent Garden, I did sometimes think that the two o'clock to nine thirty shift to which I was consigned, while exciting in its way, was robbing the current media and social scene of a potential big hitter. ITN was all very anonymous. I had in fact, surreptitiously applied for a couple of other things. For example, a new magazine was about to appear called *London Life*, backed by some bright boys from *The Sunday Times*. This promised extreme trendiness and, at the time, all of London who cared about these things, was talking about it. Through a Cambridge contact, I secured an interview with the features editor who was not overtly impressed with my CV to date. After all, soccer results, motorway pile-ups and scripts on snowstorms around the regions don't exactly provide the best shop window for one's literary or creative ability. But he gave me a task. A sort of literary audition. Apparently, Orson Welles was coming into town. Why didn't I go and interview him, and do a piece for the magazine, after which he'd consider me for a job. Orson Welles! Fancy little me going to interview Orson Welles! It's like asking someone nowadays to interview the Queen. Absolutely impossible. While I had heard of him, of course, I hadn't seen any of his films and remember, these were the days before PR handouts, promotional interviews and eager publicists easing your way into the presence of greatness.

'He's staying at Brown's Hotel.' That was the only information volunteered by my putative employer. 'He's arriving today.'

There was little time for an action plan. I rapidly began to long for the anonymity of the newsroom and the quiet comfort of merely having to type a few lines for Andrew Gardner to read about the latest horror in Vietnam. However, I felt I had to do something, if only at least, to get out of his office with dignity. So I reasoned I should go to Brown's. That was a feat of daring in itself, never having experienced such poshness. The Station Hotel at York had been the summit of my sophistication until then.

On my way there I began to entertain a morbid desire that when I arrived, I would find the hotel had been burnt down, thus making the arrival of Mr Welles unlikely and thus rendering the chance of me interviewing him understandably and excusably impossible. When I turned the corner it was still standing. I arrived without either a notebook or a game plan, or indeed the will to survive. I crept into the hotel and pretended I was on the way to the lavatory. Indeed, I was deeply shocked and confused to find an attendant there who seemed to expect two shillings for the privilege of running the tap for me. So, expensively cleansed, I sat in the lounge and waited, trembling slightly, trying to overhear conversations in case they should be discussing any Orson Welles films, which would give me a clue as to the line my subsequent interview should take. Alas, the muffled American conversations seemed to reveal nothing more than the price of lingerie at Harrods. Eventually, there was a kerfuffle, a slamming of doors, great activity from the uniformed flunkies, and the entrance of this huge man, Mr Orson Welles, I presumed. I sat, shifty eyed, and terrified.

Well, any great ITN reporter for whom fear is an unknown four letter word, would have been straight in there. Imagine Sandy Gall just sitting there and letting the great man march past. Any great newspaper writer would have been in there. Would Jean Rook or Lynda Lee Potter have sat there pretending to read the afternoon tea menu? Of course not. Mr Welles would have been well and truly doorstepped, and the story would have been well and truly delivered. As for me, soccer results king about to turn ace feature writer, I just sat there and froze. There was absolutely no question of me even being able to stand up, never mind approach him with a request for an interview. In fact, even if he had come and sat next to me and asked my opinion of what he should do in his next film, I would have been incapable of competent speech. Even if he had said, 'Young man, I hear you are after a new job, which depends on getting an exclusive interview with me. Well, you look a decent chap. What exactly would you like to know, and would you like a glass of champagne while we talk in my private suite? Time's no problem, I've got all day if it suits you.' I would still have found it impossible to open my mouth.

155

The huge man made slow and regal progress throughout the lobby, so slow in fact that Sandy, or Jean or Lynda could have leapt up and got enough material to write his life story if they had wanted to. But not me. I just sat there, hoping that he hadn't noticed me and wishing I had never heard of the words 'career in journalism' and had become a country parson. So, naturally, there was no story, no interview and no future for me in *London Life*. I also vowed there would be no more job interviews. Hence the letter for Donald which had just suggested a 'chat' (but I think I did point out that I was born in Bradford, I had been mad on TV since I was nine, and was one of the privileged who had been selected to be a trainee at ITN, where, of course, I found myself at the cutting edge of television journalism. Oh, yes, of course I am sure that he would be staffing Yorkshire TV with as many Yorkshire people as possible, just in the same way as the Yorkshire County Cricket Club was made up of a team born solely in the broad acres). So, as you can see, it wasn't really a letter of application it was just a letter which covered several eventualities and which might interest Donald Baverstock.

It was, therefore, quite a surprise, when the phone in our office at ITN rang one afternoon in February of 1968. On the desk next to me sat a very clever ex Winchester and Oxford scholar who, while utterly charming and deliciously witty and mischievous, nevertheless filled me with awe with his high intellect and deep knowledge of all things economic, political, philosophical and cultural. His name, funnily enough, was Richard, and not just that, his surname was Wakely. He was several classes above me in the ability stakes and I knew it. So when his phone rang that afternoon I took little notice. It was probably someone from the Institute of Economic Affairs or the World Bank or the Arts Council, or the Institute of Applied Psychology. I took little notice. He was always getting such calls. After a muttered conversation he replaced the receiver.

'Donald Baverstock wants to see me at three o'clock on Friday,' he declared. He seemed totally mystified by this summons and, I felt, not a little flattered. He, like everyone, was aware of the rat race going on for jobs in the new ITV companies, and I sensed he looked rather pleased with himself. I could see some reason for the summons. He was, after all, a high flier. 'Baverstock on Friday. Fancy that,' he chuntered. 'Well, well well. Didn't know he'd even heard of me.'

I frankly, was not pleased with myself or certainly not with him. In fact, I was furious. It was I, Richard Whiteley, who had deviously written to Baverstock. It was I, Richard Whiteley, who was stressing my Yorkshire roots. It was I, Richard Whiteley, who had coyly decided to move my career on a bit. It was I, Richard Whiteley, who was prepared to give Donald Baverstock the best advice my Yorkshire credentials could provide. Not Richard Wakely. Why did Baverstock ring him out of the blue? Richard Wakely is a southerner. Richard Wakely is doing fine at ITN. What does he want to work for Yorkshire TV for? So, without prolonging this miserable saga for the reader, what happened was easily explained. Baverstock's secretary had correctly asked the switchboard for Richard Whiteley, but had been connected to Richard Wakely. Easily done, of course, but strangely, due to the excellence of Jo Redding and her hello girls on the switchboard, rarely done.

On realising this I did breathe a sigh of relief when we sorted out the fact that Donald wanted to see me, and in fact had never heard of the other Richard W. Mind you, I often think YTV would have been better served if the other Richard had turned up for the interview and had got the job.

In later years when I was driving hell for leather through Knottingley and Goole to report on a bus strike in Grimsby, I used to feel guilty that it was I, and not Richard Wakely on this plum assignment. Would he have just loved it, or would he rather be where he was, attending Prime Ministerial briefings and being sent out to cover peace talks in Rhodesia. I felt as guilty as hell. How would Richard ever forgive me? In fact, Richard Wakely continued his career blissfully unaware that he could have been doing vox pops in Barnsley high street and, having reached a senior position in ITN, he eventually left to pursue a career in the Civil Service.

And so, I duly turned up at the London office of the infant Yorkshire Television grandly situated in Portland Place, just opposite the BBC. As far as I was concerned, of course, it was not a job interview as such, just a general chat about the state of television as we know it, a few observations from me as to how current affairs and television news could be improved, and an opportunity to acquaint Donald Baverstock with some needed tips on Yorkshire, Yorkshire people, and the Yorkshire accent. Tips which he would surely need, Welshman that he was, and thus probably not too familiar with the route of the Leeds-Liverpool canal, or the state of the shoddy industry in Batley. Definitely not an interview. I was quite happy at ITN thank you Mr Baverstock. Just come for a chat.

Donald Baverstock, that whirling dervish of BBC television in the Sixties, was, I have to admit it, not only a daunting character, but something of an icon. Donald Baverstock had invented *Tonight*, the nightly magazine programme which bridged the so-called toddlers' truce, when TV shut down for an hour to let the mums put their kids to bed after tea. The format and technique of current affairs programmes today, nearly forty years later, owes everything to what Donald and his young team pioneered in the mid Fifties. The down the line interview, the film report, either hard hitting or gently humorous, the studio debate between different protagonists, the spoken piece to camera, the topical calypsos of course, and particularly the personality presenters and reporters – Cliff Michelmore, Alan Whicker, Fyffe Robinson, Julian Pettifer. As Head of BBC1 he then commissioned *That was the Week that Was* under Ned Sherrin, a programme that had us all out of the pubs and in front of a television set on Saturday nights at Cambridge. He was the hero of the hour in TV terms and, of course, in my non-applying for a job mode, I just wanted the chance to meet this great man.

However, Donald must have got the definite impression that by sitting supplicantly before him in his office, I *was* actually applying for a job. He was brisk. He said that having been in the job now for six weeks, he was suddenly convinced that God is a Yorkshireman and chortled. He then observed that someone on a train from Leeds had told him that the proper way to eat Yorkshire pudding was on its own before the beef ... that couldn't be true, could it? Being pathetically ingratiating, and also, feeling increasingly nervous and incompetent in the face of this loquacity, I half agreed.

'They used to,' I volunteered, 'in the days of Victorian and Edwardian families. After chapel, the father of the house would serve Sunday dinner and announce to the children that them as eats the most Yorkshire pud, would get the most roast beef ... ha, ha, ha.'

Donald careered on, asking me a question occasionally, 'Had I seen the article in *Encounter* last week by Professor A.J. Ayer about the fallibility of nineteenth century philosophy? Had I read the biography of Balfour by Roy Jenkins? What was my opinion of the Giacometti exhibition at the Tate?'

Good job this wasn't an interview I thought. There were certainly no questions about the fishing fleet in Hull and the prospect of a cod war with Iceland, Yorkshire Cricket's chances in the championship or even J.B. Priestley's importance as a social commentator in the Forties. Anyway, all the questions that Donald asked, he answered himself. He seemed to have little interest in my opinion, thank goodness.

'Well boy,' I heard him say, 'Geoffrey Cox says you're reasonably competent so we'll give you a go. Let's say a two-year contract as assistant producer starting in April. Is that OK? I'll have to check it with Ward. I'll get him to come down.'

I felt well and truly Yorked. There was this top man offering me a two-year contract when I hadn't even applied. These things only happen in novels or Sunday papers. And who, or what was Ward? This was one Yorkshire institution I wasn't aware of. Ward duly arrived, in the person of Mr G.E. Ward Thomas DFC, the managing director of YTV and one of the influential men behind the franchise bid. He was a quiet man to those who didn't know him, with a deep face, black hair and an endearing habit of seeming to suck as he spoke. Over the years I was to realise that Ward Thomas was not only a skilled businessman, but a shrewd and tough television operator and, indeed, a visionary of great quality, masterminding a team which put Yorkshire television at the top of the tree for many years. Ward sat down and looked at me. I was frozen, not unlike my Orson Welles encounter.

'This is Whiteley from ITN. He comes from Bradford. Geoffrey says he is not bad so I am offering him a contract.'

Ward looked me up and down and seemed to suck on the roof of his mouth. I remembered, fatuously, how I worried that ITV was not very posh until I saw the name of Diana Edwards Jones in the *TV Times* credits. Ward Thomas seemed very posh to me.

'Well, if he seems OK to you, it's OK by me,' he breathed.

And that was it. Bingo, by heck, Shazamn, Izzy Wizzy let's get busy. However you wish to phrase it, I was in. I couldn't believe it. I hadn't bargained for this. I almost said, 'There must be some mistake, I just came here for a chat you know, I am a trainee at ITN, on the fast track hoping to produce the election results programme by the time I am thirty. That's my ambition, not to report on the price of tripe in Cleckheaton.'

This of course I didn't say because Donald was barking out his next statement. 'HowmuchyouonatITN?' One word. Must be Welsh.

I had heard that you were always meant to inflate your own salary in these felicitous circumstances when they apparently want you more than you want them. 'Seventeen hundred and fifty,' I replied and immediately regretted it. I felt both slick and guilty.

I had, in fact, added the fifty. I bet they knew. I bet Geoffrey Cox had told them what I earned. They'd cancel the contract and think I was untrustworthy. Perhaps they'd even send for Richard Wakely in his own right. There was a pause.

'Howstwothousandfivehundred?' Another one word question.

This time I really was frozen. This was riches beyond my wildest dreams. The Orson Welles moment was nothing compared to this. Not only did I seem unable to move my lips, my throat was dry, my face was pale, my hands were paralysed, I'm sure my bottom was stuck to the seat and I was equally sure that the way they both looked at me, all my fly buttons were undone as well. This feeling of total shock and paralysis lasted half an hour. In fact, it didn't. It probably lasted a couple of seconds. But it was the most pregnant pause I was ever to make.

Donald Baverstock, a sensitive man beneath the bluster, took thought. Perhaps he felt I was unhappy with this mediocre level of salary, and the inconvenience of moving out of an expensive flat in noisy London, to live rent free at home with the parents, with a two year contract as an assistant producer, when clearly I wasn't going to get anywhere at ITN. After all, I was hardly Sandy Gall, and Peter Sissons was above me getting all the good jobs and, so what about swinging London? I never saw any of it anyway, and those white Triumph Herald Convertibles look really nice, better than an old Ford Anglia that I was running at the time, and two and a half thousand pounds a year thrown in. I was indeed the Viv Nicholson of my time. So hence the pause.

'Well,' said Donald. 'If you're not keen on that, what about another hundred. Two thousand six hundred all right for you, boyyo? So agreed Ward?' Ward nodded, hands were shaken, grins were exchanged. 'Well, boy see you in April. I've enjoyed our chat. It will be nice having you aboard. Goodbye David.'

TROUSERED

It was my first day at Yorkshire Television. I parked my two-tone grey Ford Anglia, which I had bought from my mother, on adjoining wasteland. The entire YTV operation was housed in a modern industrial shed where until recently three thousand pairs of trousers had been made a week. Consequently it was christened by those pioneering staff, the 'trouser factory', and there was a huge expectation of the new programmes which were to be invented and produced from here. A giggling list emerged: 'Zip Cars' – the gritty police series, a late night discussion programme – 'Late Night Turn Up' and, of course, two soaps – 'Crotchroads' and 'Coronation Seat'.

Everything therefore was temporary and increasingly cramped as the number of staff grew daily. At reception you encountered two things: a security man named John who would give you a tip for the 2.30 at Redcar (I, chastened by my salutary experience of the whole horse racing business at ITN, always declined), and an Orwellian notice which said 'Keep it moving, we're on air in eighty-three days', or whatever it was, counting down every day. The actual studios and, grand they were to be, were being built on a site right next door. Leeds City Council had been unseemingly co-operative and speedy in helping to set up this venture with YTV having to get on the air in a mere thirteen months, assembling programme staff, air time sales staff, and most of all, technicians to run the studio centre, then the first in the world designed and built for the latest development – colour TV. Getting on air was a massive task, especially as YTV was the fifth 'network company'. A new road was built, endearingly named by the council, 'Studio Road'. I have driven up and down it so many times now, it should have a more relevant name like 'Whiteley's Way', and no, before you ask, it's not a dead end!

On arrival there was a note for me. It was from Tony Essex, the much admired documentary maker poached from the BBC. He was sorry he couldn't be there to meet me, but could I put in a bit of work researching the trawler tragedies which had benighted Hull that winter. He gave me a few numbers to phone and suggested I might even want to spend a few days in Hull to really get to grips with the job. Well, by now I had reconciled myself to not being in Harrogate, and, in fact, Leeds was going to be OK. But I had hardly given up London life only to be sent to Hull!

'Hello, I've arrived at YTV all flash from London to get you on the air.'

'Go to Hull,' said YTV. Very funny.

As I rather soulfully read and re-read my battle orders, I heard a large sniff behind me, then a cough and smelt the whiff of cigar smoke.

'Sending you to Hull are they?' he observed. 'They've been looking for some-one to go for a fortnight.'

This was the voice of a man who with such perfect eyesight, he could read memos at fifty yards, and even better if they were upside down on someone else's desk. It was the man to whom I owe so much, Michael Partington. I was delighted to meet up with him again. He had left Anglia last summer and had joined Yorkshire Television as one of the early staff, as senior presenter, senior reporter, and political editor – that's what it said on his business card. He had every right to be there, being the son of a well-known Harrogate doctor and, indeed, having been editor of the *Pudsey News* at the tender age of twenty-two. Michael, as befits an early arrival, had the best desk in the trouser factory. It was always very neat and tidy with his Samsonite briefcase on top and blotter and pens tastefully arranged. He also had a Toblerone type triangular wooden name plate which said 'Michael G. Partington, Senior Presenter, Reporter and Interviewer'. I eventually was to get one too. It just said 'R. Whiteley'.

I never did manage to get to Hull on that assignment. Michael was magnificent. From ten o'clock that morning, he immediately took me under his wing. Coffee, lunch, teabreak, drinks at early doors. Michael, a super teller of tales, always punctuated with a huge snorty laugh at the end, regaled me with a history of YTV from the July of last year when he joined, to the present day. And this one-man show took from Monday until Friday, the first week of my career with YTV. Michael should be writing this chapter. He had an opinion on everybody and everything, certainly a name for everybody, some of them even complimentary!

So those early days passed, me listening to the story of the sackings so far, the rows, the sex, political chicanery, all the things indeed which make life in the media so delightful. In truth, Tony Essex did not know what to do with me or why I was there. I was not an obvious film maker, nor I fancy, was I assiduous enough to be a researcher. I think he thought of me as one of Donald's boys destined for the local programme, which I suspect I did too. I always imagined I would end up doing the six o'clock magazine show, although certainly never on the screen. Chaps like Michael Partington were earmarked for roles like that.

As the spring days gave way to the lengthening evenings of summer, so the cast of characters who would open YTV grew and grew. Work was already in progress. Tony Essex was creating a children's series, filmed in the Yorkshire Dales, about a farm lad in the First World War called *Tom Grattan's War*. Michael Blackstad was making a schools series seductively called *I am an Engineer*. He was looking for a presenter, but somehow I didn't fancy that. Peter Willes had moved in as Head of Drama moving the whole of the Rediffusion drama department to YTV, but the lack of completed studios in Leeds required him to carry on making his top class productions in London. The outside broadcast vans had arrived. These were being used already by Jess Yates to produce hours of children's programmes from a nearby church hall. *Jimmy Green's Time Machine* was one and another, a puppet show intriguingly called *Mr Trimble*. I know it's cheeky, but whenever I see the Ulster politician, it takes me back. Jess Yates was an old showbiz hand, both as a performer and a very efficient producer. He was able to bring in scores of programmes with all star casts, consisting mainly of old friends who owed him a favour for giving them a break, and he always brought them in cheap. He is still remembered for *Junior Showtime,* in which a procession of precocious but talented youngsters from nine to sixteen, paraded themselves in various guises of costume, singing songs from the shows meant for people three times their age. From this troupe emerged Mark Curry, later of *Blue Peter*, Kathryn Apanowicz of *Angels* and *EastEnders,* Rosemarie Ford of *The Generation Game,* Joe Longthorne of world-wide fame, and many others.

Jess took over presenting *Stars on Sunday* when his original choice, Liz Fox, decided she was to be a serious newswoman at ITN.

It became a huge show, and while the executives couldn't decide whether it was a religious programme or an entertainment, the audiences loved it every Sunday night. The cast was top quality. I met Gracie Fields in the studio corridor, I met Dame Vera Lynn in make up, and Shirley Bassey too. In fact, I can reveal how I nearly achieved what the Germans couldn't – incapacitating Vera Lynn. I was interviewing her on the *Stars on Sunday* set, walking up a big, sweeping staircase. We were singing 'We'll Meet Again' looking into each other's eyes, when I noticed the stairs ended in two steps' time. I grabbed Vera by the hand rather clumsily but stopped the Dame plunging twelve feet to the studio floor, and certain injury. On one famous visit, while appearing for two weeks at the nearby Batley Variety Club, Shirley Bassey was every inch the superstar while recording a number for *Sez Lez* on the Thursday and the Friday. The fee was totally in line with her superstar status and so were her demands. A sigh of relief was heard round the studio when she finally left after a traumatic two days, to go off to her late night show at Batley. Surprisingly on the next Monday she was found sitting meekly in the staff canteen munching a salad. Without fuss or palaver, she had agreed to record four songs for Jess Yates because they went back a long way, all for the standard fee and accompanied not by a thirty piece orchestra but by Jess Yates himself on the organ.

Not everyone liked that standard fee. When informed what it was, Gregory Peck apparently replied, 'Well no thank you Mr Yates, my chauffeur doesn't need a haircut this week,' but the money didn't deter the likes of James Mason, Princess Grace, Bing Crosby and other world class stars. Rumour has it that, before Jess' ridiculous and undeserved exit in the boot of a car from the YTV car park, he was on the verge of signing up the Pope. Yes, Jess was a player like anybody else. He had lived apart from his wife for many years. He was one of the most interesting men around, with a wealth of showbusiness experience under his belt. I remember one evening when, at the very top of his powers as presenter of *Stars*, and fast becoming a national treasure, and giver of comfort and succour to millions, he was also still in charge of *Junior Showtime*. He came into the bar, saw Michael Partington and me in our usual position in *Calendar* Corner and said, 'Here you two, come to reception with me. There's something I want to show you.' We looked round reception, to see youngsters being met by their parents. 'Look at that fourteen year old auditioning for *Showtime*, she's got the

172

biggest pair of tits I've ever seen.' If the multitude had ever known! But he never pretended to be anything else but an organist who read out requests from the elderly and certainly he was never referred to as 'The Bishop'.

Donald Baverstock made an error of judgement when he put Jess Yates, one folk hero, as executive producer over Hughie Greene, another folk hero. Hughie was doing *The Sky's the Limit,* a son of *Double your Money,* except air miles could be won instead of cash. It was inevitable that these two old troupers would not get along. Things allegedly came to a crunch one night in the studio when Jess didn't like Hughie's tie and told him to change it minutes before recording. Hughie refused with, he felt, some justification, and he was sure his stand would be supported by senior executives. It was, after all the YTV company tie. Now, of course, we all know the real reason for the spat between the two, in that Hughie Greene was the real father of Paula Yates. This situation, had it been crafted into a sitcom or feature film, would have been frankly unbelievable.

By now the nucleus of the team for the daily local magazine show had arrived. Not that Donald Baverstock had actually decided there would definitely be one. I still have a memo which is headed 'The proposed thrice weekly news and current affairs magazine programme'. Inevitably, there would be a nightly show – and he himself would produce it at first. We were thrilled by this prospect, to sit at the feet of the man who invented *Tonight*. Having dreamt up the title *Tonight* which still exists in various guises in various networks, he invented another excellent title for the daily programme, *Calendar*. Never bettered in my view as a daily title. Strong. One word. Saying it all. Who was to be the anchorman of *Calendar*? Not me, certainly. Having passed an audition at Leeds University studios (we had none of our own) by giving a twenty second piece to camera about buttercups – 'He'll do,' Baverstock muttered to a henchman – I was to be a news reporter. In fact I was to be *the* news reporter. Donald said he wanted an older man to be the presenter and mentioned Ronald Eyre, a distinguished drama director, who I knew had been Russell Harty's English master at Blackburn Grammar School. But then enter Jonathan Aitken.

Jonathan had made his name with the book *The Young Meteors* in which he identified young people of his generation whom he reckoned were going to make it big. He was also Conservative candidate for Thirsk and Malton, then the safest Tory seat in the country, conveniently placed some forty miles up the road from Leeds. He was grand, tall, handsome, drove a blue MG and gave dinner parties at his rented house in North Yorkshire, served by his housekeeper, a Mrs Ricketts. He once told me he liked to keep in with world leaders and politicians who were currently out of office, because one day they would be in office. Shrewd and cunning, even then. A TV natural I'm afraid he was not.

The newsdesk staff arrived.

John Wilford, a reporter from ATV. I had seen some of his reports, while editing regional contributions for ITN, rail crashes and the like. He had never edited a news bulletin.

Graham Ironside, who had. He came up the hard way in Aberdeen, and greatly impressed me by not only knowing shorthand but by being able to place a pencil behind his ear without looking a prat.

Sid Waddell, a volcano of Geordie energy, albeit he was strictly Durham, from Ashington, where he grew up with the Charlton brothers. A top scholarship to Cambridge University endowed him with an immense vocabulary and a unique way with words and phrases, but did nothing for his Geordie accent. Stints in Tyne Tees and Granada qualified him superbly to be one of the most inventive and energetic young producers.

Simon Welfare arrived. Twenty-one, just three weeks down from Oxford and in that time married to Mary, the eldest daughter of the Earl of Aberdeen. He'd met her while taking his touring drama troupe to perform in their Scottish seat, Haddo House. Flaxen haired, chubby and beaming, not completely at ease with his trousers (I now know this feeling), he was handpicked from that Oxford generation by Baverstock. He was to be a star. His wedding, by the way, covered two pages of the September edition of *Tatler*. The YTV opening got just one picture in the same issue.

Liz Fox, the most bubbly and infectious girl on the team. A continuity announcer at Tyne Tees and former actress, she had a lovely musical lilting voice, a big smile and personality to go with it. She became YTVs first homemade celebrity.

Barry Cockcroft. An early arrival and a refugee from Granada. He had worked on the famous *Scene at Six Thirty* which would shortly be replaced by Yorkshire's *Calendar*. A true son of Rochdale, Barry declared his intention of never moving into Yorkshire. He extolled the virtues of the great men of Granada – Bill Grundy, Gay Byrne, David Plowright, Tim Hewat, Mike Scott, and his lookalike, Michael Parkinson. He was always passing on share tips and once tried to explain to me what a P/E ratio was. I still

176

don't know. Barry was known as 'Dino' to most of us, after epic film director Dino de Laurentis. He was a good thirty-three and that was old. Fancy having passed thirty and not being a millionaire! Mind you, Barry tried hard. Legendary expense accounts read 'Attacked by footpads in Rome', or 'Shoes ruined while walking backwards to set up shot and fell into moorland beck'. Crews loved filming with him, as not only was a good lunch and four star accommodation assured, but Yorkshire's Beaujolais lake just shrank and shrank under his patronage. He, of course, discovered Hannah Hauxwell, and they both lived happily ever after.

A late arrival was John Fairley. Baverstock recruited him from the Today programme where he produced Jack de Manio. John entertained us all with crazy tales of the wireless, including his favourite. He was on duty when the news of the sad death of Alma Cogan came through. A tribute was hastily prepared and he called the record library for one of her numbers. Without looking he played it in after the spoken tribute had finished. He was alarmed and, I suspect, ashamed to hear her singing the words 'Heaven ... I'm in heaven...' I knew on the first day that John was going to be important. He too was older, and although he had no television experience at all, would be a natural leader. He was also the tallest member of the team. On his first day he was sent out with me, like a student on work experience, to watch me filming a story about cutlery craftsmen in Sheffield. He would soon find out how the TV professionals got to work.

In the cramped workshop in Sheffield though, it was difficult to accommodate me, the craftsmen, the camera, the mike and the crew of eleven who we were obliged to take around, let alone a six foot two rubber necker. So with the initiative, forward thinking and tact for which I have always been famed, and thinking of lunch, which I occasionally do, I dispatched John Fairley to go out into the centre of Sheffield and find a place where fifteen of us could have a good lunch. I don't think it was a particularly good career move, especially bearing in mind that he was to be my boss for the next twenty years, although I think he has now forgiven me. Looking back, it was not exactly the sort of way an ex Midshipman, an ex Oxford scholar, an ex *Evening Standard* sub, an ex senior producer at the Beeb, would expect to be treated. Except that I knew what he didn't. That thanks to my stammering performance earlier with Mr Baverstock, I was on a hundred pounds a year more than him, although not for long! To cut a long, i.e. a twenty-five year, story very short, John became editor of *Calendar*, Head of Local Programmes, producer of *Whicker* and other popular network documentaries, Head of Factual Programmes and Current Affairs, Director of Programmes and Managing Director. In those positions he could, and has, taken lunch at many exotic locations around the world, where he has doubtless got people like me to find restaurants for him. His career blossomed, particularly under Paul Fox in the Seventies and he became a very real contributor in the creative and political maelstrom that is ITV. He now runs Channel Four racing with the kind of flair that only a lover of horseflesh can bring to bear. By the way, the place he found for us in Sheffield was actually very good except there were no oysters.

Thus the small team got ready for the big day, augmented by people that Donald knew or had just met on the train. He met a top London model between Leeds and King's Cross, who came from Halifax – thus Jane Lumb was recruited. Of limited journalistic skill, at least she looked good and she was local, so that would do nicely. Andrew Kerr, a charismatic, soft spoken scholar, had been writing with Randolph Churchill and he brought a friend, a wistful lady named Eithne O'Sullivan.

With three days to go, as the notice said, we were keeping it moving and had our first rehearsal. Remembered over thirty years later, it is a bit of a blur, but I can recall Jonathan Aitken, the anchorman, sitting on a mushroom stalked chair that trendily adorned the set, enquiring, 'When the red light comes on on the camera, what exactly does that mean?' Oh dear, I thought, we have a lot of work to do.

Monday 29 July 1968. Opening day. The Duchess of Kent, our Yorkshire Royal, was due to throw the switch at 11.30 and take us on the air and live to Headingley for the Test Match. The goodest and the greatest were there in the foyer awaiting the big moment. Yorkshire's Prime Minister Harold Wilson was due to make a surprise appearance. There was live coverage and a commentary, but because ironically YTV was not officially on the air, it only went out in Granadaland. How they must have laughed over there. Guests were late, cars were delayed, board directors were hovering and the commentator bravely slogged it out with one of those 'we are still waiting for Nelson Mandela to be released' type commentaries. I looked at the tape recently and marvelled at his stamina. There was a classic moment when over a shot of Harold Wilson chatting benignly and smoking his pipe, he said, 'We are now waiting for the Prime Minister to arrive so that the ceremony can begin.' Ah well, things could only get better.

I saw none of this because, as ace news reporter, I was on the track of a missing person in York, that day's top story. Rather feeble for an opening night but what can you do? Ferrybridge cooling towers couldn't collapse again to order. Back at the ranch, the *Calendar* running order, written personally by Donald Baverstock, was taking shape. An intro from Jonathan Aitken. The news read by John Fairley. This was to be read standing up at a lectern, so that shot from waist up, it would show the newscaster upright and erect, not hunched over a desk. It was yet another great Baverstock invention which was to be kept secret. The news would include my story from York, a feature by Simon Welfare on stainless steel underwear, another one by Liz Fox surrounded by old school desks, which apparently were making a bomb at local sale rooms, more news from Michael Partington, and a prefilmed feature from me about a chap in Sheffield with the biggest hat size in the country. Charming! Oh, and because of the cricket, we would not be on at six, it would be half past, so we could record the programme to be on the safe side. The equipment, remember, was brand new, untried and unbeknown to us all, was being silently infiltrated with deadly brick

181

dust from the ongoing works. Nothing, it seemed, could be relied on, from the presenters to the electronic widgets. Certainly not the presenters.

I returned from York with my story. Alan and Sandy would have been proud, I thought. So, it's only a film report about a missing person, but thanks to my ITN training and natural creative and journalistic skill, it would be a winner. It had all the elements. A powerful and vivid piece to camera at the start setting the scene. A bit of hand held camera work foraging through the bushes in the park where he was last seen. A tough 'come on now Inspector' interview with the police chief. Well chosen vox pops with worried residents and a concerned and mature end piece wrapping the story up. I reckoned I'd soon be off parish pump, or bent fenders as the Americans called such reports, and on to the big documentaries. Watch out Mr Whicker! I returned to the editing machine with the film. This, by the way, was processed in a laboratory conveniently placed on the other side of Leeds. Coping with rush hour traffic when delivering the can of film and its subsequent despatch to the studios, did little for tight deadlines and up to the minute coverage. Never mind the nerves. So my film arrived back in negative. That was the way we did it. Shoot and edit in negative, project on telecine machines and electronically reverse phase – that is turn white into black and black into white. This system worked at ITN for years. I had the epic report well sketched out in my mind as I sat with the film editor. He didn't seem to share my Hitchcockian view of the report. Out went the hand held. Out went the moody shots of the park. Out went all but the most basic of questions to the chief leaving such masterpieces as 'what is your latest theory as to what happened?' and 'What advice have you for local residents?'. Out went the mature thinkpiece at the end. We were not left with much. Nevertheless the clock was ticking and the film had to be in the telecine for our 5.30 deadline. After that, there was little I could do for the programme except watch it, as I was definitely not wanted in studio.

I'll tell you this now, and so as not to drag out your patience or indeed sympathy any further, the programme was – well, let's just say 'memorable'. The opening statement from Jonathan, in which you might have expected a warm greeting from your new teatime friends on YTV, and some indication of how glad we were all to be here, and what we were going to do in the years to come. At long last Yorkshire, this great county of ours, would have its own dedicated great TV station. Not so. Donald, who frankly saw *Calendar* as a cross between the Home Service, *Panorama* and the Reith Lectures, had written the following opening script to be delivered by Jonathan. 'With the Australians playing for a draw at Head-ingley, the Russians giving no concessions to the Czechs, the Pope refusing to withdraw his latest encyclical on birth control, it's been a good day for non-events. Here's John Fairley with the news.'

Non-events! Yorkshire's own TV station opens up and he says it's a good day for non-events! However, I had no time to ponder as John Fairley, standing at the lectern but shot so that nobody would know, firmly and clearly intoned the first story, with that knowing nod he used to give before beginning. Michael Deakin, a witty producer and old friend of John Fairley's later observed that John read the news as though he knew more about it than he was prepared to tell you.

'Police in York are still investigating the disappearance of a middle aged man who was last seen in a city centre park. Richard Whiteley reports.'

Wow, this was me. I was on. First reporter on YTV on opening night. Little old me. All the top brass of ITV in the Queen's Hotel watching prior to the opening gala at Leeds University. All watching me. Family and friends at home, all watching me. Fairley's face disappeared as they cut to film. A strange vision replaced his fine features. A face, grey to black looking, with white hair, black teeth, black shirt and white tie. The face spoke. It was mine. And then I realised. There I was in glorious white and black. They hadn't or couldn't reverse phase. Neither could they cut away from it and back to the studio. The next bit of film on the running order would surely have the same problems. So, for nearly three minutes, the viewers of this much heralded Yorkshire station were treated to the spectacle of some black toothed, white haired, nasal berk asking a stiff policeman if local residents should be worried.

And to think only on Friday, forty-eight hours earlier, they heard Grundy and Parky and the likes wishing Yorkshire viewers good luck and a fond farewell. The technical standard did not improve greatly as the programme progressed. Jonathan soon learnt that when the red light came on the camera was on, and he was on. And with the film obstinately refusing to oblige, he was on an awful lot. (Brick dust in the French telecine machines was the reason. Ah well, it's the machines. They were French.) At one point, a film item previously pre-recorded as a standby item, finished earlier than expected leaving the director in some confusion.

'Get me a shot of Partington at the newsdesk,' he shrieked.

His call was answered by camera three, which happened to be positioned at the farthest end of the studio. Mike, the director, had to cut to that shot. There we saw Michael Partington dimly in the corner of the set, a speck among all the paraphernalia of backstage television. As camera three zoomed in, we saw and the viewers saw, that Michael was standing as erect as Nelson on the plinth, at a lectern to read the news. Long before Kirsty Young and Jon Snow, we saw the newscaster's legs. And the secret of how to read the news without hunching over the desk was finally out in less than fifteen minutes on Yorkshire TV's first night.

At one point, in the control room, the harassed director got up from his chair, and paced the length of the gallery saying, 'It's going to be a disaster.'

'Sit down,' said Juliet Vallans, the PA who had taken over directions. 'It *is* a disaster.'

It was soon all over. But the joy was it was recorded, we could do it again. Do it live this time at 6.30. But Donald wouldn't hear of it. He wouldn't allow it. No, the recorded programme, fandango though it had been, had to go out as it was. We could only watch ... helpless. Now search as I have, I cannot find that tape. It would be priceless.

Afterwards, the feared post mortem. Donald in charge. Not a pretty prospect. He'd been known to make great men shiver in their shoes. My item came up. 'York missing story. Little imagination. No atmosphere. Why no hand held of leafy wood? Why no vox pops with worried residents? Why not a tough interview with a policeman? Why no authoritative upsum at the end? You'll have to do better than that David.'

No mention at all of the report appearing in negative. Perhaps he thought I always looked like that. I opened my mouth for the right to reply, but Donald had moved on to the next item. Just as well Donald thought I was someone else. Perhaps some new boy with a black face. Anyway, I was to be David in his eyes for the next two years at least. I didn't mind too much. It didn't do Frost, Coleman or Dimbleby any harm. However, David had been invited to the opening night live, nationally networked party at Leeds University. Nigel Ryan, I remember, came over saying he thought *Calendar* had had a pretty encouraging start. Come on Nigel, it's very nice of you to say that, but you must have been seeing too much Ugandan television. It was terrible. We soon forgot about our troubles and laughed the evening away with Bob Monkhouse and co, going to bed in the early hours. Tomorrow is another day, especially in the news business.

I was woken at seven o'clock by the news on the radio. There had been a huge hotel fire in Ilkley over night. At least five dead. It was to be the biggest story in Yorkshire for years. And on our second day. Hell's Bells! What does a fire look like in white and black? It didn't bear thinking about.

CALENDAR BOY

I don't cry easily. I cried regularly at the end of school term – not at the prospect of going home, but because the end of term at Giggleswick was orchestrated for such emotional outpourings. Big boys cried. Little boys cried. Even masters cried. Well, you would. The end of term service was held in chapel, totally dark, save for two candles on the altar. The service was always the same, which meant you had to learn the hymns and psalms. The organ voluntaries were the 'Londonderry Air', which for years I thought was the London Derriere, and Elgar's 'Nimrod' at the end. You just had to cry. But, of course, in the dark no one could see you, so nobody knew you did.

I cried at most episodes of *Upstairs Downstairs* in the Seventies, although I suspect I cried for myself really, going through a stage of solitary weekends in my little country cottage in the Dales. And I cried when Austin Mitchell left Yorkshire Television to become an MP in 1977. And I don't know why. Not for him, he was happy enough, having secured a famous victory at Grimsby. Nor even for me, after all, with his sudden departure, I would be kingpin on *Calendar*. I suppose I cried because the departure of Austin meant the end of an era – and I always hate ends of eras, whether the eras in question are long or short. I shall cry when I've finished writing this book. You might well cry long before finishing reading it!

In this case, the era was almost ten years, and it was the suddenness of Austin's departure that was so brutal. His political career began when he was out at lunch. There was to be a by-election at Grimsby following the death of Anthony Crosland. There was no doubt about where Austin's political sympathies lay, but he was impeccably impartial in his interviewing, and hardly active on the local political scene. Shortly after Crosland's death, the phone rang on Austin's desk. Christine Wilkinson, his secretary answered. It was Les Bridges, the Regional Organiser of the Labour Party in the East Midlands. Was Austin there? Well, could he please ring back when he returned from lunch. Christine dutifully composed a note, and put it on Austin's typewriter. 'Ring East Mid. Lab Party. Reg. Org.'

Austin duly arrived back, saw the message, dialled the number, and the following conversation took place.

'Labour party – Hello.'

'Hello. Is Reg there please?'

'Reg ... Reg who? We don't have a Reg.'

'Yes you do. It's Austin Mitchell. I was told to ring Reg at that number ... Reg Org.'

'I think you need to speak to Mr Bridges, our Regional Organiser.'

And, out of such delicious confusion, began Austin's highly individual political career. He was speedily selected and adopted and was off to fight the campaign just three or four days later. His desk, as you would expect, was a permanent tribute to the art of detritus. The director of Tate Modern would have been highly excited. Want a *Yorkshire Post* of eight weeks ago? Try Austin's desk. Want a cassette of last year's Christmas special? Ferret around Austin's desk. Where are those free tickets for the opening of Leeds' latest niterie? There'd be a wadge of them on Austin's desk.

Mind you, his desk was well fortified. During his academic period at the University of Canterbury, New Zealand, he had authored a great tome, *New Zealand*

Politics in Action – The Election of 1960. Worthy, and a standard work this may have been, but frankly, there wasn't a large market for it in Britain in the mid Seventies. So his desk was surrounded with twelve cartons containing the remainders of the book. Having arrived at Goods Inward at YTV, they found their final resting place all around his desk. This to the frustration of everyone who wanted a passage through the already crowded newsroom.

I remember Austin's final words as a YTV employee. Rushing out of the office to Grimsby, bound to fight the election, he grabbed a pile of papers from his desk, and bejeaned and sunglassed, made for the door.

'Mitchell ... tidy your bloody desk before you go,' was the cheerful message of support booming out from the *Calendar* editor, Graham Ironside.

'I'll do it when I come back,' panted Austin. And he was gone. But he genuinely believed he wouldn't win.

Austin was, without doubt, the saviour of YTV in its early days. He was discovered by Sir Geoffrey Cox at the high table of Nuffield College, Oxford in the summer of 1968. YTV had been on the air for a week – a disastrous one at that, with failing technology and an unskilled, untried, uncertain group of performers. Luckily, after we came off the air, mentally and emotionally drained, on the first Friday, we went to the pub across the road to watch the opening of London Weekend at seven o'clock. No sooner had Frank Muir said 'we have ways of making you laugh', than the screen went blank, and the whole of ITV was off the air for a two week strike. This gave us some breathing space, and when we came back, Sir Geoffrey presented his new signing, Dr Austin Mitchell. He couldn't have fitted the bill better. He was a Yorkshireman, from Baildon, my own village. He had presented the New Zealand equivalent of *Panorama* for a year, he was an academic of some achievement, but he was also thoroughly likeable and amiable. He immediately won over the viewers, who had been so put off by the stiff performance of Jonathan Aitken. And he took the region by the scruff of the neck – joshing about Heckmondwike and Cleckheaton, taking the mickey out of old Yorkshire games like Knurr and Spell, as well as conducting razor-sharp interviews with the big hitters of the time. He had the old senior common room manner of addressing interviewees by their surname, 'What do you say, Scargill?'

I, later, impressed by this, tried to do the same in a political forum I was chairing. It consisted of the following MPs – Joe Hiley, Dennis Healey and Frank Hooley, MP for

Greenhill, Greencliffe Avenue.
The house with the pond,
where I dearly wanted to live. I
did – from 1954.

Right So was I a sweet child?
Judge for yourself, as I was on
my trike, aged 5.

The unique and beautiful chapel at Giggleswick
School. Everyone loved, and was haunted by the
magic of this place, with its green copper dome and
Byzantine architecture. It dominates the Yorkshire
Dales for miles around, and kindles deep feelings
among all of us who worshipped there. The
watercolour is by Margaret Blackburne.

The scorer – in training for the numbers game. The Heather Bank team of 1956. Note the handsome knees, even then.

Prep in the study after chapel. I do not have a halo, it is my straw boater hanging up. Brian Marr is my study mate. I would shortly be opening a tin of mandarin oranges and eat them segment by segment.

Sunday afternoon out in the Giggleswick countryside.
Bunny Empsall, RW, John Hansen and Ted Reay.

Below left Age 16. Watch out, Mr Dimbleby. My first
OB commentary on the gruelling cross-country run,
Scarrig. Luckily, because of my asthma, I was "off
games". *Below right* My front page dedicated to Sir
Winston, January 1965. Lady Churchill wrote to say
she was deeply touched. Such tabloid layout was bold
at that time.

Was I ever a journalist? The editor of *Varsity* at work on the stone at the printers in Bury St Edmunds. We lived in awe of Len (right), whose patience often grew thin. But it was always all right on the night.

What Lord Butler saw, on his first visit as Master Elect to Trinity College. I carried his bag, and *Varsity* photographer Patrick Eager got a scoop.

Calendar boy 1969. "Where's his blooming ears?" the father of my then girlfriend had remarked. Didn't he know we all looked like that then.

Austin Mitchell's expression says it all. So he didn't get a T-shirt. Well, it wouldn't have fitted him anyway, and he was about 42 at the time...

I often think that Carol and I are the Wilfred and Mabel Pickles of our time. "Give 'em a consonant, Carol." Wilfred recreated *Have A Go* for my chat show *Calendar People*.

Brian Rix and I never knew Ian Carmichael could be so funny.

"Who's the nicest person you've ever interviewed?" they ask. James Herriot, I say. This was in 1975.

A man's best
friend...

Ferret man, the
highlights, 1977 –
scenes famous the
world over. This
blooper clip goes on
and on and still makes
me laugh. Brian
Plummer is the
intrepid ferret tamer.

Calendar team ten years on: Austin Mitchell, RW, Liz Fox, Jonathan Aitken. Variety Club lunch for *Calendar* in Leeds, 1978.

Collective noun for this quartet? A tongue, perhaps. David Frost, Michael Parkinson and David Jacobs, 1978 – all chat show hosts – and one trainee.

All smiles with the second Mrs Thatcher and the innocent Mr Whiteley, unaware of the rumpus in the YTV boardroom after I'd asked her if she'd taken elocution lessons. 1978. Jeff Druett, *(left)* asked the tricky political questions.

Spot the difference. My hero and role model – but Sir David still hasn't asked me to his summer garden party.

With Dennis Healey on the Moors above his childhood home in Keighley. The pictures he took may have been black and white, but the language that day was blue when a jobsworth tried to stop us filming. 1980

Ready for the
countdown, November
1982. I suppose I
thought saucer-sized
spectacles were trendy.

Countdown team photo
1985 – Gyles Brandreth,
Carol Vorderman, RW
and Cathy Hytner.

The Master. We recreated a classroom scene with me
and Russell Harty for a *Calendar Tuesday* programme
in 1985. He was saying "Whiteley, what is your nub?"
I replied "My nub is Whiteley J.R., sir" We were both
adenoidal.

"And the total so far is..." My proudest moment at YTV – presenting *Telethon '88* – 27 hours at the helm wearing a different jacket every half-hour to do my bit for the Yorkshire tailoring industry .

Stephen Fry likes to watch *Countdown*, he says, with his feet up on a pouf.

Kenneth Williams took over from Ted Moult in Dictionary corner. He brought a lot of wit and sparkle to the show, but he hated the lunch breaks, and thought I was "smug".
Smug – moi?

Coated in dust, reporting from outside the Grand Hotel, Brighton at 5am, two hours after the blast in 1984. I had been in the foyer, about to leave, when I was delayed for a few moments to refuse a glass of champagne!

Reporting live as more of the Holbeck Hall Hotel in Scarborough falls into the sea, 1995. I am obviously not very good with hotels!

The original *Calendar* team 25 years on in 1993. Back row, left to right: Barry Cockcroft, John Wilford, Graham Ironside, John Fairley. Front row: Michael Partington, Liz Fox, Himoff! Paul Dunstan, Simon Welfare. Austin Mitchell was late for this photo call!

"*Countdown*? I do believe my sister watches it after the racing."

Her Majesty seems delighted... "Now where have I seen him before...?"

Hockney, Bennett, Whiteley – what have they got in common? Must be the chins.

With my leading ladies 1995 – Carol Vorderman of *Countdown* and Christa Ackroyd of *Calendar*, the two nightly programmes I presented. Hence my nickname "Twice Nightly".

Is *This Is Your Life* – well some of it, anyway! The rest is in this book!

His dad just presses a button! Well, a few other things besides, perhaps. With my son James in the studio, 1996.

With my sister Helen on her silver wedding at Turnberry, 1997. It was her smiling personality that everyone loved, together with a sparkling wit.

Subject's mum on *This Is Your Life*, 1997. She was the biggest hit.

Women eating out of my hand? My *brand* image!

Right With John Meade in Monte Carlo. Does he look the kind of chap who would even think about sacking me?

Below My coronation as Mayor of Wetwang in 1988 – in borrowed robes, courtesy of the Mayor of Beverley. One day, perhaps, Wetwang may get its own – but with only 300 people...

Heeley. Hiley, Healey and Hooley of Heeley. Don't even ask what sort of a mess I got myself into.

Although possessed of great intelligence, Austin saw his job on *Calendar* as an opportunity to catch up with the decade he lost being an academic in New Zealand. He loved dressing up, or dressing down, prancing around in the snow in underpants, in and out of the newly arrived phenomenon of sauna baths.

At one morning meeting, John Fairley said he'd fixed up for Austin to do a film in a new Jacuzzi. Austin, to the surprise of the rest of us, looked horrified.

'No, I can't do that,' he said.

'Why?' enquired an incredulous editor.

'Because I can't ride a motor bike,' pleaded Austin.

Ah, such innocence. But give him a chance to dance with a gogo girl in a cage, he wearing hot pants, he'd grab it ... and would return to the studio to do a devastating interview with a cabinet minister about the Public Sector Borrowing Requirement. Paul Fox, arriving at YTV in 1973, took a dim view of this split personality, and banned him from tomfoolery. Mind you, that was after Austin, who had been conducting an end of programme interview with some professional party organisers, was handed a news flash about the death of the IRA hunger striker in Wakefield jail. He had just got the words out when he was whacked in the face by a custard pie. Austin's hyena like laughter brought the programme to a close, and very nearly the careers of all involved.

I, meanwhile, carried on as ace news reporter, finding that the only story of any significance in those early days was one which very nearly finished us all off, the collapse of the Emley Moor transmitter in 1969. This, of course, was our lifeblood, and with this huge mast lying crumpled on the ground like a dead dinosaur, the end of YTV looked imminent. Naturally, no one had thought of insuring against not being able to broadcast. But I survived, by, I think, just surviving. Ambitious people began to leave.

Jonathan went on to do some good documentaries. Liz Fox, hugely popular, went off to become only the third female ITN reporter. My mentor, Michael Partington, went off to become top anchorman at Tyne Tees, Simon Welfare went off to produce science programmes with Magnus Pike and Arthur C. Clarke. So, in effect, only Austin and I were left. I think, actually, we worked quite well, and *Calendar* was always in the local top ten with over two and a half million viewers. We had a programme which combined good film reporting, tough studio confrontations, and still had time in part two for a chap to come in and play the piano while standing on his head. 'Get them talking in the pubs tonight' was John Wilford's mantra – John being the second editor of *Calendar*.

Every night on *Calendar* was like a first night. There was fun, loads of it, but never any complacency. And there were some hard taskmasters. On many occasions I would dread coming out of studio two. There, after a bad night, would be John Fairley leaning against the wall in the corridor, waiting for you. If he had found fault with your performance, he was there to tell you why. Tall, with piercing eye contact, and chin as sharp as a dagger, you felt the steel going in. Ouch. And John Wilford once had occasion to reach up and grab Austin by the lapels and shake him vigorously. Why had he ignored one councillor who had driven a hundred and twenty miles from deepest Lincolnshire and not allowed him a single word in a three handed discussion?

'Oh,' Austin had replied. 'I spoke to him in the Green Room before and thought he hadn't anything interesting to say.'

Then, as we walked from the newsroom to the bar, we had to pass a further hurdle. Paul Fox's office, with the imminent thought that we could be horned. Michael Deakin had christened Paul Fox the 'Rhino'. His office was the Rhinorium, and if you were to be bollocked you were 'horned'. Not a pleasant experience! Sometimes we skulked shiftily past his door, hoping he wouldn't hear us, or drag us in for a horning.

When Paul arrived from the BBC everybody was terrified and apprehensive about their careers. In his first week, I remember Wally Lowry, the number cruncher who served Paul, came down to the bar. He'd been watching *Calendar* with the big man. And his verdict? We hung on every word. All I can remember was him saying to me 'You're all right ... he likes you.' Phew.

I am delighted, and, actually, proud to say that Paul and Betty Fox have been great friends and supporters ever since.

Eventually, Austin was poached by the BBC and went off to join Ludovic Kennedy as presenter of the pre *Newsnight* programme *24 Hours*. So that just left little old me as the main presenter of *Calendar*. Every day, John Wilford produced, I presented, Gary Ward directed and Ros Boothroyd was the PA. We were the core team for months and months on end. And the team developed into a slick and successful operation.

Eventually, John Wilford took me aside, and said that after all these months of effort, he thought we'd both benefit by going to a health farm. This we duly did. To the quaintly titled Shrubland Hall in Suffolk.

Now, John had always been a determined and athletic character. Sunday football, squash, jogging, doing all the things which make me have a panic attack. So his agenda at Shrublands was mightily different from mine. He was in the gym, he was weight-lifting, he was swimming, he was power walking round the grounds, early morning tennis, even late night snooker. I settled for a few gentle massage sessions, a stroll into the next village, some group exercise in the shallow end and five minutes on an exercise bike. However, superfit John and I did share saunas, heat rooms, cold hoses, steam cabinets, and many other delights of the place. We spent a week in most agreeable circumstances, and as producer and presenter, had as excellent and as cordial a time as one could. I, always bearing in mind that, godfather to two of his children I may be, he was still ultimately my boss.

There were never very many official titles at YTV. Once, when I thought I should have some status, I ventured to ask Paul Fox for a title, or at least something I could put on my business card.

'You've got a title,' he said. 'Your title is Mr Richard Whiteley.'

But, Mr Richard Whiteley took nothing for granted, and always sought to reassure himself by checking when the daily running order was issued at about 3.00 in the afternoon, that his name was on it. It usually was, in the handwriting of John Wilford, as 'Opening link ... Ric'. Or 'Coal Interview ... Ric plus two'. So Ric was always to be subject to the whims of Wilford as his editor. But we were on a roll, and we would, I thought, arrive back from Shrublands duly refreshed, knowing each other even better and marching on to greater triumphs.

It was, therefore, with some surprise that driving home on the Sunday, after seven solid days in each other's company, he chose a stretch of road between Wakefield and Leeds on the M1 to make the following statement.

'Oh, I meant to tell you, there's a new kid starting next Monday.' I was driving. I stared intensely ahead.

'Oh really,' I said, as casually as possible, and, knowing there was a vacancy in Hull, 'In the Hull office – a Humberside film reporter?'

'Oh, no, Leeds. A main studio presenter. He's from ATV. Bob Warman. His brother Mike is one of my oldest pals. He's a great presenter. You'll like him.'

In my week at the health farm, I had lost two hundred and fifty-seven pounds. Two hundred and fifty pounds sterling, and seven pounds in weight. I had felt good.

Suddenly, all the good the two hundred and fifty pounds had done me, began to seep away. So, after a week together, he waited till we were ten minutes from home to tell me the brother of his best pal was coming to take over my job. Well, that's how I saw it. Very straightforward we TV folk.

'Oh,' I said meekly, and delivered him to his front door. He jumped out of the car, told me he felt fantastic. His wife told him he looked fantastic, and I drove my solitary way home in a state of agitation. Not that I was worried, of course, I could stand some competition, I'd already seen a few off, but – well – you know. The next morning, John Wilford was not there to take the morning meeting. At midday, when he still hadn't showed, I rang his home. A worried and anxious wife came on. John had been terribly ill overnight – the doctor had just left – and guess what? John had got shingles. Definitely not funny. Well, not funny, perhaps, but ironic. He goes to a health farm, gets himself frighteningly fit, and immediately falls over with shingles. Bearing in mind his disclosure of the previous day, I must say I had mixed feelings.

John was still away when Bob arrived, but he must have sent word about his status. Bob was allocated the desk next to mine, in the senior corner of the office. He was, indeed, a terribly good presenter. Tall, blond, square jawed, beautiful voice, clear blue eyes, in short, very professional. He was also the most secretive bloke I have ever met. Every phone call, and there were many, because he also seemed to be running several businesses in Birmingham from his desk in Leeds, was made with his back to me and his mouth as close to the receiver as he could get. Where he went in the evenings, no one knew. The only thing we did know was that he had the top of the range, brand new Rover 3500, and that when the phone rang on our desk – a phone which John Willis working quietly and solidly on his documentaries, christened the sex phone – we both made a grab for it, and it was inevitably for Bob. Annoyingly it was usually some female I had previously introduced him to.

In his second year, the ice melted and we started to speak a little more as it somehow caused him endless amusement that my car had changed from third hand Jag to Ford Escort Ghia.

'I know your flat will be all smoked glass and chrome, Ricco,' he once said.

'How could he know that?' I thought, knowing he was spot on.

Bob and I became great friends, even friendlier when he said he never really felt at home in Yorkshire, and he'd got a better offer to go back to ATV where he was at home. I was genuinely sorry to see him go, as he had become a great soulmate, and was gracious enough not to mind that I had withstood his challenge. My greatest memory of Bob was his leaving night. At the Flying Pizza restaurant, he managed to dive under the table, and emerge a few moments later, grasping in his teeth the knickers of one of the girls sitting opposite. I still don't know how he did it. Every time I try, I find they aren't wearing any.

I was with *Calendar* for twenty-seven years – half a lifetime in any profession – surely an aeon in television.

Twenty-seven years is an awfully long time to be involved with anything, let alone a commitment as demanding as a live daily current affairs programme. For years my body clock, both physical and emotional, was tuned in to that witching hour of six o'clock in the evening. Even on holiday, I was aware of the run up to that hour, the half hour itself, and the inevitable, and hugely enjoyable relaxing time afterwards. On a typical day, I could have been in the office from, say nine-thirty for a ten o'clock production meeting, found myself volunteering for a hundred and ninety mile trip to Cleethorpes, rushing to bring the film back, editing it, and briefing myself for the studio presentation of the programme. I always thought it strange, that while most people wind down in their last half hour of the working day, my last half hour, was the most critical. By rights, I should have been shattered after the rigours of the day, but I was called upon to be bright, reactive, sparkling and quick, presenting on live television.

Mind you, the picture painted above of my working day is fairly atypical – purely for the benefit of luncheon club question and answer sessions, and journalists doing 'A day in the life of'. Normally it was thus: in at one minute to ten. Morning meeting. Throw in some ideas and comments, hoping the producer would not throw them back at me to get on with. Read the papers all morning. Seek out a lunch companion, or better still attend a personal appearance. Come back for haircut, or a pre-record. Watch *Countdown* in the Green Room with a cup of tea. Into make up, talk to studio guests, and bingo, on the air, having first scrutinised, and criticised the script which was written by others for me to read. Yes, I have to be honest, that's how lots of daily anchormen live their lives. Most of those years, I was presenting both *Calendar* and *Countdown*, sometimes nipping out of the *Countdown* studio at 5.30 to present *Calendar*, hence the nickname 'Twice

Nightly Whiteley'. (At least I think that's what it means.) But there were golden moments in my *Calendar* career. The programme meant everything to me, and I think for many years it was, to quote Dickie Bird MBE, 'more important than life itself'.

I got a reputation as something of a cheeky interviewer who could get away with quite a lot, as well as someone who could get right to the point if the occasion demanded. All those years provided me with a unique opportunity not only to bang the drum for Yorkshire but also the name of Yorkshire Television, of which we were so proud. The name was a two-edged sword. Hundreds of thousands of people in North Yorkshire couldn't receive us, their sets picking up a strong Tyne Tees signal, while hundreds of thousands more in Nottinghamshire, Derbyshire, Lincolnshire and even Norfolk, could only get Yorkshire. It was a great tribute that over the years, whenever the sensitive subject of the name was approached, all non-Yorkshire viewers said they liked the name. We, though, tended to regard all our viewers as one big family in *Calendarland* – not original, but I do think we were a little bit more user friendly and cuddly than the father figures of the old *Granadaland*.

Calendar built up a huge reputation in the Seventies. Our every night was a first night, the philosophy being that if you, at home, missed *Calendar,* then you really did miss something. Arthur Scargill was always too good to miss. Bernard Dineen, the formidable columnist on the *Yorkshire Post,* fulminated against YTV for twenty years for creating the Scargill monster. In a way he was right. When we came on the scene in 1968, the NUM in Yorkshire was run by ageing heavyweights, more interested in the traditional power of the pick, than the modern message of the media. Enter one A. Scargill, branch secretary at Woolley. His novelty was that he was available. He and I once drove round the Barnsley coalfield in my Triumph Herald, with Arthur rooting out people he thought suitable to interview. Arthur would knock on doors, and drag them out of the Welfare Clubs at lunchtime. I filmed on top of a tram at the NUM conference on the Isle of Man. That was real money. He was demanding twenty-five pounds a week for face workers. He became a master of the studio debate ... often finishing some tour de force, and then when the cameras had cut away, asking me how I thought he had done. On the way out of the studio, he would say, 'What did I say?' I would tell him what I remembered. 'I never can remember what I've said,' he told me candidly.

To this day, Arthur has seldom been

mastered in a TV studio. Bernard Dineen himself was the only person who could remotely stand up to him on a clinical and debating basis, while Philip Simms, a chunky and articulate Conservative Chairman, weighed in with eloquence and sheer physical size. During the most intense moments of the year-long miners' strike, I saw top interviewers like Sir Robin Day, the Dimblebys, the Snows, Frost, Sissons, all go red in the face trying to get one over Arthur – while he remained calm and polite, and won every time. He has actually a smiling, cocky and somehow vulnerable persona. He will enter a studio all smiles but his face will turn serious the moment the red light is on. I always loved my jousts with Arthur, especially face to face. Down the line interviews lack that physical presence, and in the most bitter years, I was strangely nervous of such encounters. It was a case of Mr Whiteley and Mr Scargill, each of us wanting to score points. Me wanting him to squirm before my incisive questioning – him intending to take no notice of the questions at all, and just saying what he had come in to say. What a master. It could be a Barnsley thing. Which brings us to Dickie Bird, again.

Dickie is, of course, a poppet, but his habit of arriving anywhere three hours early can be as tedious for TV production teams as it is for gatemen at Lords or guardsmen at

Buckingham Palace. This is what usually happens.

'Dickie, it's Richard Whiteley. Can you come on *Calendar* tonight to discuss Boycott?'

'Aye. What time do you want me master?'

'Five-thirty, Dickie.'

'Right.'

Two-thirty in the afternoon. Newsroom. Everybody busy. Phone call to Anne Monks, the meeter and greeter.

'Mr Bird in reception for *Calendar*.'

Three hours early. Dickie wanders round the newsroom for three hours, nice chap though he is, but getting in everybody's way. But I used my cunning to crack this, and here is my tip to others who book Dickie.

'Richard Whiteley here Dickie. Can you come on *Calendar* tonight to discuss Boycott?'

'Aye. What time do you want me master?'

'Eight-thirty, Dickie.'

No reaction. *Calendar* is at six.

'I'll be there.'

Five-thirty. Everyone frantic. Half an hour to transmission. Call from reception.

'Mr Bird here for *Calendar*.'

Perfect. He still hasn't realised.

I've met writers great and small. James Herriot, who had just published his first book at the age of fifty plus, surely the nicest and most modest bestseller there ever was. On an early interview, we did what TV crews from the world over subsequently did ... follow him on his rounds, up hill and down dale. I am sure I can remember the following incident taking place. We were filming in a farmyard on a hill farm high up above Wensleydale. Nearing lunchtime, I asked the farmer we were interviewing for the time. He bent down, lifted up the udders of the cow, with his horny hands, and said, 'ten to one'. I was as amazed as James Herriot himself, who said he had never seen anything quite like that in all his years. I asked if he could do it again for the camera. He agreed but made me do it. As I bent down, and grasped the swelling milk sack with my dainty hands, farmer George urged me to lift the udders higher and higher.

'There,' he said, 'you should just be able to see the church clock across the valley.'

But James Herriot and his wife Joan, were very special. Going to America in 1976, I realised just how big a name he was. They were wild for him. Coming back, I found him so infuriatingly modest and oblivious of the great affection the world had for him, I almost wanted to shake him. His son Jim, is now carrying on the practice and the Herriot tradition, and his daughter Rosie, a doctor, completes a truly lovely family. I stepped out with Dr Rosie for a while. I remember once sitting in an empty Cambridge cinema on a stunningly sunny Sunday afternoon, watching the second Herriot film which was released that day. It ends with the birth of Jim, her brother, and I have never forgotten the magic of that moment, to sit with someone who is seeing a recreation of their own family life. Rosie and I had words about something silly and I shall always regret that I never turned round and said sorry.

Authors great and small. Well, Herriot was not small, but I suppose you would call Sir Peter Ustinov great. He arrived at the studios to plug his autobiography *Dear Me*. Five hundred pages of riveting stuff about the life and very influential times of this truly iconic man. Dickie Bird style, Sir Peter arrived far too early, but he was treated to a boardroom reception. Would he like tea? No. A drink perhaps? No. Would he like the papers? No. Would he like to watch TV? No. He'd just mooch around the boardroom for two hours on his own until transmission time.

I was geared up for this interview, not, of course, having read the book, but aware of enough about Sir Peter to do the five minute interview the running order had suggested. In the break at 6.15, the great man was brought into the studio and sat next to me on the sofa. It had been a busy news day, and items were coming in and going down with all the usual activity of a live show. Eventually, I started on the intro to Sir Peter. Words like, 'great man, unique view of the world, role model, wealth of experience, highly influential' poured out of me.

'Sir Peter,' I began, when through my earpiece the stern voice of the PA asserted 'one minute twenty-five on this'.

Surely some mistake. Sixty years, and five hundred pages of a great man's life, to be considered in just a minute and twenty-five seconds! I wished I was dead. His first answer to the question, 'Does it seem sixty years ...' took one minute ten seconds. Only fifteen seconds for another question and answer. It was a nightmare. What would you do? Ask another question, and have no time for the answer. In the event, I heard myself apologising for having to curtail the interview, on account of some late film arriving of a fire at a tyre dump in Scunthorpe. Let's just say he was courteous but not amused. He was out of the building quick sharp, en route to the BBC studios of our rival *Look North. I* noticed they gave him the whole of their second half. Ah yes, but then they didn't have any film of the tyre fire in Scunthorpe.

There was a perpetual rumour threading between London and Yorkshire every so often, that I would be standing for Parliament. I would, said the rumour, be taking over from Sir Marcus Fox as MP for Shipley, my own constituency. There was no truth in this, at all, but it ran and ran, and every so often the *Yorkshire Post* would ring me up to ask if it was true. I did think momentarily of standing against Austin in Grimsby. *Calendar* was then so popular, and the two of us so identified, it would have been a hilarious beauty contest between us. But then I realised, if that was the case, Austin would win.

It was in the *Calendar* days that there occurred the notorious incident with the ferret. We ran an easy going interview show on Tuesdays called, enterprisingly enough, *Calendar Tuesday*. This was a loosely produced show, mainly featuring celebrities on publicity tours, or local celebrities and personalities talking in relaxed afternoon style. So relaxed was Des O'Connor, that he, on being invited to come to the studio half an hour before air time, asked what time he was on. The second half. Well, he'd stay in his hotel until he saw the programme start, and then come in. Cilla Black did the whole programme without knowing it was going out live. Frankie Howerd and I sat on the newsdesk swinging our legs, because a strike by props men meant there were no chairs. I did the programme week in week out, until one Tuesday I went out filming on Spurn Point. Marylyn Webb took over, only to have a member of the studio panel collapse and die live on air.

My own nemesis occurred in October 1977. The main guest on the show was Roger De Courcey, famous at that time for his double act with Nookie Bear. Anyway, the producer, Kevin Sim, didn't think that Roger and Nookie could justify a whole show, so a hastily arranged item was put in at the top. One Brian Plummer had published a book entitled *Ferret and Ferreting* and was booked for a six minute interview, and would he please bring a couple of ferrets with him? I approached the programme in my usual way, casually reading the dust jacket, not being wont to do any research before such gentle interviews. Brian was genial, talkative, amusing and extremely knowledgeable. We conversed easily, as I didn't know anything about the patron animal of Yorkshire, the questions were naïve, perhaps, but genuine, as I sat and stroked a ferret he had given me to hold. On the question 'are they easy to look after?', I was aware of a piercing pain, as if someone had stuck two needles through the fleshy part of my index finger. Please don't try this at home. Take my word for it, it's pretty painful. Live on TV we may have been, but this was no time for pretence, cover up, or even professionalism. Everything was at stake, including, it seemed, my finger. The exchange is now well known.

Me – 'Ow, ow, ow.'

Him – 'Keep still, it won't hurt you.'

Me – 'It is hurting me.'

Him – 'Here, hold these.' (Offers two ferrets he's holding.)

Me – 'I can't hold on to anything.' (Drops ferret onto slippery glass coffee table. Studio soundman's arms reach in to take ferrets. Thank you Alan Stormont.)

Me – 'Ow, ow, ow.' (Close-up of ferret with teeth firmly embedded in index finger.)

Him – 'Now this is the conclusion of the matter.' (Does something unspeakable to the personal parts of the ferret. This, if you like, made the ferret go 'ouch' in ferret speak. Thus the mouth was opened, and the finger released.)

Me –'Phew.'

Him – 'Don't worry, it's playing with you. If it had meant business, it would have been through to the bone.'

Hardly Kay Mellor, or Denis Potter, but surely one of the most spontaneous and genuine exchanges on British television in the last century.

There are two post scripts.

In the commercial break which followed, the studio nurse, Shirley Whittaker, having seen the happening, rushed into the studio, screeched at me to take my trousers down, and administered a tetanus injection there and then.

Brian Plummer was replaced by Roger De Courcey ... the supposed star turn. Roger was less than amused that he, a man who earned his living by putting his hand up a stuffed teddy bear's bottom, had been totally overshadowed by a real live ferret who fancied fingers.

From my point of view, the whole thing took half an hour, although as the tape reveals, the experience only lasted just over twenty seconds. That clip, thanks to Paul Lewis at LWT and Denis Norden, has become a classic. It is featured on all the 'best of' shows in the *It'll be Alright on the Night* series. It featured in the title sequence of Dick Clark's *Blooper* show in America, and I even received six hundred dollars for it being in the top five of his *World's Greatest Ever Bloopers* compilation.

So the legend of the ferret lives on. The ferret, of course, is long gone. Brian Plummer was last heard of in John O'Groats, and I expect I will always be known as the ferret man. Certainly, the headlines will be 'Ferret man dies' over my obituary. Not 'Perceptive TV interviewer', or even 'Cuddly afternoon TV host'. Certainly not 'Best selling author'!

COUNTING UP TO COUNTDOWN

In the beginning there was the word, or to be precise, the two words *Calendar Countdown*. For that is how the little, simple, low budget parlour game which has now become one of the most successful and longest running of its genre in British TV history, was born.

It began its life as a regional programme on YTV, a filler for the summer season. Frank Smith, an ex editor of *Panorama*, had been brought into Yorkshire Television by Paul Fox as Head of Factual Programmes, after the departure of John Fairley. John had felt that he should leave the company to whose great success in documentary and current affairs he had so creatively contributed. He was masterminding a franchise bid, indeed seeking to create a new franchise area carved out of the East Midlands, based on Nottingham. This was part of the mighty ATV empire of Lew Grade. The politics of ITV at the time demanded that Mr Fairley should go, as his presence on the staff of Yorkshire was a great embarrassment to Ward Thomas, who, as MD of a fellow 'Big Five' company, was a close working colleague, indeed friend of Lew, then, of course, a towering force in the world of television and entertainment on both sides of the Atlantic.

So enter Frank. He didn't have the best of starts. Three weeks after joining in the summer of 1979, the whole of the ITV network went on strike, and there was total shut down for three months. At one time, both BBC channels were also off the air due to an unrelated cause and for several days that summer all three channels were showing apology cards and playing music. One of the best pieces of writing I shall always remember was that of the then editor of the *Yorkshire Evening Post*, Malcolm Barker, who, without any television to review, did in fact review the three apology captions, making judgements on wording, graphics, shades of blue, and the music which was played endlessly as the days wore on. However, I digress.

In the spring of 1982, Frank started talking about a game show he had seen during his years working in France. A words and numbers game called beguilingly *Des Chiffres et des Lettres* which being translated is quite simply, Numbers and Letters.

Running six days a week just before the main news on the second channel, it attained a huge rating and indeed was a national institution. When it came off the air once for a break, questions were asked in the French Parliament. Frank had thought it might work in Yorkshire in the summer and a team of three, not including me, went over to Paris, to *regardez,* or so their expenses said. Why it was necessary to stay Saturday and Sunday to watch a Friday recording, can only be assumed, although England were playing France at rugby that weekend.

A deal was done with the French and work was done on reformatting it for our Yorkshire audience. Looking at the French tape and certainly as one not fluent in the language, I must admit I had to wonder just what the appeal was. It was bottom achingly slow, technically crude in the extreme, but especially in production values. Microphone cables trailing everywhere, loose camera work, much extraneous studio sound. There was a minimum of chat and a total lack of humour, just a cold Gallic feeling of getting on with the business with little of the Oh là là you might have expected from the French. When time ran out at the end of the show, the next edition just picked up where it had left off. The tension element which has become so important to *Countdown* these days, was totally non existent. I was brought in at a relatively late stage of the planning, and I don't know if I was the first choice, in fact, I'd rather not know. But I suppose I was a fairly obvious candidate as the main presenter of *Calendar*. Most of the presenters had little spin-off half hours suiting their interests – sport, fashion, country life, politics and so on. So *Calendar Countdown* fitted me well. After all, I was an English graduate and, therefore, bound to be fluent with the words. Did someone mention a numbers game as well? Well, I certainly didn't volunteer the fact that I had failed O level maths twice. Anyway, the Yorkshire concept also called for a modicum of spontaneous wit and an element of literacy and knowledge of literature. If someone else had been chosen, I suppose I would have been very annoyed.

Some major decisions had been taken. We would have a big clock ticking down to zero for each round. How long the countdown would last, we weren't sure. The French had forty-five seconds, with no clock on the set, just one inlaid on the screen towards the end of the time with lift muzak playing dimly in the background. We would have a celebrity wordsmith as well as a professional lexicographer to bring some personality to the party. We would have a definite games span of nine rounds: six letters, two numbers and then a conundrum – our most significant departure from the French – which would signal the end of the game, and often, given the way that we reorganised the scoring, produce a definite winner at the end of the programme.

Their numbers girl clanked up the numbers, and the dictionary man was also clever enough to work out the numbers game. We didn't know a person of such dual skills and looked for a girl (it was OK to do such things in those days), to work out the numbers. Oh yes, there was the small matter of a presenter. Theirs was a dark, sanguine, fine featured, fairly monosyllabic, but nevertheless charismatic monsieur called Patrice Laffont. Apparently he had presented every edition for the whole eleven year history of the programme. 'Call that a job,' I thought to myself. Of course it is, I now tell myself after eighteen years and three thousand editions doing exactly the same thing. While the French ethos was one of muttered relaxation in which you felt the participants could be just about bothered to take part, and the presenter could be just about bothered to turn up and present it. ours was to be lively, spontaneous, earnest, competitive, witty, confrontational, fought against the clock, and instructional too. We finally agreed that the countdown would last only thirty seconds both for words and numbers, and the jangly jangly theme would ensure no one slept when that tick tock started. We left the decision as to the length of the countdown to the very last minute, and as the set designer got more and more agitated, the compromise was made that the clock should be a full minute, therefore giving us all options for the allotted time span. That is why, in answer to one of the most asked questions, the famous count-down clock shows a whole minute, while only half that minute is used. One thing was made absolutely clear by Frank. I was to start the clock with the phrase, 'The countdown starts now' and he was con-vinced it was to be one of the catchphrases of the decade.

Eighteen years later, I have to admit, this has not yet become a national catchphrase, while the nine notes of the irritating clock music certainly have. You can sing it now, as you read this, everyone does when they see me in the street, here are the words Boo, boo, boo boo boo boo boo boo boom! I often feel rather sad on reflection that after the eighteen years and three thousand editions, I do not have my own catchphrase. Goodness gracious I have tried, but somehow 'that's the end of part one, see you again in part two', has never really caught on. So I have had to reconcile myself to the joys of nine notes of music and an exclamation mark.

A pilot show, rare in those days, was scheduled. I was due to go to Portugal on holiday, and would therefore miss the recording date. In fact I very nearly went, thinking the show was nothing really special. We were always putting new series on in the regional transmission slots that we had available. This one would doubtless come and go. There would be a political or a chat show coming along soon. Oh the blaséness and confidence of youth! But I remember saying to my putative host, a Yorkshire businessman, Stuart Barr, that I felt I should be around in Yorkshire for this pilot because, come to think of it, I did believe something might come of it.

What did come was indeed *Calendar Countdown*, first transmitted on Monday 6 July 1982 at 6.30 in the evening, straight after the nightly *Calendar*. If you ever come round to my place, I'll show you the tape and we can squirm with embarrassment together. The set was brown, the letters were yellow on grey. For some reason we only had eight in the selection. Dictionary Corner was staffed by a lexicographer from Leeds University, and the affable and ubiquitous Ted Moult. Between them they rarely topped the average efforts of our contestants. And the numbers girl, named in splendid pre-political correctness, 'vital statistician', was totally unable throughout the run of solving a single numbers game. If neither of the contestants were able to work it out, she was also incapable, but made it worse by remarking, 'Well, I can't get it and I bet no one can at home.' There was news for her. They certainly could – in droves, and they certainly let us know. As for me, I floundered around trying to explain the relatively simple rules, reading out made up cod letters from nonexistent viewers, and trying to point out the origin and first usage of some of the words. Looking back it was toe curling and in spite of our production efforts, it did seem so slow and naïve. And yet ... and yet...

It had something. Just as the French lot seemed to get on with no fuss, their team emerging as everyday friends, although somewhat dull, and inviting you to have a go and play along, so that feeling began to develop with our viewers in Yorkshire. I can tell you that if you are on TV every night, then it's no big deal for friends, family, people in the neighbourhood, certainly in the local, and even more certainly your colleagues, and those who you pass in the corridors at work. They seldom mention your onscreen appearances, except when you are out of context. For example, I was featured for about thirty seconds in the famous fly on the wall docusoap about the

Adelphi Hotel in Liverpool. It was when the IRA bomb hoax sent us all scuttling out of the Grand National at Aintree. I was one of the first to arrive at the Adelphi and I was filmed ordering two bottles of Premier Cru Chablis from an already harassed old bird of a waitress who was to get considerably more harassed as several hundred thirsty oiks like me staggered in. When this went out later in the year, there was a huge number of people who subsequently said to me, 'We saw you on TV the other night'. Why did they say that when I am on TV every night as it is? Of course they saw me on TV that night. I'm on TV every flipping night aren't I? Yes, of course I am, but that's not remarkable. But thirty seconds of me behaving like Michael Winner probably is, it is untypical, and thus noticeable.

And so it was with *Calendar Countdown*. Normally, a performance on the previous night's *Calendar* would never draw any comment at all from anybody. Why should it? I was just doing my job. People don't come up to barbers or bank managers or barmen in the street and congratulate them on having done a great job the day before. No one has said to me, 'Richard, you put on a terrific show with the Prime Minister last night. Thought you really pinned her against the wall', or 'Hey Richard, you really trounced that Arthur Scargill last night, don't think he'll want to come up against you again'. Or 'Hey you and Les Dawson. It was so funny. He couldn't hold a candle to you'. None of that is ever said. I had realised this several years ago when I had a series of half hour chat shows in front of a studio audience called *Calendar People*. This went out in the excellent 10.30, post *News at Ten*, slot. After the first one had finished, I sat at home waiting for the phone to ring, issuing congratulations from friends, family, colleagues, ex girlfriends, future girlfriends, even my ex wife, just ordinary viewers. I waited and waited and the phone never rang. Incidentally, twenty-five years later, after a showing of my *Richard Whiteley Unbriefed* on the BBC, I similarly waited at eleven o'clock for phone calls. I got two. One was from my brother-in-law saying they'd watched the show and they liked the all-girl saxophone band and the second from Sir Paul Fox who boomed into my message machine, 'Well, it was certainly better than the first one but that's not saying much'. So believe me, I am used to not getting a reaction.

But the reaction we got for *Calendar Countdown* convinced me that we were on to something rather special. For example, after each edition, the canteen ladies you'd meet the next morning would comment while I was in the salad queue, 'I got a five letter word last night.' Taxi drivers would do the same thing. It certainly made a change from their usual mantra, 'Does that *Calendar* come live or do you record it?' Depending on my sense of humour at the time, I'd often reply, 'Yes, we record the news several days ahead, especially the soccer results.' People in shops whose previous policy had been totally to ignore you with no eye contact, all made comments, and there was just something in the programme, naïve and bumbling as it was, that seemed to strike a chord. Who knows why? Anyway, we did our series of nine, setting a trend by recording three a day, and we all went off on our summer holidays.

But Frank Smith got to work. To this day I don't know how he did it but I'm sure glad he did. He had shown *Calendar Countdown* to Cecil Korer, the first Commissioning Editor of entertainment at Channel Four which was due on the air that November. Cecil, who had previously worked with the great Barney Colehan on the unforgettable *It's a Knockout* and numerous beauty competitions, had been based in Leeds for the BBC. Actually he did seem a rather out of place choice for the somewhat eclectic team of commissioning editors which Jeremy Isaacs was assembling at the Charlotte Street headquarters. Cecil was a good old fashioned end of the pier song and dance man. Not, you would imagine, the sort of chap destined to brand the new channel with distinctive and innovative comedy and entertainment. However, Cecil you'll do for me. So hats off to Cecil for recognising the show for what it was and for selling it to Jeremy Isaacs on that basis. Mind you, Jeremy was the man who had run several series of *Love Thy Neighbour* produced by an ebullient ex floor manager called William G. Stewart. Where is he now I wonder? Probably retired I expect at his great age.

One day Frank came in with the news that Channel Four had commissioned five weeks' worth of *Countdown* and they were planning to run it four days a week, Monday to Thursday at 4.45 in the afternoon. This was known as stripping and was, in those days, a relatively new departure. Only *Crossroads* had achieved such a stripping schedule in its heyday. While we, of course, were humbly grateful for the commission, the time of quarter to five in the afternoon did seem less than happy. It seemed to us the ideal time was six thirty in the evening when people, certainly up North, at home for the night, had had their tea, washed up and were putting their feet up ready for an evening's entertainment. However, five weeks on Channel Four was five weeks on Channel Four and we were all very excited. Channel Four liked the educational element of *Countdown* (ah, thank you Jeremy), but the old trooper Cecil liked the game show element, so the trawl was on for ex beauty queens who could assume the onerous duties of selecting the numbers and the letters and putting them on the board.

I gather a good time was had by all involved in this interesting exercise. Cathy Hytner was chosen as the letters girl. She had served as well on *Calendar Countdown*. Although she has not been on the show for well over ten years now, people still ask me 'Where's Cathy?' The numbers were to be selected by a former Miss Great Britain, Beverley Isherwood. We had the luxury of two numbers girls to do the working out, Dr Linda Baxter from Leicester University and one Carol Vorderman, a Cambridge graduate of engineering, who lived up the road in Headingley. In addition to this, Ted Moult was brought back and so were a series of professional lexicographers, this time from Oxford University to sit in Dictionary Corner. So that only left me.

Well, I'm not daft. I don't think anyone was exactly knocked out by me or my performance as quizmaster. Certainly no one in Charlotte Street had ever heard of me, but I was available. I knew the rules, I looked reasonably the part with a pair of glasses and an English degree. But most of all, I was considerably cheaper than Bob

Monkhouse or Tom O'Connor. In fact, much cheaper, virtually free. *Calendar* paid my salary. *Countdown,* as the Channel Four version was conveniently to be called, was something I nipped out and did on my days off, or in the afternoons, while combining it with my *Calendar* duties at 6.00 in the evening.

Our first recording dates were due in October to get ready for delivering the first programme on time. The set had been changed from brown to a combination of brighter pastel colours. The Heath Robinson of the French game was given the high tech treatment of the time. The big clock. The big letters made out of linoleum tiles. A random number indicator to give us the target figure to which I sycophantically gave the acronym Cecil – *Countdown's* Electronic Calculator in Leeds. In fact, it was nothing of the sort. It was not a calculator at all, just a standard number generator used in numerous studio productions.

Incidentally, the French version is now awash with high technology – computer selected letters, touch screen displays for working out the numbers game, not a felt tip in sight. Meanwhile, we have stuck to our basic 1982 arrangements, and eighteen years on people seem to love its nostalgic retro look, and, music and all, we would never think of changing it now. Talking of music, the *Countdown* theme has emerged as one of its strongest points. I am frequently asked, 'Can the contestants hear the music as the clock ticks round?' The answer is yes. 'Does it not drive them crazy?' The answer is probably yes, but by gauging the beat of the music, they can have some idea of how the thirty second time limit is progressing. The music itself was written for the pilot by Alan Hawkshaw. Legend has it that on the morning of the pilot he suddenly remembered while doing his morning ablutions that he had yet to deliver this thirty second motif for the pilot at Yorkshire TV. Now, of course, I am not privy to Mr Hawkshaw's movements but I gather as he sat on the loo that morning, inspiration suddenly dawned. He grabbed the back page of the *Daily Telegraph* and wrote down the vital notes. Hence can be explained the plippety plop nature of the *Countdown* theme. This turned out to be a good bit of business for Alan, who not only composed the *Countdown* theme, but also the theme for *Channel Four News* and the theme for *Channel Four Racing*. All these three programmes have been broadcast on an almost daily basis for the last eighteen years. Who wants to be a millionaire? Easy. Just invent a theme for a parlour game!

John Fairley had returned to YTV by now as Director of Programmes and came in one day with some interesting news. We were scheduled as we knew, to go out at 4.45, but we didn't know the exact date of transmission. Now, it had all been fixed at 4.45 on Tuesday 2 November.

'It looks Mr Whiteley as if yours will be the first face on Channel Four. Good luck to them.'

ONE SMALL STEP

'As the countdown to the start of a brand new channel ends, a brand new *Countdown* begins.'

The first words spoken on the first programme transmitted on the first day of Channel Four on 2 November 1982. These days the opening of a new channel is something of a 'so what' event ... can anyone remember who opened Channel Five? Actually, I desperately wanted to, and Dawn Airey, the Director of Programmes, got so fed up with me pestering her about coming on and doing it, which would have been a unique double for me, that she left a tart message with her faithful PA Elspeth, 'Tell' him that not only is he not opening it, but he will never, ever even appear on it.' But Channel Four was big news in the Eighties.

It was Britain's first new channel for sixteen years, preceded by as much debate as there was about the opening of the BBC television service in 1936 and certainly as much as that which set up Independent Television in 1955.

There were great expectations of a new channel which, like any media start up, was going to be all things to all people. When we were proposing a commercial radio station in York in the Nineties, I heard myself, as putative chairman, standing up at a public meeting and committing the station to a regular programme on fifteenth and sixteenth century music, for which York is rightly famed in certain charmed circles. As far as I know, *Top of the Pops 1556* has yet to be transmitted on Minster FM. But like many openings, there were problems. For a start, Channel Four transmitters didn't cover the whole country and a dispute with Equity kept most adverts off the air, resulting in long captions for minute after minute, where commercials should have been. This did not add viewer appeal to the mix. However, for me that opening night was a great thrill and perhaps the one achievement of which I am most proud in my television career. After all, it's one thing they can never take away from me. Even if the series had bombed and been axed after the first few weeks, I would still have been forever the first face on Channel Four. Long forgotten and completely unknown, perhaps, but still the first face on Channel Four. Indeed, I am now a well known trivia question, usually coupled with 'What was the first advert ever on commercial television?' Well luckily, Gibbs SR after forty-five years, and I, Whiteley J.R., after eighteen years, are still gleaming!

We had, as I said, recorded the first edition of *Countdown* some weeks previously. Apart from the majesty of the Neil Armstrong like words, the programme was cringeworthy in the extreme. As is the practice these days when several editions are pre-recorded, we could have started with a later edition which would have been a little more honed. But the very nature of *Countdown* denied this. You end each show with a winner and the winner goes on to the next show, so you have to progress sequentially, and obviously show the first one.

Countdown, of course, like any programme did not just happen, and there are some key players in the whole saga. The first element is the game itself. It is, of course, a devilishly simple game, and one which every one of us thinks we could have invented. It perhaps is the most obvious of all parlour games. Just choose nine letters and make a word, the longest correct word wins. Do a similar thing with the numbers and there you have it. Absolutely nothing to it. We all could have invented it. I remember playing a game in the Sixties called the Dictionary Game. Someone chose a long word from the dictionary and we sat around composing definitions. It kept us quiet and amused for ages. Surely there is a TV series in that. Oh, yes, of course there is ... it's called *Call my Bluff*. So there we are.

People are always asking me did I invent *Countdown?* The answer, sadly, is no. Well, do I own the rights? Do I own the rights? No, mes amis, I do not own the rights. They belong to our friends across the channel, the French. The *Countdown* père is Armand Jammot. Monsieur Jammot, who passed on recently was a journalist, turned radio producer working in the heyday of French commercial radio in the Fifties. He turned to television where he was famous for creating programme formats. For many years the credit '*Une emmission d'Armand Jammot*' guaranteed a successful show. He became Director of Programming for the second French network Antenne 2, now called FR2. It was for them that he developed the simple formula of *Des Chiffres et des Lettres*. It was this that had intrigued Yorkshire TV's Frank Smith while he was working in Paris.

Frank sought to do a deal with Armand

Jammot, and here enters another exotically named character (this show is nothing if not romantic), Monsieur Marcel Stellman to be the go-between. Marcel was not a Frenchman but spoke the language very well as he was born next door, in Belgium. In fact, I would seriously claim that Marcel Stellman is without doubt the fifth most famous Belgian born and that includes Hercule Poirot. In fact, Marcel who's mother was a Scot, is a long naturalised English man, a magistrate for seventeen years and a Freeman of the City of London. Marcel goes back a long way BC – that is before *Countdown*. He was a senior executive with Decca Records, producing singles, albums and the like when plastic was giving way to vinyl, and we were all marvelling that our turntable had three speeds and we didn't have to wind it up. Marcel worked with Edmundo Ross, whom I saw arriving at Nice airport in 1957, and was by far the most famous person I had ever seen apart from the Queen Mother and Len Hutton. Stephan Grappelli was one of his colleagues and close friends, but his greatest claim is that while employed at Decca, he discovered a lovely catchy tune on the Continent, and thought it would be ideal for Max Bygraves who was under contract. He reworked some totally new lyrics, coined a catchy title, and Max cut the disk. The rest is history, which is why he is the fifth most famous Belgian. Did I say fifth, fourth, third, second? No, I think we should hear it for the *most* famous Belgian. For that song was 'Tulips from Amsterdam'! Yes, hands up all those reading this who bought that record? And even if you are too young, hands up if you know the words – I bet you all do. Bravo, Marcel!

So Marcel was the link between YTV and French television and we have enjoyed a très magnifique relationship over the years. He is the most elegant and dapper of characters and having resided in London for over forty years, is more English than a lot of us. Purely for our own in-group amusement, I try to mention 'Tulips from Amsterdam' at least once a series. Sadly, I don't think he gets any royalties from the mention!

And then there was John Meade. John was assistant producer, and a member of the expeditionary team to France, and we had worked on hundreds of editions of *Calendar* together, as well as my chat show *Calendar People*. He was a great character round the building and indeed was the bedrock of *Countdown* in production terms. Much of what we take for granted on *Countdown* – the opening banter, the puns, the 'last time out of Guardian of the Dictionary' routine, the pieces into the break by the celebrity, the general fun and yet competitive aspect of the show – stems both from his ideas, and his acceptance of the ideas of other people, including me, who had to pretend that the ideas were indeed John's in the first place. He was punster, a wordsmith, an accomplished practitioner at crosswords, and thoroughly into the concept of *Countdown*. He also directed the show from the gallery for many years, having taken over as producer when Frank left YTV. I was grateful not to be able to hear his juicy comments through my earpiece. I had what's called 'selective talkback' so that I could only hear anything that I really needed to know. Our John was no respecter of personalities or positions. You expected blunt talking when John was in the gallery and, had a sensitive soul like me heard his words of wisdom in my shell-like, I might well have not only lost the will to continue into the next round, but might have been put off a life of television altogether.

On many occasions in the early days, we had to stop recordings in mid-take owing to some technical fault, or indeed a fault with the very lifeline of *Countdown*, the big clock. These interruptions, which would often last up to an hour and a half, did nothing for my frame of mind. On more than one occasion, I was in the full flow of verbal activity when the floor manager would order us to stop.

'Oh, why have we stopped this time?' I would flounce dramatically. 'Not bloody sound again is it?'

'No,' said the floor manager. 'Only because you welcomed us back to part two of *Calendar*, and not *Countdown*.'

What a dumb dumb. I also used to get the letters mixed up with the numbers, seemingly not being able to tell one from the other. On one blessed occasion, I said, 'Well now let's move on to choose your letters,' when I meant numbers. I said in frustration, 'Oh why do I always get the numbers mixed up with the letters?'

Straightaway came this thick Yorkshire crisp monotone down my earpiece, and indeed down all the headsets of all the camera crew. 'Because you're a pillock.' Although I don't think the words he used were as sympathetic as pillock.

All this creative energy was marshalled by the first studio director, David St David Smith, a lively and garrulous Welshman, who gave the show its initial look and technical feel, a formula we continue to the present day. We feel we change anything at our peril. What was high tech in 1982 is pretty low tech in the year 2000, but we believe the viewers have come to love what is now the retro look, and wouldn't have it any other way. Two competitors appeared in that first series, a former bookies clerk from Edinburgh, Michael Wylie and a sixteen year old schoolboy at Latimer Upper School,

Hammersmith, called Mark Nyman. The rest is history. Both of them are now producers of the programme. Mark having run a parallel career as a King of Scrabble – he is even a former world Scrabble champion. They were later joined by another champion Damien Eadie, who when he became *Countdown* Champion was working as a Civil Servant in Blackpool. These three chaps backed up by Cindy and Dianne, complete the full time team. The very compactness of the team and the great sense of history that its members carry around in their brains, all contribute to the present day success of the *Countdown* operation. Brenda Wilson directs the affair, with deceptively calm authority. As the vision mixer for many years, she knows that each programme has over three hundred cuts, a lot for twenty-four minutes.

I owe much to this team, especially to Frank Smith who put me into the show in the first place, and John Meade who kept me in it, and David St David Smith who got the show on the road. It is painful to have to record that both the Smiths, David and Frank, left us at far too early an age. I do think though that it is wonderful for their families to know that a programme they helped to create is still in such rude health, and is an ongoing testimony to their contribution. We never let one of our anniversaries go past without a toast to their memory.

All this success that we have now enjoyed, nearly never happened. The opening night was hardly a success. Channel Four chiefs had decided that the opening would be low key. No pressing of buttons by Her Majesty, no speech by Mrs Thatcher to turn the channel on (and on!). No, they would just, well, start at 4.45 pm on 2 November. At 4.40 that evening, crowds were gathering round TV sets wherever in the land the signal could reach. Expectation was high. The landscape test pictures which had been running all day to the accompaniment of jolly music abruptly went off. There was a terrible darkness over the screen for one, two, three, four endless minutes. Oh dear, everyone thought, including all of us watching in the *Calendar* newsroom. Something has gone terribly wrong. And then, when the technicians had done all the switching they apparently had to do, out of nowhere came the famous few notes, and then the image of the Four logo which self destructed and then reformed. Paul Coia, out of vision, announced, 'This is Channel Four' and next thing the *Countdown* titles were on. And suddenly, there I was, looking thirty-eight, which indeed I was (incidentally, more or less the same age Carol is now, depending when you read this). And so into the magic words. Now, I'm no Neil Armstrong and I'm certainly no John Kennedy, but I tell you this. A lot of people tell me exactly where they were when they saw the first *Countdown* go out. Many of them had just come back from school, in fact. They also tell me they remember exactly where they were the day the second *Countdown* went out ... as far from a TV as possible – even staying late at school!

But few remember those portentous words. So, for the compilers of trivia quizzes and books of quotations, are you ready Nigel Rees? Here they are once again, and I shall say them only once.

'As the countdown to the start of a brand new channel ends, a brand new *Countdown* begins.' Come on now, it's not that bad. We only thought we were doing twenty little teatime programmes, and anyway, *Countdown* wasn't our main job, we all had proper ones. We certainly didn't envisage it going on for twenty years. The first night got over three and a half million viewers for that opening programme. Encouraged by this, we had high hopes for the second which turned out to be just eight hundred thousand. And the third – well, just don't ask me. Carol has worked out that the ratings slide over those first three nights was the biggest ever recorded in the history of television in the Western World. It wasn't just us, we comforted ourselves. The whole of Channel Four got off to a pretty bad start didn't it? Luckily, most reviewers had more important things to say about the rest of the evening's output than to worry about us. I was upset, though, to be personally branded as Wally of the Week by Nina Myskov in one of the tabloids. Mind you, I don't blame her as we had disallowed the word 'wally' on the Thursday edition. I'm glad to say that that word is now well and truly in the *Oxford Dictionary*. The first two contestants were a young chap from London, Geoff Andrews, and an accountant from London, Michael Goldman. Michael, in fact, went on to win six editions. Our lexicographer from Oxford was a lady of a certain age, slim if you like, nervy if you like, intellectual certainly. And therefore, finding it rather difficult to fit in with us unashamed showbiz types. But unbeknown to us she certainly set a trend. When I referred to Dictionary Corner, she came out with a word, which would better those offered by the contestants.

'So what have you got Alice?' I cheerfully said.

'I have an eight,' she said. 'Rogering.'

Gasps all round. This, of course, is exactly the sort of tittering word that so many people tune in for these days, but at the time we weren't to know, and I have a feeling that particular contribution ended up in the video graveyard.

Well, perhaps those early shows weren't the greatest. Although we really wanted them to be and we all tried our best. Marcel famously said to his wife Jeanne on the way back to London on the train after watching the opening recordings, 'Don't hold your breath.' I often wonder if he had penned another hit for Max on that journey home. He must have thought he was going to need it. On that November evening I sat at home and waited for the phone to ring. It did indeed ring. My mother thought that Ted Moult was such a nice man and why didn't I have a haircut. And then the *Bradford Telegraph and Argus* rang to ask what I had thought of *Brookside*. Well, not encouraging, but so what? In a way it was only a hobby, it was not our proper job. Besides, no one in Ilkley where I lived could even get Channel Four, so I could still walk down the Grove unmolested every Saturday morning.

But truth to tell, of course I wanted it to work. Really I did. I was proud, proud, proud of being that first face, and naïvely perhaps thought it could lead to other big things. just as when getting one of my *Calendar* news reports networked on *News at Ten*, I thought I would be bound to be spotted. 'And were you?' I hear you ask. 'Er ... no.' Even at the Channel Four opening party on the Thursday, nobody spotted me.

I had thought that at the very least Sir Richard Attenborough, the Deputy Chairman, would stand up and present me to the other guests.

'And now my dears, the man, yes, the man whose face was seen by those pioneering and privileged millions, the man who will surely become a flagship for this station, as she sails elegantly and steadfastly and, thanks to *Countdown*, launched so beautifully on to a golden horizon, the man about whom people will for ever say, this man, this humble Yorkshireman is forever to be remembered as long as television people gather together, they will, with one voice, remember him as the first person to appear on Channel Four ... Richard Whiteley, we salute you.' Actually, I don't seem to remember this happening. In fact, I wondered why there were so many people at the party, about five thousand, it seemed to me. What had they got to do with Channel Four? And then I thought, perhaps they were the viewers.

Anyway, I didn't know anybody there, so I told a waitress I'd been the first face on. She politely pretended to be impressed but quickly made an excuse and left saying she must take a drink to Peter Sissons who she could see had just arrived.

Well, as you know, we did survive. The lesson of *Countdown* for subsequent television bosses is 'keep the faith'. Shows do take time to develop and win the affection of the public. It would have been very easy indeed to have axed *Countdown* after the first series. By now, it would have been long gone and forgotten. Mind you, the show was no great shaker. It was all blonde bimbos; Ted Moult, bless him, who had appeared in every panel game going in those days; me, who nobody outside Yorkshire had heard of; irritating music and a format looking as though it had come from Alexandra Palace, rather than from the new cutting edge radical, much longed for, TV channel. But we staggered on and eventually Kenneth Williams took over from Ted. If you have his diaries in your house, put this chapter on pause now, and just reach for them, look up *Countdown* in the index and he will tell you all about his experiences and his thoughts on the personalities involved.

Right have you done that? Well, you see that's his version. He didn't like the show, he didn't really like anyone in it. He certainly didn't like me, especially me, with my appalling puns and in his view, I was terribly smug. But he did rather like John Meade. Now, I in no way seek a right of reply, indeed I was thrilled to bits to be included in his diary, but I will say this, Kenneth was marvellous for the show. He gave it a style, he delivered a class act, both on the screen and in the studio with the audience between recordings. His presence on the show gave it a credibility and while we could hardly claim that gravitas was what we sought, his presence certainly brought the programme to the attention of the newly forming chattering classes. By appearing on *Countdown,* he gave it a status that set it apart as something just a little bit different from other panel type games.

He may well have hated it and he was certainly awkward to have around the place. We recorded morning and afternoon in those days. He used to go mad at the lunch break which lasted a minimum of an hour and a half. Why did we have one? Couldn't we start before two o'clock? God, did you expect me to eat this! Why are we still hanging around? John Meade became his minder and comforter, indeed court jester, keeping him just this side of walking away. But Kenneth gave us that status and we were on the map at last.

After Christmas, Channel Four experimented with a raft of other teatime shows – *TV Scrabble, Jeopardy,* the American hit and so on, but nothing seemed to work particularly well at this time of 4.45. So they kept, in desperation I suspect, coming back and ordering more editions. As we ploughed on, Gyles Brandreth joined in Dictionary

Corner and was immediately at home. He revelled fulsomely in the definitions and the origins of words and their quotes, and it was a great platform for his outgoing personality. Sadly, it wasn't to everyone's taste, and it looked as though if he persisted with his woolly jumpers, we'd all be outgoing as well. Going out of the Channel Four schedules!

Actually Gyles was a terrific asset to *Countdown* in those early years. For while some viewers did mistake his somewhat theatrical eagerness for an irritating mannerism, he was just right for the job, and it meant that I, as host, did not have to worry about doing two jobs – that is mine and his. Some of our guests in Dictionary Corner have arrived ill prepared, which in turn has meant that I have had to shoulder the additional burden of shoring them up. No such bother with Gyles, who brought a genuine enthusiasm to the game.

The Brandreth charm is legendary ... almost as much as that of Sir David Frost. And it works. After all, if someone seems genuinely delighted to see you, says he thinks you are wonderful, and suggests a further meeting in the indefinite future, then it is impossible not to warm to that person. So with Gyles. Everything is marvellous, super, wonderful and he is always so grateful for everything. This manner endeared him to producers, crews, audiences, hosts and hostesses.

One day, my partner at that time, Jeni, suggested he came home for a kitchen table supper. On the way Gyles was ecstatic. My car was terrific and so stylish. The scenery going out of Leeds was marvellous. By the time we got to my little lane on the edge of Ilkley Moor, he could hardly control himself. The countryside was stunning. My lane so exquisite ... the old stone built cottage magnificent. Jeni was beautiful ... the shepherds pie smelt fantastic ... the white wine he knew to be of the best ... and the wine glasses! Oh, the wine glasses so perfect.

'Tell me Jeni. Where did you get these?'

'With six gallons of Shell.'

'Wonderful petrol,' he would surely have said ... but by this time even Gyles had run out of superlatives.

In February of 1984, only eighteen months into the programme, there was great excitement. There was talk of us being invited to Monte Carlo by the French to watch the grand final of their programme, *Des Chiffres et des Lettres* direct from the principality. We were to be their guests, and to be treated to the very best – hotels, restaurants, formal dinners, best seats at the final itself, in the presence of Prince Rainier and his family. Now, this was a super freebie. You couldn't get this type of treatment with any old gameshow. Where did Terry Wogan go with *Blankety Blank?* Did Eamonn Andrews get further than Shepherds Bush with *What's My Line?* And what about Nicholas Parsons doing the *Sale of the Century* from Norwich. He'd be lucky to get to Great Yarmouth. No, this was the big one. Even Whicker would have loved this.

I had been contemplating going in to ask for a rise. Incidentally, when *Countdown* first started, I was paid an extra two hundred pounds a show, in addition to my *Calendar* salary. This was a deal previously arranged by Paul Fox which covered my doing any specials or anything not strictly related to the daily *Calendar* programme. For the first series YTV did indeed pay me two hundred pounds a show. Very useful money indeed for the twenty that we did. When Channel Four kept coming back and commissioning more, I was called in by the contracts man to be told that there was no way they could go on paying me the two hundred pounds.

'Why not? YTV makes money out of selling it to Channel Four.'

'Yes, but there are so many shows now on order that if we paid you two hundred pounds a show, you'd be the best paid member of the staff at YTV.'

'Well,' I said, rather dumbfoundedly. 'Why shouldn't I be? Someone's got to be. It's either me or some union member on massive overtime, so why shouldn't it be me?'

Well, call me old fashioned or just plain stupid, but I sat there meekly and heard him say, 'Yes, but you must understand, every pound we pay you is one pound less profit for the company.'

'Quite.' I somehow accepted the logic of this, and I heard myself being grateful for the offer of sixty pounds a programme, a drop of one hundred and forty pounds for presenting a show which was becoming a nice little earner for YTV. I was disappointed, obviously, but then, I have always been a company man. Anyway, when we heard about this French trip, well, I'd have done *Countdown* for nowt. In fact, I'd have probably paid them.

A couple of days before, I went up to John Meade's office to put some expenses on his desk for signing. As a graduate of the Michael Partington school of reading memos upside down on other people's desks, I saw some notes that John had taken during a meeting with senior executives to discuss *Countdown*. 'Ratings – sluggish', he'd put. Then things like 'time slot' and 'set design'. Finally, I could see that he had written 'New Presenter'. This was underlined twice with a couple of question marks.

'Oh, dear, poor old Carol,' I thought, as I

left my exes and went to the cash office to draw my francs for Monte Carlo. On the way I met Graham Ironside, the Head of Regional Programmes. Knowing that he was on the lookout for a local weather girl, I asked him if he'd have a look at Carol Vorderman.

'She's very good at standing in front of boards,' I said, eagerly advancing her cause, 'and drawing with a felt tip pen.'

'Whiteley,' he replied, 'I've seen that wee lassie on your programme and I can tell you this. That girl has got no future in television.'

Oh, well, I thought. Poor Carol. At least I had tried. She'd probably do very well going back to selling computers. After all, it's a tough world ... television ... survival of the fittest. Meanwhile, Monte Carlo with all its charms beckoned. This story now divides into two ... what I did know, and what I didn't know.

What I didn't know, until years later in fact, was quite simple. While it was relatively early days in the history of Channel Four, and while certainly there was no benchmark to assess the ratings of a teatime intellectually based programme, the situation was under constant review. Channel Four were obviously looking for a sound programme to fill that slot, and were naturally looking at several other options.

YTV, conscious of the fact that they had a low budget, potentially hugely profitable product, were anxious to keep *Countdown* in the frame. Indeed, while general disinterest greeted the initial series, I do remember John Fairley, the Director of Programmes, saying to the team that there was no reason why this programme shouldn't run and run and run. Prescience indeed. But at that time nobody was confident. Consider. It was an uphill battle. We were on the air at quarter to five, only later being moved to four thirty. We started from virtually a blank screen, only a test card and music preceding us. We were never promoted, either on air, or through any other Channel Four publicity. We were virtually ignored in the listings in the papers. 'Countdown – word game' was as good as we could hope to get. Only one, Tony Pratt, in the *Daily Mirror* of all papers, used to write carefully crafted little straplines. The first critic to recognise us. And let's face it, *Countdown* carved out that teatime slot, which at that time was a no view area for our target audience, no one viewing at all apart from children. The scheduling did us no favours – on for six weeks, then off for six weeks, then on for four and off again. It was very difficult to get a head of steam going. Nevertheless, there had been a meeting in which doubtless, time slots, new sets, and the like, were discussed. New presenter. Double under-lined. How naïve could I be? The first rule of TV. If you're in trouble, sack the presenter. Plenty of them around. They're expendable. While producers live, pre-senters die. So, the plan was this. Send Whiteley to Monte Carlo with the team, make sure he has a good time, and, John Meade as producer, while you're there, you sack him. Meanwhile, we'll get on to Bob Monkhouse's agent to check his availability.

I was blissfully unaware of this cunning plan as I arrived in the Eurolounge in Heathrow that Saturday morning. It was, in fact, a lovely sunny February morning, and with only a couple of flights scheduled it was fairly empty. For some reason I did what I try to avoid doing at airports which was to go to the loo for big jobs. It must have been the early departure from Leeds Bradford airport that had upset the body clock. Or perhaps it was just good old childish excitement about the days ahead. If I had known what was really intended for me, then I genuinely would have had the need to spend more time where I was.

As I sat thinking all was well with the world, I thought I heard my name. Yes, there it was. 'Would Mr Richard Whiteley of Yorkshire Television, passenger to Nice, please contact the Air France desk immed-iately.' Hell's bells, I thought. It's bad enough having your name tannoyed when you are late for a flight, but sitting here with my pants round my ankles is ridiculous. What could be the matter? Bad news from home? Trip called off? Big newspaper story over Carol being sacked, and my comments required? I didn't know. I hotfooted it to the Air France desk. There I was given an envelope. Knowing of course what I do now, it could have said, 'Dear Richard, don't bother coming to Monte Carlo. You're off the show. Love John.' I opened it with trembling fingers.

'Dear Monsieur Watley,' (so it said) 'We are very glad to upgrade you to first class for the flight to Nice. Hope you have a very Nice journey.'

Good old Marcel, I thought. He must have fixed it. These Gallic types aren't that bad really. I arrived at Nice airport – all marble, chrome, glass, and full of girls in beige uniforms meeting people off the London plane and escorting them to limos en route for the Monte Carlo TV festival, which was running at that time. I had expected to make my own way by taxi, when I saw a girl at the barrier whom nobody seemed to want to know. I only gave her a second glance because the card bore the inscription 'Monsieur Twatly'. No wonder she was standing by herself. Who on earth would want to acknowledge a name like that? I don't know what possessed me but I found myself going over to her and saying, *'Etes vous pour moi peut-être?'*

She said, *'Etes vous Monsieur Twatly?'*

And I heard myself saying, *'Oui. Je suis Monsieur Twatly.'*

If there ever was a real Mr Twatly on his way to the TV festival, well I hope he enjoyed the taxi ride. *Moi et mon amie nouvelle* got into the top of the range Citroën and it was a case of Monte Carlo or bust. We arrived at Loëwes Hotel just in time for lunchtime cocktails. It was a terrific few days. Our French hosts invited us to corporate dinners at the best hotels. We had afternoon tea in the Hermitage with Gilbert Bechaud. We drank large amounts of our own special drink: Campari, orange juice, ice and soda, with a hint of bitters which we christened a 'Countdowner'. We ate out at lovely pavement cafés in the sunshine by day, and I bought the regulation male accessory, a navy blue cashmere scarf. The highlight was to be the grand final of *Des Chiffres et des Lettres* in front of the most glittering audience Monte Carlo could produce.

What a life. Terry, Eamonn, Nicholas, Robert Robinson – hey ... where are you? I don't think I can see you here. How was I to know that as I sat on the front row so close to Princess Stephanie I could have given her my last Rolo, that J.B. Meade, producer and friend, sitting right next to me, had still to perform his devilish duty. Certainly, looking back at his behaviour, or his manner towards me, there was no hint at all that such a dastardly deed was on his agenda.

Consider the position for JB. There he is, a cross between the true Yorkshire grit of Freddie Trueman and the weathered craggy determination of Charles Bronson. At times he had all the tact of Norman Tebbitt, the confidence of Margaret Thatcher and the sense of humour of Les Dawson. But in quiet and private times he had the genuine kindness and concern of an inner city vicar. He was a true hometown boy who enjoyed his success and was a thoroughly decent guy whose company I enjoyed, and with whom I greatly enjoyed working. He wasn't a major interferer, he let me get on with *Countdown* doing it my own way (which I think, pompously is one reason for its longevity). He was a real character and his name will long be connected with the success of *Countdown*. Well, that said, unknown to me, he was a double talking little sod, who in order to protect his own precious job and programme, was under orders from his boss to sack me. Allegedly. I am sure the burden that he carried to Monte Carlo would have affected him deeply. It was not a task he would have relished performing.

It was a great night, with a swelegant and elegant party afterwards. I danced with the great Armand Jammot's daughter, who was married to a champagne grower in Rheims. It all looked very promising. The next day was to be our last, and early Countdowners were to be consumed at Loëwes before the trip to the airport and home. I thought JB was looking pale, but well, last night had been party night. A hotel bellboy arrived. There was a 'Massage for Monsieur Mid'. Gosh, I thought, a massage. Old smoothie. Why hadn't I thought of having one? Too late now, I suppose. It was, of course, not a massage, but a message. He tore it open and a fax fell out. It was from Paul Fox.

'Congratulations to you and the team on getting two editions of *Countdown* into the Channel Four top ten. Business as usual.' There was great excitement as the fax was passed round. This really was something. A teatime show getting into the top ten, taking its place along with *Brookside* and *Film on Four*. Wow.

'What does business as usual mean JB?' I asked.

'Oh, it's a code,' said JB.

'A code for what?' I persisted. I was uncomfortably close to things for JB.

'Oh, it's just that Paul wants us to have another bottle of champagne on him before we leave.'

And so we did. In fact, over the subsequent sixteen years we have had several bottles of champagne. And we all went home and those two places turned into three, four and then eventually all five in the top ten, and we all lived happily ever after. And I was no wiser about what nearly happened that weekend in Monte Carlo until John Meade himself, in jolly mood, blurted it out at our Christmas lunch. Mr Twatly indeed!

INTERVIEWING MRS T

My first encounter with Mrs Thatcher was shortly after she had become Tory leader in 1977. YTV were running a series of half hours in which Geoff Druett – an innovative double hander, now so beloved of sofa TV – and I interviewed leading regional political figures. The YTV area had five cabinet members at that time so we were spoilt for choice – Roy Mason, Denis Healey, Merlyn Rees, Fred Mulley, Anthony Crosland. We didn't do too well for great Tories but we had Sir Keith Joseph, Marcus Fox, and the new leader, who was born in Grantham, which counted for us, as it was just inside our transmission area.

Mrs Thatcher was to arrive at the studio at seven o'clock. There'd be the boardroom reception, then the interview, and back upstairs for the drinks. All the signs we know now, and which became so familiar, were there that evening. She got out of the car, largely ignored the welcoming committee of top brass, having seen the faces of the canteen ladies peering and waving out of an adjoining window.

'I *must* go and speak to them,' she humphed and duly disappeared into the canteen, leaving the suits and party hacks flummoxed. She was not one for small talk in the boardrooms over gins – in fact she wanted to get on as soon as possible, which suited Geoff and me.

It was a simple set up. I kicked off, and did seven or eight minutes, and then Geoff took over for a bit and back to me, as directed by the producer John Wilford. Hardly Mr Nice and Mr Nasty, but I was known for being a bit of a cheeky interviewer and getting away with it, while Geoff, as ever took the more intellectual approach. I go hot and cold now, especially when I look at the archive tape. Geoff would talk about her political philosophies and hand back to me. I heard myself asking her about taking elocution lessons when she left Grantham. Was it true? She elegantly and politely denied this, speaking, if I may say so, quite beautifully.

Upstairs, the boardroom party were watching, in a smoke-filled room. In fact the room was a tribute to Cuba. Paul Fox, the managing director, had a huge Havana and was puffing away. So was Gordon Reece, half the size of Paul, puffing away on his trademark cigar, although his looked bigger, given the size difference between the two. Reece was uncomfortable with that question ... and, as the nation's first spin doctor, voiced an opinion. All eyes stayed on the screen – no one daring to react.

At one point, Mrs Thatcher told me, 'My dear, I am old enough to be your mother.'

Emboldened by this previously unconsidered matriarchal bond between me and Mrs Thatcher, I ploughed on. 'Why wasn't it revealed until very recently that you are in fact, the second Mrs Thatcher.' Only a few people then knew Dennis had been married before. How did I know? How did I dare ask her that? I don't know.

She remained calm, and smiled ever so sweetly. 'Oh, quite simply. Because no one had asked. If one had been asked, of course, one would of course have said one was the second Mrs Thatcher ... but one just wasn't asked.'

Downstairs in the studio, all was calm. Upstairs in the boardroom it was not. I am told that Gordon Reece nearly had apoplexy.

Yanking the cigar from his mouth, 'This is outrageous,' he barked, leaping out of his chair. 'I won't allow this ... stop the recording immediately.'

All eyes in the room averted their gaze, and remained steadfastly on the screen. There was only one man who could reply. Gordon Reece was on his feet.

'Be quiet.' growled Paul Fox. 'The recording goes on. Now sit down.'

Gordon was in a state of high excitement. Paul Fox was a big man. Gordon Reece was not. Nobody picked a fight with big Paul. Gordon duly sat down and puffed furiously. After the recording, Mrs Thatcher posed willingly for photographs and Geoff and I made our way to the boardroom, to be met by a decidedly chilly atmosphere. It was as well that Mrs T didn't want to linger – she and her party soon departed. There was certainly none of the 'that was terrific' atmosphere that TV luvvies wallow in after any show these days. The lady herself, it has to be said, seemed totally unphased by what had been said.

But Eric Ward, just starting as the Yorkshire Conservative agent managed to whisper to me, 'They don't like the second Mrs T bit. Don't expect a Christmas card.' The official party hurried downstairs to the main entrance. At the swing door Gordon Reece hissed a message to Paul Fox; 'We won't be darkening these doors again.' Politicians, of course, never keep their promises and this one was duly broken, as we shall see.

I knew nothing of these ructions till years later, when Eric admitted that my bold approach had been held against me and was noted in files and memories. Certainly, as a political interviewer, I never set foot in Number 10, but spookily, whether she knew it or not, every year while she was in power, I got a Christmas card from Number 10. And Paul Fox, who so robustly and typically stood up for a member of his staff, went on to receive well deserved honours from the government.

I did, in fact, survive the Prime Ministerial purdah, and interviewed the lady several times afterwards. The big one was very big indeed.

She planned a Friday foray to the regions in February, 1982. It was to be Leeds. Mrs T, being Mrs T, decided that only four hours' sleep at the Queen's Hotel would be necessary to cope with whatever Yorkshire flung at her the next day. And then it was off at six o'clock, to visit the Leeds wholesale market, which it seemed she had some urgent desire to inspect. I suppose, once a grocer's daughter ... always a grocer's daughter. Anyway, the plan was then to come to YTV, where she would do a set piece recorded interview with me in the *Calendar* studio at 7.30 am. This was doubly remarkable. For a start, it was BBTV – before breakfast television. No one did interviews at that time in the morning, certainly not on sofas. And second, as PM, interviewers had always to go to her. Messrs Day and Dimbleby and Frost had to troop off to her place in Downing Street, and set up the gear there. She would never contemplate visiting their studio. She always sought to claim the home advantage.

This early audience presented problems for YTV. Studio crews were called in at 6 am. This was to their great delight with eager anticipation of the mammoth overtime payments this would trigger. Bravo, Mrs T! But as it turned out, this invocation of lucrative 'backward ghosters' was to be of transient value. The lady was learning fast about restrictive practices and overmanning in TV and later she was instrumental in their abolition. Equally aware was Paul Fox, who ordered that Studio Two be cleared of anyone but three cameramen and a floor manager. The barest minimum, lest the lady should glance round and notice a crowd. The other twenty sat in the canteen having breakfast on quadruple time. They, of course, later voted Conservative in gratitude for their unexpected bonus!

For me, the whole thing was a nightmare.

For a start the Downing Street apparatchik would ring a week beforehand to ascertain the area of questioning. How can you know a week beforehand. 'The general economic situation,' I unhelpfully and vaguely replied. It calmed them for at least twenty-four hours until the call came again, and again with ceaseless and menacing regularity. This served to whip me, and editor John Wilford into a total state of intense nervousness.

The night before, I slept fitfully like Lady Macbeth. Not only worried about my confrontation with the lady, but ridiculously worrying in case it snowed overnight, and I couldn't get the car out of my lane, which was devilishly steep. I, too, should have stayed at the Queen's, I thought. In the event, her four hours' sleep was considerably more than my twenty minutes.

At 7.00 the next morning, the PM was closeted in dressing room number one with Bernard Ingham. They were not to be disturbed. They were going through the papers, and he was apparently briefing her on my line of questioning, and trying to second guess what I would throw at her. When I heard what they were doing, it terrified me even more. The Prime Minister of this country and her trusty aide pre-arming themselves to take on me – little old me, little Dickie. It was ridiculous. If they had been fashionable then, I would have had a panic attack. As I'd never heard of them, I was just panic stricken. 'Please God, let it be over soon.'

At 7.30 she entered the studio ... and sat on the sofa beside me. Sofa – remember this was BBTV – my sofa in my studio where I sat every day, and here was the Prime Minister sitting beside me.

'The Prime Minister likes ten minutes to get used to the studio lights,' Mr Ingham had decreed.

So, we went through the process of miking up and voice levels, making small talk for ten minutes. We chatted away, she saying her throat went dry when a microphone was attached ... me asking about daughter Carol who I found amusing on Ned Sherrin's *Loose Ends*. I sensed that, unbelievably, she was as nervous as I was. It also occurred to me that little Dickie was in fact having a no-holds barred natter to the PM in a totally relaxed and chatty situation. It was like talking to your auntie. 'This will all change when I tackle her about the unemployment figures,' I thought to myself. 'Then she'll turn true to type.' In the event the lady was not for turning.

'I thought I may begin with the regional unemployment figures,' I said, giving her just a hint of the deadly armoury of questions which had been concocted for this encounter 'and then, perhaps move on to local government funding...'

'Now look, dear ... don't tell me what you are going to ask. One always answers better if it's spontaneous... I don't want to know what you are going to ask me.'

Oh yes, so why did Number 10 hound me to a state of shaking anxiety asking me the questions, if, in the end, she doesn't want to know? Just protecting their jobs I suppose, in case she suddenly turns and says, 'What's the little Yorkshire chappie going to ask me?' So we did the interview. Ten minutes. We could have gone on forever, I thought. A most pleasant experience, with no mention of elocution lessons or second wives. I bet she wanted to make sure that wasn't on my list. She then went off to breakfast in the boardroom with Paul Fox. I hung around the newsroom, and at the earliest opportunity took myself off to the Flying Pizza and had a very, very enjoyable lunch from which I returned, deservedly in my view, tired and extremely emotional.

There were two more interviews. One when she was not half as nice. She was in the middle of the poll tax revolt of early 1990 and was in Bradford for a TV link up with several big cities, which I hosted. In return, YTV got an exclusive interview in a rigged up studio in Bradford City Hall. It was a big day for me ... the five hundredth edition of *Countdown* to be recorded later that afternoon, and a VIP dinner, including Carol Thatcher in the evening.

Mrs T was late into the Bradford studio. She was fired up. She seemed neither to recognise me from that morning link up, nor was she the slightest bit interested that Carol was ten miles away in Leeds at the *Countdown* bash. She just wanted to say what she wanted to say. Never mind a list of questions. Never mind she wanted to answer spontaneously. Never mind that I may actually open my mouth during the interview. She had her own agenda, her own message.

When I did manage to get a word in, and try to ask a question, trying to move on to a different subject, she just looked at me with angry and piercing eyes, let me finish, and continued where she'd left off. No relaxing lunch for me after that. She went off to do other things, planning to go to Leeds and then home. A blizzard descended on Bradford and the only way to Leeds was by train. It's a little known fact that Mrs T was reduced to travelling on a commuter diesel after being 'grilled' by me!

But the real horror was reached at the party conference of 1990. She had for the first time agreed to be interviewed by the regional hacks – four minutes each, straight after her Friday 'end of conference' speech. An amazing coup. Only four of us were chosen, the ITV company being favoured, I suspect, not the interviewer personally. We watched in the makeshift studio. Llew Gardner of Thames TV was not chosen. Thames had no news show on Fridays, it was LWT, but he was there for the event. As she thundered on, Llew treated us to his laconic and cynical comments on her speech.

'That's hypocrisy, sheer hypocrisy,' he would yell. 'That's just not economically possible. We'd be bankrupt in a month. That position's untenable, everyone knows that.' And so on.

For all I knew, it might have been true. Llew's political knowledge and experience went back over thirty years. He'd been a Communist hadn't he? Mrs Thatcher finished, to the unique reception only the ecstatic Tories used to be able to give. And you have to say, that even as hard bitten political neutrals, it's a moving occasion, the flags, the singing, the elation.

We watched the screen as she and her party left the conference hall – out the back to those makeshift backstage nether regions. And, before you could say Saatchi and Saatchi, there she was, bounding into our area, applause still ringing in her ears, high as Blackpool tower, except this was Brighton.

'Well, then, who's first ... is it YTV?'

It wasn't actually, it should have been Reg

Harcourt from Central. But don't argue with a lady on a high. I hardly had time to form any questions, mentally having been prepared to follow the line of the other three, thinking I was last. With the blessed organ still grinding it out in the hall below, I began.

'Prime Minister ... your statement on education ... some people are already saying this is untenable.'

'On the economy, Prime Minister, critics are saying we'd be bankrupt in a month.' Thank goodness for Llew Gardner. Must buy him a large one. 'People are already accusing you of hypocrisy...'

'People, people, who are these people ... what do you mean, people...? I've only just finished my speech, who are these critics, these people...?' She ranted on, quite justifiably, for so long, the time ran out. As I sweated it out, from the corner of my eye I saw not 'these people' but the person, Llew Gardner, falling about with laughter in the corner. Bloody Communists.

And then, quite suddenly, it was all over for Mrs T. On the final night of Mrs Thatcher's reign, the Thursday, Carol Thatcher had defiantly thrown a dinner party, and invited me. Sadly I had to refuse because we were doing a live programme about her mother's fall. In 1990, satellite trucks were a novelty. YTV splashed out to hire one, but because we didn't have a permit, the parking wardens wouldn't let us on Abingdon Green, conveniently just across from the Houses of Parliament where all the interviews take place. The nearest we could get was a parking lot behind County Hall. Imagine the scene, Geoff Druett and I ready to go live at 10.40, the signal travelling via twenty-six thousand miles of space to get to Leeds two hundred miles away. And with minutes to go – no Tory guests. No problem with Labour MPs. They were queuing up to gloat, but we needed Tories, especially Sir Marcus Fox, Chairman of the 1922 committee, and a crucial figure in the Thatcher downfall and the subsequent battle for succession. But where was he? Co-operative as ever, he was with producer Charlotte Milligan in Old Palace Yard trying to get a cab, like dozens of others. Eventually, in the coolest bit of operating I've ever seen, Charlotte dragged him out to Parliament Square, flagged down a passing car, and told the surprised lady driver... 'I've got Sir Marcus Fox with me. You've got to drive us to County Hall as quick as you can.'

She did and Sir Marcus was duly on air. Well done, Charlotte. Mrs T would certainly have approved.

Later when the lady wrote her much

heralded memoirs, she decided there were to be only two public events to mark publication – one meeting at the Barbican, chaired by Jeffrey Archer, and one in Leeds Town Hall. Brian McArthur of *The Times*, which was involved in a sort of sponsorship deal, rang to ask me to chair it which I was delighted to do.

In the afternoon I interviewed her in the Queen's Hotel for that night's *Calendar* and it went pretty well. No poll tax nonsense, just good old fashioned Maggie. Afterwards, I proffered a book for her to sign. Now, the funny thing is, that through all those interviews over the years, she never called me anything. Never any sign that she knew my name, or any acknowledgement that she'd met me before (names aren't her strong point ... remember the Mr Day episode to the good Sir Robin). No, 'My dear Mr Whiteley', or 'Now look Mr Whiteley'. So when she signed the book, I wondered what she'd put. Did she actually know who I was?

'I'm going to say "All good wishes",' she purred. 'So much better than just best wishes, don't you think?' I, of course, agreed, still wondering if she knew my name. Out came the fountain pen, and job duly done, out of the room went Mrs Thatcher (now a Baroness), with ne'er a word about our date later in the Town Hall.

I gingerly opened the book ... and there it was 'To Richard Whiteley... With all good wishes.' Bingo. I was in luck. Hardly anybody, I learned later, got a dedication in the book. It took up too much time.

That evening Leeds Town Hall was crammed with nearly two thousand people. The plan was, an intro from me, a speech from her, questions from the audience chaired by me, for the time limit twenty minutes, and after that, sheer unadulterated book signing. As we waited backstage, with two thousand fervent fans out there, and just herself and me at the bottom of three steps waiting to go on, I looked at her, and suddenly saw her as a faintly frail granny, bowed shoulders and clutching her handbag like grannies do. On an impulse, perhaps remembering her words of fifteen years earlier, 'My dear I am old enough to be your mother,' I put my arm round her shoulder, and whispered 'Good luck'.

I wondered later why I had done that. Who am I to wish one of the strongest leaders of the Western World good luck and give her a hug? As if she needed it. But I did, and that was that. At a quarter past eight, the book signing began. The faithful came up row by row like communicants, to have their ten seconds maximum ... and no dedications. I left, my job done, but discreetly returned at 10.15. They were still queuing.

PARTY ANIMAL

I've always enjoyed my attempts at being a political interviewer, indeed I can proudly say I've interviewed every Prime Minister since Harold Wilson. Verdict on them all as follows...

Harold – very civil, used to take big puffs of pipe which would let you get in with a question.

Heath – as Opposition leader he already had great media skills when spin was what the Bedser twins did. He'd ask how long the interview would run, either filmed or live, say three minutes. He'd proceed to answer the first question in three minutes precisely, and that was that. Interview over. As PM, he perfected this art and would brook no interruptions. As an author, e.g. Heath on Sailing, Heath on Music he was affability itself. By the way, if anyone has an unsigned copy of these books – hang on to them. They are rare indeed.

Sunny Jim Callaghan – not as avuncular as his image, rather crusty and impatient.

Mrs Thatcher – see previous chapter.

John Major – makes you feel sorry for him halfway through the interview. You don't, of course, want to be beastly, he's such a nice man, but you've got to do your job, and hate yourself for doing it.

Tony Blair – very slick, very matey, but strangely cold eyes, at least when I interviewed him.

The joy of political interviewing is that what seems so important at the time, is so much claptrap as time passes. I have chaired hundreds of round tables, panel discussions, open house forums, one to ones, studio confrontations ... and to what avail? Important on the night, and in truth I tried to work hard on them ... but years later, what does it matter? What has such telly talk ever achieved, for the participants, the audience or the country at large? At the time though it did really seem to matter for MPs to appear on their local channel. Conversations often went like this.

'Hello ... is that George Carruthers MP ... Richard Whiteley here ... *Calendar*. I'm ringing about our political programme on Friday.'

Carruthers, 'What time do you want me?

Twelve thirty in Leeds. I'll be there.'

No interest in what we're discussing. Just to be on was the thing. As one MP so frankly admitted, 'I approach each TV appearance in my usual way. Open mouth and closed mind.'

'Hello ... Richard Whiteley here ... I'm ringing about our political programme we're recording on Friday at 11.30, we're discussing the Common Market, and the fee is twenty-five pounds'.

George Carruthers MP, 'OK, who do I send the cheque for twenty-five pounds to?'

Often MPs weren't as keen to be on. Jeffrey Archer (then MP for Louth), 'If you think I'm giving up all my Friday to travel the one hundred and eleven miles from Louth to Leeds and back to appear on a little regional programme that goes out on Sunday lunchtimes when everyone's in the pub, then you are much mistaken.'

Dennis Skinner (Labour – Bolsover), 'George Carruthers ... I'm not coming to sit in a studio with him ... he's a blooming Tory... Do you realise that he should be sitting in the House of Commons on Friday morning, not skiving off to a studio for a free lunch ... and there's men working down the pit who don't earn in one week what you lot get in one day,' and so on. It was a brave and determined producer who dared ring Dennis Skinner when he was on song. But wonderful moments abound.

Two Tories facing two Labour for a discussion about European Monetary Union. With the countdown to recording underway, and ten seconds to titles, I heard one Tory Knight of the Shires whisper to another on his left... 'This European money thing we're discussing. I've been shooting in Scotland all week, are we for it or against it?'

Me to Yorkshire Regional Chairman of Conservative Party after 1976 defeat, 'Mr Simms, you're an extremely pompous Conservative,' meaning to say 'prominent'. Collapse in fit of laughter by Arthur Scargill, also in studio.

Also, merry chuckle by Phillip Simms, 'You're right, dear boy, I am pompous.'

But the highlight of the political year is the party conference season, so called for a very straightforward reason: one big party. While the season for some may involve Ascot, Henley and Wimbledon, mine was Bournemouth, Brighton and Blackpool. And they were the days, my friend. Nowadays it is all changing. The Liberals have more MPs and are more businesslike. Labour, disappointed that Blackpool hoteliers and restaurateurs have yet to grasp the importance of ciabatta, polenta and a good virgin olive oil, have abandoned their heartland resort as well as the card vote, and the Tories, who always put on the greatest show, are clinging together for warmth and are trying to make a half full conference hall sound as triumphant as former years. But still, these conferences continue to be most enjoyable, and the arrival of the conference season does mark the re-emergence of political life after the summer spent with John Prescott running the country, and the rest of the politicians hibernating in Tuscany.

Thirty years of conferences, going to almost every one – and do you know, I cannot really remember a single one individually. They all melt into some mass of sameness. Three weeks a year for thirty years, that's ninety weeks, damn nearly two years of my life spent at party conferences. And for what purpose? If you said to me, Labour Brighton '72 or Tories Blackpool '76, I just couldn't tell you a thing about them. It's like trying to remember every meal you've ever eaten at a restaurant.

Before my time, important things did happen. Gaitskell at Scarborough and Fight, Fight, Fight again. Wilson at Brighton with his white heat of technology speech. Lord Hailsham paddling in the sea at Brighton and ringing his bell. And where I would have liked to have been most – the Tories at Blackpool in 1963 scrabbling around in panic trying to find a successor to the ailing Macmillan.

To be fair, there have been moments I can

remember. The Benn/Healey leadership contest, Kinnock shouting at the Lefties, and Hatton shouting back. Denis Healey turning back at the plane steps en route to borrow money from the IMF in Washington, and storming up to Blackpool, where red faced and angry he denounced the extremes of the party and all its works in the four minutes which, as a mere delegate, he was allowed from the floor. The Parkinson affair which broke at Blackpool, the Brighton bomb, the William Hague experience, and for the Liberals – well, didn't someone once tell them to go back to their constituencies and prepare for Government. I always wondered what they actually did when they got back. How did they prepare? Look up the train times between their constituency and London? Sell the Sierra in the hope of a Government Rover turning up in the front drive. Cancel the caravan site in expectation of future weekends being spent at Dorney Wood? The reality was probably a lot more stuffing of envelopes.

All the political hacks love going to the Liberal conference. It's the smallest, and over the years, the one with the least likely impact on the world order. But it is friendly, well meaning and attracts genuinely committed delegates. For the hacks, though, it's like the beginning of the school year.

Friendships are renewed, faces light up with genuine pleasure as old pals heave into view. The bars are alight with gossip, new innuendos, new ten pound notes, leering looks at new young female hacks joining the circuit. In fact, the manifestation of all the things that make journalists such a thoroughly attractive and endearing species. Everyone is fresh after the hols, and a gentle four days with the Libs is just the tonic – generally oiling the wheels for the big ones in the ensuing weeks.

By the time the Tories meet, the hacks are tired, bored with each other and jealous of their scoops, exclusives or conquests, fed up with living out of a suitcase, and working in sweaty and cramped pressrooms. They feel their creative and critical faculties draining away with each late night meal taken with a politician, real or imaginary, as yet another set of receipts is stuffed into a Filofax. White wine, four pounds twenty a glass at the Grand. It's outrageous. 'Two large ones, please.' Ah, the gay abandon of that time honoured feature of a journalist's expenses 'Recip. Hosp'.

But it's the parties within the party that are a growing attraction. Nowadays, it is perfectly possible to party all day at other people's expense, and even rarely meet a proper delegate or representative, with whom to share legitimate 'Recip. Hosp'.

The people you meet are other hacks, and the guests of whoever's hospitality you are partaking. The company PRs are genuinely glad to see you, in fact, they often really want you to come to their parties, not least to fill the room and impress their bosses. But, while gushing over you, they will be constantly glancing over your shoulder towards the door in the earnest hope that any minister, however junior will turn up, and thus justify the expense.

'Well, Sasha ... how do you think that went?' the MD might ask, having just turned up that evening and been stuck for half an hour with two well lubricated delegates from the T and G in Liverpool telling him about the old days.

'Rather well ... we had Meg Rawlinson, just promoted to Junior Overseas Aid Minister, and John Prescott said he'd come, although I didn't see him. And there was a very nice guy from Yorkshire TV. Your wife watches him every afternoon.'

'So you think it's worth doing again next year eh...?'

It's only human nature after all to get perverse enjoyment out of summat for nowt. Hypocrisy therefore abounds in glassloads. How I enjoy being welcomed to the bash given by, say Southern Electric, while I consume their Australian Chardonnay, and Yorkshire Electricity at home.

My presence there is of absolutely no use to them at all, although I suppose I could tell any pals I've got in Lymington what frightfully nice people they pay their electricity bills to. Or Connex, the French owned rail company. I've heard journalists making oily remarks to the girl PR while she makes sure the next glass arrives clean, on time and certainly not empty ... then, with her back turned, make highly slanderous comments about what do the French know about running railways? And best of all, food conglomerates or supermarkets. There's often a goody bag to be had, which you later see being touted round the conference centre stuffed with leaflets, like teenage car nuts at the Motor Show.

From, say a Channel Four breakfast, to the Kingfisher late night reception, it is quite possible to garner the mood of the conference without ever entering the conference hall – the simple trick is to be room rooted. This involves merely staying put in one room, and then letting the various parties happen all round you. For example, you find yourself at the Meat and Livestock Commission's lunch, you can with a bit of luck stick around until the Irish Embassy cocktail party at 5.00. Then, stay put while the room is cleared and set for the next do at 7.30 to 9.30, possibly with food. The radio station GWR is very obliging in this way. And then it's the late night receptions where guests arrive in generally good humour as a result of the generous hands of friendship and fraternal love which have been extended, not by their fellow delegates, but the PR companies and lobbyists. The trick of the art of room rooting is to con the head waiter or under manager that you are an official of the incoming host company checking the PR sign boards, not a tail end layabout from the last. He'll even, if thus fooled, offer to let you taste the wine!

Each year the list of hosts gets bigger. In the beginning there was only one – the ITN party was legendary. Because it was unique, ITN, generally impoverished and, frankly, not all that worldly unless it was covering world affairs, secured the presence of the greatest and the most good. Rank and file delegates could only marvel at the political glitterati of the day who passed through the doors of one of the Imperial's or the Grand's finest suites. Legend has it that at one such party the late Bill Grundy, known for his pioneering live commentary of the party conferences with Granada TV in the Fifties and Sixties, and his splendid ability to relax after the chores of coverage were over for the day, once peed in the copious jacket pocket of the benign and sociable William Whitelaw while he was holding court with colleagues, and in his booming and bluff style he did not immediately notice. When Willie did find out, he was pretty annoyed. The bonhomie turned to malhomie. ITN chiefs were naturally terribly embarrassed, with the result being that Mr Grundy was banned from all future parties, although his antics had earned the general approval of hacks and politicians alike, in a mischievous schoolboyish sniggering way that we all enjoy, like laughing in prayers.

The next year, duly banned, legend has it that Mr Grundy reportedly took up a position on a chair right outside the reception room, nodding cheerfully to invited guests as they were admitted to where he could not pass. His presence outside was quickly turned to his advantage as there was a continuous succession of guests who, one glass in their own hand, and a glass in the other for him, drifted out of the room to converse with and succour the inner man. So the party devolved to Bill Grundy. And to think, it was no politician, but a punk group called The Sex Pistols that brought about the sad decline of Bill Grundy. Well, that's showbusiness! And a good tale, whether true or false.

The idea of the ITN parties was not to curry any real favours, such matters were barely contemplated in those naïve days. It was a way of getting grandees together after the rigours of the week, a chance for newsmen and politicians to appreciate their mutual problems, and, in a purely innocent way, a gesture to thank politicians for so often inconveniencing themselves to meet the then inflexible technical and logistical demands of television news. This is a very pompous way of saying it was a chance for Alastair, Reggie, Ludovic and Ian and the rest of the company stars to have a good piss up at the company's expense.

Nowadays, corporate entertaining exists on a scale second only to Wimbledon fortnight. And if any MD is reading this, my advice if he were to ask what benefit the company might reap from such hospitality is, in Wimbledon speak, 'love all'. But eager companies are increasingly hopping on this drinks trolley turned brewer's dray, much to the delight of hotel managers. Invitations, or stiffies, though nice for the mantelpiece, and for jotting down useful phone numbers, aren't strictly necessary. The pin board in the foyer of the conference hotel is a God given guide to the gatecrasher eager for a freebie. Gatecrashing is not frowned upon, indeed it is becoming an expected ritual. One of my best years was spent on an evening party tour in the company of a director of a PLC who had so many gatecrashers at his reception, he was determined to get his money back by drinking as much of other companies' booze as he could. And, apart from the obvious thirst quenching exercise, gatecrashing does bring its own vicarious thrill. My habit has usually been to hang on to a friendly MP who generally has a pocket full of stiffies, indeed some have lists printed by their secretaries telling them whose drink they are meant to be consuming at what time.

'I'm just looking to have a word with John Birt,' an MP might bark at a PR girl with a badge. 'I don't think he's here, Sir ... this is the Scotch Whisky Association party.'

Mind you, the presence of riff raff like me is counterproductive to the aim of the party. The real movers and shakers keep away, lest they be assaulted by some emotional hack, or even worse by a genuine delegate. So most influential parties take place in private rooms in security guarded suites. And in the Tory heyday, the champagne parties given by Lord McAlpine, and later Lord Archer, were like an off the record briefing. Everyone knew they were happening, but officially they were not taking place. Ah yes, you Tory toffs, I've witnessed you slinking away from a more public reception pleading an early night or a big speech on the morrow, knowing too well you were skulking up to the first floor for some shepherds pie and Krug.

For years the social high spot, apart from the ITN party, which still goes on and must cost a war or two in terms of annual budget, is that given by British Airways. And under the aegis of Lord King, it was a spectacular affair, the top attraction. Gatecrashing this one did require a little subterfuge, after all BA do know a thing or two about security. With the Tories in power, it was an all champagne affair, from 10.00 till late. There was also a ticket raffle to win a trip for two to New York on Concorde. We wiseacres who toured the circuit sniggered to ourselves, as the Tories slurped their bubbly, because we knew, what they did not, that the week before, the Labour lot had to quench their thirst with plain old red or white wine. Likewise, the Labour guests didn't know that it would be champagne all the way the next week. However, with the pungent, and to Lord King, I fancy, rather repugnant smell of the wind of change in the air, champagne generously appeared a couple of conferences before the Labour victory.

Receptions at Labour conferences are now, actually, far posher than during the Tory years. Naturally companies want to court the party of Government, so their perceived alignment changes. But, hitherto I rarely took a suit to a Labour conference for fear of looking out of place. Now I take five.

In those glory days, my partner in these junkets was Sir Marcus Fox, a social animal if ever there was one. Every year, Lord King would stand at the door, glass in hand, welcoming his chosen flock.

'Hello John, my guest Richard Whiteley,' chortled Sir Marcus, the cheeriest of chappies and influential too. 'I'm sure you know him,' knowing perfectly well he didn't.

'Yes ... the numbers man ... numbers and letters ... that's him isn't it Geoffrey?' he boomed to a bemused and even more owl like Sir Geoffrey Howe who until then had been the subject of his Lordship's attention.

'Numbers ... no ... all I know is that whenever I go to Leeds, he interviews me,' he countered.

'No, no, no, Geoffrey, he doesn't interview ... words and numbers with that girl.'

And so on, both talking at cross-purposes. Both were right, of course, but only I knew that, and it would have been too complicated to explain the difference between *Calendar*, which Lord King had never seen, but Sir Geoffrey had been interviewed on, and *Countdown*, which the Foreign Secretary somehow seemed to have missed. Afterwards, chuffed that Lord King was a *Countdown* viewer, I had this confirmed by an aide, who told me the TV in his executive office was turned on at 4.30 pm. 'Good time for him. Just getting over lunch and getting ready for the cocktail hour.'

Lord King and I have met on many occasions since. He has entertained Carol (ironically called Mrs King in real life) and me, at lunch at Wartnaby and he often rings up to add his suggestions to the way we run the programme. Once, when we had a BA employee on as a contestant, I referred to the fact that the BA President, Lord King, was a faithful viewer. Next day, he rang. He'd been watching at Wartnaby with his son, just within hours of him flying in from America ... and I had mentioned his name. The man who had turned round one of the greatest businesses in the world was thrilled to hear his name mentioned on television in front of his son.

Final word on Lord King, of whom I am greatly fond, although I wouldn't have wanted to work for him! (Mind you, he sacked thousands, so I probably never would have.) He has a hesitant manner, but a biting wit. At Wartnaby, he was pottering about, serving the pre-lunch glasses of champagne to guests sitting in the drawing room. As he entered the room, drinks duly dispensed, Lord Hesketh, with his usual immaculate breeding, jumped to his feet and said, 'My Lord, am I sitting in your chair?'

After a pause, the lordly walking stick was brandished in all directions round the room. 'They're all my chairs,' was the response.

CONFERENCE TALK

There was however work to do at the conferences. 'Are you covering the conferences?' If I heard that from one delegate or representative I heard it a thousand times. 'Yes' I lied, because the real answer was 'No'. For years, genuine reporting was not possible. Live, gavel to gavel coverage was provided by the BBC and in short transmissions by the local TV company. But for regional bods like me, coverage meant using a four minute slot between six o'clock and half past to conduct a live interview with a senior figure. This was injected into *Calendar*. Four minutes a day didn't seem exactly what you'd call hard work. Of course, it wasn't just that. You had to study the agenda for that day, discuss and agree who to go for at 6.00, then fix it up. All before the spin doctors and research assistants were there to do it for you.

There were days when the team regional hacks, Michael Partington of Tyne Tees, Geoff Druett of Anglia, me, from Yorkshire, Brian Shallcross of Southern. Max Perkins of HTV and the redoubtable Reg Harcourt of ATV, would all decide to go for the same man. At 6.00, the chosen one would sit miked up and earpieced, and a procession of earnest and self important regional political correspondents would parade before him each having their four minutes to reduce the Cabinet minister to tears, offer his resignation, or at least get him to admit that he had been wrong about his convictions all his life. It rarely worked. Most did as their instinct served them, which was to ignore the question totally, and just say what they came on to say. Competition was fierce among the hacks as to who would do the most perceptive inter-view. This was usually judged by the make-up girl afterwards, who had seen each one, and who I am sure told everyone while wiping off their slap, that theirs had been the best interview. So we all went off to the drinks parties feeling even grander.

One day, we all decided that Denis Healey should be honoured by being in the regional hot seat. It was, in fact, quite a coup. He was Chancellor of the Exchequer, no less, thus welcome on any occasion. What we weren't to know when we booked him was that later that day he would be thrown off Labour's National Executive Committee after many years of service. He was not a happy Chan-cellor. No Silly Billy remarks or funny faces in the studio before going on air, as was his usual wont. A florid face. A tight mouth and a distinct lack of bonhomie. I was, that night, the last in the queue. The others had worked their political nouses to the limit, and got him more and more worked up and angry. This was Denis Healey who pioneered the use of the phrase 'with great respect' to the interviewer, when clearly he had absolutely none.

By my turn, at 6.25, he was not a pretty sight and I was nervous. But Yorkshire TV was his home station ... he is a Leeds MP. I comforted myself with this thought. He can't be beastly to his home team – and I'm sure he likes me. How wrong I was. He laid in to me with some panhandle. No use even of the word respect. My facts were wrong. The question was misguided. I didn't understand. I was naïve. And so it went on. I was relieved when we lost the line to Leeds, and he stormed out of the studio. The other hacks had made themselves scarce, sensing the atmosphere would not lend itself to ITV hospitality. I sat chastened in the make-up chair, still trembling and dry mouthed. The make-up girl, unusually, said nothing. The floor manager muttered 'Goodnight' and disappeared.

Only my old mentor Michael Partington remained. 'Well, I've always thought he was a xxxx anyway.' He tried to reassure me. It didn't actually help. Michael's favourite summing up of many people was that they were xxxxs anyway. Besides, he'd have been first in the 'let's get Healey really furious' queue, and he wouldn't have been human, let alone slightly competitive, if he hadn't perversely enjoyed my four minutes of discomfort.

The phone shattered the weird peace of the empty hospitality room. It was the editor in Leeds, Graham Ironside. 'Whiteley,' he always called me that, even around the bar. But now the blunt 'Whiteley' had a sinister sound to it ... the headmaster was on the warpath. And so it looked. 'The Healey interview. There's been a tremendous reaction, the phones are still ringing.' God, I thought. What are they saying? Naïve. Rude. Unbriefed. Whipper-snapper. Fire him. He must be a Tory. Bring back Austin Mitchell... 'They're all furious,' Graham went on. I bet they are, I thought. 'Yes, they all think Healey is a real sod laying into you like that. They're saying he was rude, a bully, bad tempered and thoroughly out of order. He's done himself no favours, especially in Leeds. They're all disgusted about how he treated our Richard. Well done, great interview.'

For this relief, much thanks. But it did go to prove a point ... that people at home are capable of regarding their regular regional presenter as part of the family, and they often become personal property. Interviewees, especially politicians for whom there is conversely little love and affection, even from those who voted them in, denounce them at their peril. It sounds pompous, but I have witnessed this scenario on several occasions. The viewers side with their pals, and don't want to see them abused.

Fast forward, and Denis Healey and I had many television adventures together. We were once filming on the moors above Keighley tracing his steps as a youngster, when a jobsworth intervened with the express purpose of preventing us shooting on the moorland. To my everlasting delight he was treated to some real Healey invective and straight talking which I doubt he ever used either in Cabinet or even with foreign despots, and with a vocabulary he can neither have learned at Bradford Grammar School or Oxford. I applauded as the official cowered and retreated, and the camera rolled again unfettered.

Denis is always convinced I was attacked by a weasel! Obviously not knowing a ferret. He is inordinately proud of the achievements of Edna and his children. I was greatly touched when he invited me to his eightieth birthday party in the House of Lords. A great moment was a photo line up of Messrs Healey, Heath and Jenkins, all Oxford pals. There were only three TV people there – besides me, the other two were Michael Cockerell and Jeremy Paxman. I expect that somewhere along the line, they received the same treatment that I got at Blackpool but I am sure it did us all good.

On the Wednesday of the Tory conference of 1977, the regional hacks were of one mind to go for Michael Heseltine. He was the darling of the conference, and each year the love affair grew and grew. I too went along with the Heseltine idea and enjoyed his rant before lunch. Then, after lunch, we were treated to the now legendary speech from the Rotherham schoolboy William Hague. I listened to him with amazement and amusement like everybody else. But I had a particular interest in this lad, because, unlike the massed ranks of representatives and media, I knew him. It had only been two months ago that I had presented him with the 'Yorkshire Television Young Speaker of the Year' trophy at a ceremony in Chesterfield. I was on the judging panel and well remembered his confident, appealing and witty style. He had his first television interview with me on *Calendar* the following day. Now here he was, wowing the nation. So, I cancelled Heseltine, and showing sound regional journalistic sense, found William Hague and booked him for the YTV evening slot.

Heseltine, of course, was furious that afternoon. The prelunch cabaret had been completely eclipsed by the afternoon delight of the sixteen year old. Look at the archive footage now, and read what you will into Heseltine's body language. A gentleman, of course. Decent, of course. Human, of course, and therefore thoroughly pissed off that this sprog was eclipsing him in the evening bulletins. Hence the meeting in the hospitality room of the makeshift studio was electric, more perhaps in retrospect than at the time. Heseltine received, as entitled, the respect due, and William, the sort of attention you give on daily news programmes to one-day wonders like pools winners or parents of miracle babies. We all, including me, sycophantically crowded round Heseltine over drinks and listened to his thoughts on the conference so far. William Hague had an orange juice. As he left I wished him good luck in his ambition of getting to Oxford, told him to keep his YTV trophy clean, and probably thought I would never hear of him again.

Now, whatever became of Michael Heseltine...

THE BRIGHTON BOMB

I wasn't actually going to go to the Brighton conference that year, 1984. It would have been the first time I had missed the Tory conference for fifteen years, but the dates clashed with *Countdown* recording dates, leaving only the Thursday free, making only a quick twenty-four hour visit possible. So that morning I travelled to London en route for Brighton with Gyles Brandreth who had been in Dictionary Corner the previous day. Gyles had never been to a Tory conference, and I spent much of the journey explaining to him what went on officially, and also what really went on. He was fascinated. It must surely be as a result of what I had told him about what officially went on that he determined to become a Tory MP. I obviously must have convinced him that as a Tory politician he would have far more fun than prancing around in a funny sweater on breakfast television.

For me, though, it was to be a party day ... or PR work as I explained to my boss at YTV who was paying the train fare. After all, I had exhausted myself that week, recording eighteen editions of *Countdown* and I surely deserved a break. Geoff Druett and the political team had been doing all the serious work there at Brighton, so I could just arrive and extend the corporate hand of YTV friendship to as many Yorkshire representatives as possible. I might also extend the hand of friendship to receive a glass or two from well-meaning and generous party members. The last full day of the Tory party conference always used to have a tremendous buzz about it. Everyone always thought the conference had gone terribly well, which it always had, as every motion was carried by an overwhelming majority. Thursday evening saw the last of the receptions and the eager anticipation of the Prime Minister's speech the next day. The very greatest and the chosen few discreetly slipped up to Alexander McAlpine's champagne party in his suite, while others, dressed in black ties and posh frocks, went off to the conference ball. Hacks, meanwhile, vied for tables in English's, the fine fish restaurant, for the final all-expenses-paid fling of their conference season, before reassembling in the Grand for one last night cap.

My day was spent in a most pleasant way. Having arrived in time for a late lunch, I was eager to throw myself belatedly into the swing of things. Who better to bump into straight away, than Alec Todd. Alec, a former head of PR at Tory Party Central Office, and, indeed a former head of PR at Yorkshire Television, was now the top PR man at ICI. Alec Todd was a Yorkshireman from my own patch. Indeed, he started as a reporter for the *Shipley Times and Express,* the paper that first published my name in print. I remember it well. 'This week's birthdays ... Richard Whiteley of Baildon – 9.' I often wondered if he wrote that himself. Alec was a legend, not only at lunchtime, but in fact all the time – big, balding, ruddy faced and with a terrific capacity for gin, gossip and gusto. All the things a good old fashioned PR man should be. Not a cautious, over anxious, mineral water sipping, boss fearing, company line toeing weasel of today's ilk. Paul Fox referred to Alec as a 'wise old bird' and so he was, and indeed a thoroughly good friend to me, and a thoroughly amiable and popular man.

Alec quickly realised my plight – i.e. not yet being in the swing, or should I say, the swig of the conference, and he did the right thing. He took me with him on his unique conference circuit. He could ferret out a party like a bee finds pollen. He knew of parties which were so discreet that even the people there didn't realise they were at a party. Alec sadly died too young, but even now, years later, his great character is recognised at the conference every year. The so-called Todd Thring Hour is devoted to the memory of Alec and his predecessor at ICI, Peter Thring. Old friends gather for an hour or two of a late morning to have a civilised drink or two in the way Alec would have approved.

When I met Alec he was on his way to the Anglia TV lunch. I tagged along gratefully, thinking that with a bit of luck I would meet Anglia's greatest star – Nicholas Parsons. Sadly, no. It was full of very pleasant people and especially pleasant for me as Anglia was the company which had first put me on television. You can't blame me for wanting to drink a couple of toasts to the wise management of Anglia TV. Afterwards the day span out in happy conversation and, of course, increasing wit. An early evening reception here, upstairs at the Grand to the Yorkshire Treasurer's room there and, for some reason, a long session with Larry Lamb, the ex-editor of *The Sun*, in which we got on so well, in the way that you do when two Yorkshire people are in relaxed mood. And so a very pleasant day at the conference drifted to a close. None of it, of course, having been spent actually in the conference hall, although by this time I had absorbed, I thought, a great deal of the atmosphere. That evening I hadn't got the right dress for the conference ball but I was in the bar at the Grand Hotel when they started drifting back, around half past one. About this time, I had been introduced to a House of Commons secretary named, well, let's call her Gladys. Everyone was in great form, and I do remember that as the bar shut at 2.30 am, I looked round the assembled company in the lounge of the Grand and noticed that I was the only person who could be loosely described as a hack. I did, as a matter of fact, know a lot of people who were there, sitting around, drinking and talking – they were mainly party staff and constituency representatives. In fact, the real people that the conference is meant to be about. It was going back to hotel time. I'd done well and certainly felt I had imbibed the flavour of the conference, which was, of course, the serious point of the visit. Gladys and I, on my suggestion, decided to share a cab down the prom as our respective hotels were in that direction. Honest!

We walked away from the bar and shuffled towards the foyer, heading to the front door on our right, with the main body of reception, the lifts and the huge staircase on the left. I noticed how Greenall Whitley, mine hosts, had done the place up since last year. There were new furnishings, and new curtains, and especially, I noticed the new carpet. And then from a group of chairs well back into the foyer, I heard a booming voice that I recognised.

'Whiteley, come and have a drink with Bradford.' It was one, Ronnie Farley. Ronnie was the exuberant leader of Bradford council, my own local council in fact. 'Come on, come over here. We're awash with champagne.'

I looked at my watch. It was ten to three. 'No,' I countered. 'I've had enough. I'm getting a cab.' Was that really me saying that? Some mistake surely. But that's what I said.

'Well, I wouldn't mind some champagne,' said Gladys. Now shareholders of YTV would have been glad to know that the Whiteley reciprocal hospitality budget that night had only extended to house white wine – albeit at Grand Hotel prices.

'Oh come on Gladys, let's go,' and looking at my watch again, 'it's ten to three.'

Gladys and I were standing outside the dining room, this difference of opinion over champagne causing us to delay the ten seconds which would have taken us to the front steps of the hotel. Then, the big bang. It was the first of what I took to be three explosions. The first, a muffled and yet starkly audible thudding noise. Strangely a torrent of crystal clear thoughts went through my mind in rapid succession. Instinctively, I looked outside beyond the swing doors, somehow knowing in that split second that it was a bomb, although I thought it was a car bomb on the street outside. Then, the second explosion which sent me to the floor. I felt myself collapsing in slow motion and landing very softly and gently on that very carpet, the newness of which I had observed only seconds before. I was aware of Gladys crumpling up beside me. Lying on the floor, I thought that second bomb had got me and then there was a strange peace of mind. No past life flashing past, just an uncomplicated thought that forty-one years of life hadn't been too bad for me, I had a lot to be grateful for and, overall, I'd had a pretty good time. There was no fear, there was no anger and there was no malice. There was just acceptance that this was the end and so be it, and I suspect that I said 'Thank you God'. And then there was the third bomb. A huge, brutal, crashing sound that went on and on. The lights were out and there was just the noise, the endless noise. It was like listening to the biggest firework display. You're hearing it but you do not see, it's all noise but no baubles.

Eventually, the crashing abated and all was quiet. Very quiet. I realised I wasn't dead, although I couldn't see a thing. Relief, amazement, incredulity and sobriety were the principal emotions. I was alive, but my mind was in overdrive. Mrs Thatcher was upstairs. Someone had pointed out her suite earlier that evening. They couldn't get the Prime Minister, could they? They wouldn't. Things like this don't really happen. They just couldn't get her. And so it was, on my return from the valley of the shadow of death, my first thought was for the safety of the British Prime Minister. I later thought that if that doesn't get me the MBE, nothing will. I am still waiting.

You must remember that while it has taken several minutes to write this and you a minute or two to read it, it all happened in seconds. And, of course, there was only one bomb. That was the first explosion I heard, going off in the bathroom on the third floor. The second blast was the huge downdraft the explosion created, swooping down that regal, curling staircase that climbed the whole height of the hotel and it was that blast which felled us to the floor. And then the third. That was the sound of the hotel being ripped apart. That huge slice being taken out of the wedding cake, a slice of masonry, furniture, pipes, glass, floorboards – all the paraphernalia of that massive wound. Tons and tons fell down into the hotel. And as we lay there on that soft carpet. I was oblivious, indeed, carefree of whether the rubble would land on my head, I was dead anyway. It didn't, but it did fall right on top of the main entrance. If Gladys and I had been ten seconds earlier hailing that taxi from those steps, well, who knows. Ten seconds and a glass of champagne that never was, saved me from certain injury.

The quiet was shattered by a cry, not of anguish, but of resolve. 'We're all right.' (Pre-echoes of Neil Kinnock at Sheffield ironically.) 'We're all right, everyone here come to the back.' It was the booming voice of Ronnie Farley, whose makeshift champagne bar at the back of the foyer had kept him unscathed by the blast.

I could hear him, but not see him. Blinded, I thought. Well, could be worse. Where this stoic attitude came from I do not know. I am normally first in the queue that is reserved for cowards and wimps. Then I realised that my glasses were covered with dust. A film of dust, as fine as you'll ever see. It was everywhere. Wiping that dust off my specs with my tie, I could see by the light of an emergency bulb. But what of Gladys? Where was she? There she was, still lying on the carpet, face down in her black evening dress and in the gloom only the brightness of her blonde hair was visible. I stroked it both gently and vigorously and even called her name (ever so polite, we'd only met half an hour earlier). There was no movement. Was she dead? I thought she was. But then she stirred and sat up and in a phrase straight out of a sitcom she said in a lovely

Lancashire burr, 'What the hell was that?'

We got up, both OK. I was wheezing with the dust but my inhaler was, as usual, at hand. We stumbled over the upturned tables and chairs to unite with Ronnie, by now standing on a chair and directing operations. How he knew the way out through the back passages and kitchen, goodness knows. But shortly we were out, in a ginnel, round the back of the Grand, then across the prom, standing on the seafront looking with incredulity at the place from which we had just escaped. It was the silence that struck me. The Grand was lit up, as bright as day it seemed, by the streetlights and the moonshine. It was just as it always looked to we practitioners of 3 am journeys down the prom, except for this gaping slice of black. And no sound except, I remember, water gushing from the cisterns.

We watched in silence as activity broke out all around. First to arrive were the black ministerial limos. The Prime Ministerial Jaguar seemed to be there instantly. That says something for the security precautions which were, even then, taken. Then the fire tenders and the ambulances, but still no noise. They arrived so quietly. No sirens or klaxons were needed as the vehicles sped through the empty three o'clock streets. That is why many people in the Metropole next door slept through the whole thing.

Gladys and I just stood and watched. We could have gone home. There were taxis a plenty. But we were transfixed, and, I suppose we were shocked. What could I do, I thought? I never contemplated going back inside to help, but I did think that as a journalist I should at least do something. But what? Who could I tell at that time? I knew from my previous observation that I had been the only newsman in the bar. But obviously YTV was not on the air, and anyway the crew had gone back home. I could ring the *Yorkshire Post* but would anyone be there at ten past three? Of course, I should have rung the Press Association and given them a real scoop, a genuine eyewitness account which would then have flashed all over the world. This chance of worldwide fame sadly eluded me. I have cursed my naïvety many times since in not doing this, but in all honesty I was rather shocked and unbalanced by the sequence of events. 'So you were there at the epicentre of one of the biggest stories of the decade and you didn't even ring the *Yorkshire Post?*' No I didn't, but never mind. Now you can read the full story!

So what did I do? Well, at one point I went behind the sea wall to have a pee. I was mighty relieved in both sense that all members were present and correct. Well, you never know what can happen in these blasts, do you? After such vivid memories of these closely timed events, the next hour merges as a mass of images. I had been worried about Mrs Thatcher.

'She's well away by now in a safe house ten miles away,' some knowall pronounced. In fact she was less than a mile away at Brighton police station. I remember Sir Keith Joseph wandering round in a silk dressing gown. And Robin Day in pyjamas and no glasses, also I think in a silk dressing gown. I remember being moved on down the prom by police, fearful of another blast, and then we all took refuge at the Bedford Hotel, which by this time was serving tea and biscuits.

News crews materialised, but most were frustrated by the fact their gear was locked up in the conference centre. The crew from TVS were hovering not knowing what to do. With the YTV crew having sped off home with their job dcne, I instinctively asked the TVS men if I could borrow them if I paid for the tape. Now Mrs Thatcher hadn't sorted out the Spanish practices of the television industry by then and the rule was if you were filming for say YTV, you must use a YTV crew. Hiring another crew just wasn't on. Well, I decided it was time for action and I would have to flaunt the rules. Grateful for some action, the TVS crew willingly set up and I, like any other reporter who hates doing pieces to camera, heard myself speaking reasonably fluently into camera for two or three minutes, relating what I had just experienced. Looking at the tape now, I notice my hair and suit caked with that fine dust and with me speaking in front of that bomb gashed Grand, the tape does have a certain poignancy. Now I'm no Michael Nicolson or Sandy Gall and never would have been, but I am quietly proud of this little televisual testimony.

A real reporter, ITN's Paul Davies appeared, wondering what to do. 'I was there,' I said to him as he passed. We knew each other vaguely. 'I was in the bar. Interview me, I can tell the whole story.'

'No, no,' he said for some reason. 'I can't talk to you. You're in the business,' and passed on. Strange. Paul later went on to win several awards for brave and courageous news coverage. In fact he could have had a scoop that night.

But if ITN had problems, no one had more than TVam, attaining on that Friday morning the nadir in their reputation as a news organisation. They too had already pulled out and when they went on the air at 6.00 in the morning, they had to make do with poor John Stapleton reading out news agency copy. The one researcher they did have in Brighton somehow found me and I did a two-way, over the telephone line to

John which he was endlessly grateful for. Meanwhile, the BBC were live on the air and were crawling among the debris with the firemen.

My experience, of course, is trivial compared with the total horror visited on the casualties. I'm often haunted by the thought of the sheer randomness of the thing. So Mrs T was spared because she was apparently padding round the bedroom, having just sent her speechwriters to bed. But how could such awful fates await couples, in the same room, perhaps in the same bed, where one survives and the other is injured or killed, like the Tebbits or the Wakehams. How must it feel to be lying in bed one minute and then being sent crashing four floors down to the ground? That famous fickle finger pointing at you like an aircrash in which a passenger on one seat survives and another on the next seat dies.

So many thoughts still haunt me about this experience, and the phrase 'borrowed time' regularly comes to mine. On the Sunday Mrs Thatcher emerged on a beautiful sunny autumn morning from the local Chequers church saying, 'This is the day I wasn't meant to see.'

I, too, was in church on that sunny Sunday for the christening of my god-daughter Holly Johnstone in Chelsea. And I must confess that my thoughts on that morning wandered, as I thought that I too, perhaps only saw that happy day because of an argument over a glass of champagne.

LADIES WHO LUNCH

There must be very few men who know much about one particular aspect of the lives of their womenfolk. I am one of a select band of males who know what thousands of women get up to at lunchtimes. Not every lunchtime – I am not going as far as that – but occasional lunchtimes, midweek, when their husbands are safely out of the way, say seven or eight times a year. They dress up in their finery, suits, twin sets, pearls and best jewellery, sometimes even hats, and they set off in their cars for the finest hotel in town. They are generally going there to meet a man!

Once at the hotel, they meet up with other like-minded women, and in anticipation of subsequent events, excitement mounts and the shrill note of conversation and chatter heralds an atmosphere of unfettered abandon. Drinks are taken, confidences exchanged, gossip traded, diaries are consulted. And how few men know about this ritual, actively engaged upon now for years and years in Britain's heartland, but barely reported or commented on. This is the world of the ladies who lunch.

Ladies' luncheon clubs are indeed big business. Once a month in the season, say September to June, up and down the land, ladies gather at select locations for their very own day. It is a day when men are not welcome unless they are the barman, the headwaiter or the speaker – usually in that order of preference. If you are the speaker, and I have been on many occasions, you are always made to feel very welcome. The goodbye is often a different matter – it all depends on what has occurred in the intervening three hours.

There are many sorts of luncheon clubs throughout the country. Some are allied to Conservative ladies, others allied to the church, the golf club or just the town or community at large. They are all essentially different in feel, in character and indeed the characters who go there, in size, in age range, and certainly, in attitude to choice of menu and beverages, but all have definite similarities. The invitation to speak always asks you to commit yourself for a date so far ahead you at first feel you will not live long enough to honour the engagement. At the very minimum it is eighteen months' time. There you are merrily opening your Christmas cards and a closely typed or neatly written letter appears asking you to visit Cliffchester in October of the year after next. You haven't even bought a Christmas present for your mother, sorted out how to spend New Year's Eve, or even thought about next year's summer holidays, never mind the possibility that you may no longer be in regular employment, or indeed, on public view. And here is this eager speaker finder asking you to turn up at twelve noon on the fourteenth of October, twenty-two months hence.

You can't, in all honesty, refuse. To plead a prior engagement is patently implausible. To pronounce that programme commitments would make it impossible to fit the date, is conscience strickenly dishonest. In fact, you just can't think of an excuse, apart from getting your secretary to reply in such terms as 'Like members of the Royal Family, Mr Whiteley only plans his diary six months ahead, and therefore, is unable to offer you a definite confirmation for your kind invitation.' No, there is nothing you can do about it. You have to accept and only nearer the date can a grandmother's funeral intervene. And, even if that were genuine, it would be the act of a brave man, to let them down with only days to go. Well, it just isn't done.

Actually, it's quite comforting to be

booked so far ahead. Come the day in January when you are transferring your appointments and phone numbers into a new diary, it is in fact, reassuring to know that some people actually want to hear you and, indeed, want to meet you. But for me, who normally lives each day at a time, such a lead time is genuinely rather alarming. I know why they do it. The speaker finder has to be the worst job on the committee. Indeed, on the shoulders of the speaker finder lies the burden of the success or failure of the luncheon club itself. Yet finding speakers is a precise art. It's not just a question of having a good idea and writing a polite letter. The art of the speaker finder is as finely honed and as skilful as that of stockbrokers who issue buy or sell recommendations. Ladies' luncheon club business is exactly what it is – a business, albeit a friendly one. Subscriptions are levied, tickets are issued, programmes are printed, membership lists are scrutinised. Once a year at least, speaker finders and chairmen – most lady chairs are still chairmen – meet with their counterparts to discuss matters of mutual interest. This is generally not the quality of the inevitable honeydew melon, the breast of chicken or the fruit crumble. It is seldom to do with the quality of the venue or the price of sherry. No, they discuss speakers. Notes are compared meticulously.

Who's had who, what they were like, how was the speech, was it well received, were they interesting to sit next to, did they hold the ladies' attention, were their travel arrangements awkward and demanding, but most of all, top of the agenda – how much did they charge? Or in actual fact, what do you think we can get away with? And finally, of course, were they worth the money?

Now, I am glad I have never been privy to these discussions. I don't mind being discussed in absentia by producers, editors, executives and the like, after all, that's what my job is all about, but to think that a couple of dozen ladies are gathering in Bridlington to discuss my lunch appeal is, frankly, extremely terrifying. And so it is on the basis of tips and recommendations and, indeed, gossip gathered at these meetings, that invitations are issued or, of course, not issued. Worryingly, you never really find out what functions you haven't been invited to, just because you didn't apparently pass muster at the Bridlington caucus. It's all about word of mouth. Forget focus groups, marketing strategies and reviews, word of mouth is, in the end, the ultimate marketing machine. As Barry Cryer wittingly summed up the shortlived success of the musical *A Saint She Ain't*, 'The reviews were fantastic – it was word of mouth that killed it!'

I have to say that to attend a women's

luncheon club is an exceedingly pleasant experience. But think of it for a minute from the speaker's point of view. Few people generally relish the idea of getting up on their hind legs and seeking to amuse and interest an audience for forty-five minutes or more. And so, in my case, there is always genuine anxiety and stress. This is translated in tangible form, leaving home late, as I scrabble around looking for assorted file cards and backs of envelopes – in other words – my material. Why can't I just sit down one day and write one speech which I could flog around up and down the country? That's how the old music hall stars did it, the same act for thirty years. Nowadays, half a dozen gags on the Des O'Connor show and they're clean out of material. And then there's the hectic drive to some distant part of the country which necessitates constant referral to the hand drawn map so thoughtfully provided by the speaker finder. On arrival, everybody else is already there. The twelve o'clock starting time means that all the ladies are present at eleven thirty. Some to make sure they get a parking space, others to bag a good table, others to partake of a quick gin before the rush. The reception committee is also there – a lady looking anxiously out from the main steps of the hotel, or pacing round the foyer. I am always the last to arrive, no

313

matter how hard I have tried to be punctual. There is the introduction to the other officers, the photo for the local weekly, the invitation to wash my hands. Would I like a drink? Did I know Ned Sherrin? They had tried to get him for this lunch but he was too expensive. Praise be to the club who would dare change the running order. What joy it would be to be able to give the talk first and then eat, and more joyfully, drink afterwards, totally relaxed, the job done.

But no, rituals must be observed. And the ritual of entertaining a room filled with a hundred or more ladies of a certain age, and indeed, some who are rather uncertain, is more daunting than a live outside broadcast from the North face of the Eiger. I make it a habit on entering the room to approach every table, say hello and apologise in advance for my speech. At top table, I am placed between the chairman and the inevitable Grande Dame of the club – perhaps the founder forty years ago or the life President. The conversation is pleasant, but ritualistic.

They ...
Do you do this sort of thing often? (Yes, but mainly for the money.)
Did you find your way here all right? (Obviously, or I wouldn't be here ... ouch.)
Have you been to Cliffchester on Sea

before? (Yes, a family holiday in 1949.)

Did we once meet at the Soroptomists' Annual Dinner in 1979? (Can't remember, but I would say, yes.)

Does Carol Vorderman really do all those sums? We all think she is wonderful. (Good.)

Don't worry if some of the ladies nod off during your speech. They do get a little tired after a big lunch. It's nothing personal. We had Gyles Brandreth last year. Do you know him? He was marvellous. He had us all in tucks. No one dozed off when he was on.

I'm afraid we couldn't get a lectern or a microphone, but I'm sure you've got a loud voice. (It will be all right.)

Me ...

How long has this club been going?

Do you find it hard to attract younger members? (Looking round and stating the obvious.)

Who else have you had here? Let me have a look at your club card. (I always make a point of this. It is because the card has to be printed so well in advance in time for the luncheon season, that bookings are made so far ahead. I look at past and future speakers, often with relief. 'Janice Ravenscroft – A Lifetime of Tulips.' 'George Appleby – The Crags and Braes of Bonnie Scotland.' Well, I think I can cope with that, not much competition there. But hang on, here's a problem. 'Arthur Sandon – Secrets of the *Antiques Roadshow.*' Now, that is serious competition to 'Richard Whiteley – It's Usually Alright on the Night.' That's the catch-all title of my efforts because, apart from wanting you to commit yourself eighteen months ahead, they also need to know the title of your talk. I should be grateful that they don't want an advance copy.)

To continue. Me ...

How long would you like me to speak for? (The answer to this innocent enquiry at a men's Rotary Club in Cleckheaton was as definite as it could be – a blunt unequivocal answer from the chairman. 'Well, lad, you can go on as long as you like. But we all go at two.')

Would you like me to answer questions? (Please say yes, it cuts down on the speaking effort.)

I've brought an autographed tie for the raffle. Would it help? (Always seeking to ingratiate, besides it goes a little towards paying my fee, indirectly.)

Why don't you organise a trip with the ladies to the *Countdown* studio one afternoon? (After they have heard the speech, they probably wouldn't want to go anyway.)

No trifle for me please, I'll just have some cheese. (Twice as fattening really, but it means they can say later, 'Yes, he was chubbier than we thought, but he did try to diet at lunch.')

Yes, I'd love that little book about the history of Cliffchester written by Mary over there. Oh, and you say there's a book of poems by Kathleen, too. That would be lovely.

And so it goes. It is, I may say, a totally pleasant occasion. They always are. From their point of view, the ladies are thrilled that I am there. Eager for the speech, turning their chairs to face the top table, rapturous in their response and genuinely interested and perceptive with their questions. From my point of view, once I'm up and away – it's fine, and the forty minutes can easily turn into an hour.

Recently, as I was in mid flight, I noticed there was a certain amount of discreet anxiety and restlessness around the room. Some shuffling and some subtle wristwatch gazing. I glanced at mine. Just after three. Was I boring them to death? Most of them at least seemed awake.

I took the bull by the horns. 'Am I going on too long Madam Chairman? Or would you like me to tell you about the time I was introduced to Princess Margaret ... when she said she'd never heard of *Countdown* ... anyway, she was too busy in the afternoon to watch television. But hang on, she did think her sister watched it after the racing. And I thought, that's great but who's her sister. Well, you have to think, don't you. You don't often hear the Queen referred to as "my sister".'

'Well, no,' said Madam Chairman tactfully. 'We are all enjoying it. It's just that the ladies are getting a bit anxious – they want to be off soon so they are home in good time to watch *Countdown*.'

The closing always has a delightful ritual of its own. The warm vote of thanks which comes from someone in the body of the room, and usually written well before that particular speaker left home in the morning. Then there is the ceremony of the cheque – always left in the discreet hands of the lady treasurer. This is best done by giving you the envelope before you sit down to lunch – 'Well, I'll be on my way then... Ha, Ha, Ha!' I josh. But more often than not, it is done at the end when the ladies are crowding round the top table for a signature or a further question. Often, she will write the cheque in full view of the assembled ladies.

'How much did we say? And does that include expenses?' she will boom.

Me, 'I don't really know. I'm sure my secretary fixed it. What did she say?'

So now the deed is done and it's over. Except the reaction. Normally, they are glowingly gushing, and that feels genuinely good. The speech, or talk as I prefer, which suggests a greater degree of informality, is usually adlibbed off notes and headings such as 'Herriot Udders' or 'Rix at Ilkley', 'Wilfred Pickles and Lift'. And of course, the good old 'Himoff-Telly' line. These headlines are all cues for well-worn tales, but I do like to be topical and spontaneous, so anything can develop. But you need these notes in case of emergency.

My game plan is always to seek a motherly sympathy at the start. The nervousness, which is not always affected, is a good ploy. 'I've been so nervous I asked the wine waiter what went best with finger nails. Last week the toastmaster stood up before I spoke and announced, not pray silence for Richard Whiteley, but pray for the silence of Richard Whiteley. But things got better,' I will go on, 'I addressed the annual meeting of the Goole Haemorrhoids Society... I received a standing ovation.'

And so we go, old ones, new ones, forgotten ones, ones best forgotten. The reaction at the end is generally gratifying. After the formalities are over, they will gather round and tell me how unmissable *Countdown* is for them, for their mother aged ninety-seven, their sister in Australia – they send her regular tapes, or their grandson at university. It's all very nice to hear.

Once at the annual lunch of a charity based club, I gallantly waived my fee after being much moved by the charity and its works during my top table conversations. 'Mr Whiteley has generously waived his fee,' the ladies were told at the end. 'So you know what that means Madam Treasurer. Next year we *will* be able to afford David Jacobs.'

The greatest joy of speaking at a ladies' luncheon club is that when it is all over, I am the only person who doesn't have to queue to use the lavatory. And, going home in the car, I reflect... Funny, it seemed to go down well, but how come in all these years I have never been asked to the same club twice. Just what do they say about me at that meeting in Bridlington? Perhaps it should be tulips, crags and antiques after all.

All this is a far cry from men's dos. I take fright at these and try to avoid them. Men's Rotary Clubs and the like are to be avoided at all costs, especially big occasions like Charter Dinners. Unless you are a first class speaker, a local bank manager with a ready and unlikely wit or a sporting hero of yesteryear, keep well away. In fact, even if you are a good speaker, keep well away, because you will be in a no win situation. Sure, you may be the star attraction, with your name on the front of the menu. Sure, you might be getting a few bob, and sure, you can scan the list of speakers on before you, names totally unknown to anybody outside the select circle of the Rotarians. You might think you have nothing to worry about. It's not as if you are following Rory Bremner or Bob Monkhouse. But, be warned, *you* may not have heard of Rotarian Brian Whitehead, immediate past president, but be sure he'll bring the house down in a way with which you will be unable to compete. Lines like, 'We all remember the Blackpool trip, but the less said about that other monstrous erection, the Blackpool Tower, the better. Don't you agree, Roger?' Huge laughter. Or, 'Our masked ball was a huge success but there was nothing that could mask you, Graham.' Wild hilarity and applause. 'And what about ladies' night when Trevor stood up and said he was drinking no more than pop. Mind you, he should have seen what his pop was drinking.' People falling on the floor, convulsed with hilarity and laughter.

Try following that with a few jokes about Carol Vorderman's dress or John Prescott at the Royal Opera House. I've learnt my lesson now, only recently picking up a good line to use if things are getting desperately and seriously flat. 'Look I wasn't born here, and I'm damned if I'll die here.' It usually gets a sympathetic groan. After one event, a Chamber of Commerce dinner, a dinner-jacketed punter approached me at the top table.

'That speech. Call that a speech Mr Whiteley? Same old jokes. Badly delivered. Heard 'em all before. Could've done better myself. Tell you this – if they've paid you, then it's a damn waste of money.' And with that he departed.

'What's he say?' said the chairman, having half heard this conversation over the hubbub. I told him. 'Oh, don't worry about him – that's only old Ronnie. He's always the same. Once he's had a few drinks he just repeats what everybody else in the room is saying.'

Give me the ladies anytime.

I'M NEARLY FAMOUS

My maroon Jaguar was making frustratingly slow progress, I was going to be late. Traffic and traffic lights were all against me. Heck, I thought, why do I never learn to allow enough time to get to places. Eventually the traffic thinned and the glowering grey form of the Royal Armouries homed into view as I drove up the grandly named Armouries Drive. It was a grim and dull day. Eleven o'clock on a Tuesday morning in a

February. Not a soul in sight. A few cars huddled together for companionship in the car park. It was the sort of day when you couldn't tell where the grey façade of the Armouries ended and the grey Leeds sky began. I swept up the last few yards. It was two minutes to eleven, so I was just in time. They'd said to collect my parking token from reception, so I slowed down and brought the Jag to a halt right outside the imposing high glass entrance. Double yellows. Strictly no parking. What the hell, I thought, there's no one here anyway. Besides the Jag looks rather nice, impressive really, in front of these glass doors and anyway, I am a trustee of this place so who is there to tell me off? All these thoughts crossed my mind in the ten seconds it took to get out of the car, slam the door and, anticipating running in and out again, leave the keys in the ignition, and the engine running. How quietly she ticks over I noted.

The glass doors automatically slid open and let me through. I happened to glance back as they slid closed again. There was a man getting into my car, into the driving seat.

'That's nice,' I thought. 'They've fixed someone to valet park the car.' 'Even nicer,' I could have thought, as a second man got in the passenger door. And with one giant leap the Jaguar was off, with a screech of

323

tyres, a plume of smoke and a huge roar of the sixteen valve engine. 'It is true what they say,' I thought. 'Jags really do accelerate with the best of them.'

This whole episode lasted only moments. I watched open mouthed as my initial gratitude for the valet parking and the courtesy being shown to me as a trustee of the Royal Armouries, turned to the sudden harsh realisation that my car had been stolen from me in front of my very eyes. It was the slickest, yet the most opportune of thefts. I swear there was no one around when I parked. Where did these characters come from? And how did they realise so quickly the engine was running and the car was all systems go, and indeed ready to go. It must have been their birthday. And to steal a car in broad daylight, well greylight anyhow, from the very front door of one of the most secure buildings in the North of England, the Royal Armouries with its priceless collection of British and International arms and armour. Surely, I thought, they won't get away. Surely metal grilles will rise from the roadway and puncture their tyres. Laser beams will track on to them and demobilise the car in some high tech way. Surely even some eighteenth century musketeer will fire at them from a third floor balcony. You just can't steal a forty-five thousand pound car from the Royal Armouries.

'Morning Richard, had a good New Year?' was the cheery call of a fellow trustee, namely Rufus Bond Gunning.

'They've stolen my car,' I screeched.

'Really,' he said. 'What sort?'

'A Jaguar.'

'Ah well, you can wave goodbye to that. They stole mine a year ago, never saw it again. Yours will be in a crate on its way to Moscow tonight. See you upstairs for the meeting.'

Well, it seemed they could escape that easily. I had thought the Museum security would swing into action. In fact security was indeed in action, they were busy overseeing the delivery of an expensive sixteenth century suit of armour at goods inwards. They told me later they *had* seen a Jag going past very fast but they get used to speed merchants burning up when the car park is empty. What about the closed circuit camera? Well, as no one is allowed to park just outside the main door, that particular area is just out of camera range. I rushed up to reception desk, which was conveniently situated at the furthest possible position from the front door. I charged down the slippery tiles of the 'street', as the impressive entrance atrium is called, shouting, 'Make way, make way, I'm a trustee. Get the police.' We called the police.

'The number of the car please sir.' Blank.

325

Damn. I can remember the number of my first car, TAK 923 in 1965, even my father's car, CFS 497 in 1951, Mr Naylor's car who took young Anthony and me on the school run in the Fifties, GBL 2, but could I remember the number of my own blasted car? I shouted a number I thought it was. After a minute the reply, 'That's registered as a Ford Orion in Letchworth, Sir. Is that yours?' Eventually, having had to ring the transport office at YTV we established the car number. I should soon get it back, I thought. After all there aren't that many maroon Jags being driven around that part of Leeds at that time of a February morning.

I sat through the meeting, eagerly awaiting a message to be handed in. But nothing, and afterwards still nothing. As the day progressed, less than nothing. Anyone who has had their car nicked knows what a trauma it is. Stuff in the boot and in the glove box, keys, documents on the back seat, favourite coat, assorted tapes. What a bore.

A week passed and then two. I was meanwhile driving a YTV company pool car, a Volvo estate. Definitely not me, as I had little affection for such a tank-like school bus. Meanwhile, wiseacres in the Hermit, my local pub on Ilkley Moor, echoed the words of trustee Rufus. Stripped for parts. In a lock up in Doncaster. In a container bound for Eastern Europe. Theories abounded. As the talk went on and the rounds continued, this sage and knowing chatter reminded me of the one-liner I heard from Peter 'machine gun' Wallis, a Yorkshire comedian and king of the fast oneliners. 'The wife rang. She was out with the car. She said, "I think this car lets in water." I said, "Where are you?" "The Leeds Liverpool Canal at Rodley".' I told this and the wiseacres all laughed.

And then there was a message for me on the mobile phone. It was the police at Wetherby. They had found the car. It had in fact been parked at the Hilton Hotel at Garforth for ten days. Naturally, it being a business hotel, a Jaguar parked there was nothing remarkable. But on Friday afternoon with the businessmen all gone, and the weekenders yet to arrive, my maroon car was standing there all alone and was conspicuous. Would I come round and pick it up the next day? You actually pick these things up at approved salvage depots. I didn't know what to expect but it was fine. They had whipped my favourite Mantovani and Russ Conway tapes, they'd dropped ash in the ashtray. (Well, at least they'd used the ashtray.) They'd nicked my cashmere coat and worst of all, they'd retuned the radio from Radio Four to Radio Aire, the local commercial. And I noticed, with huge relief, that the file containing the minutes and private documents pertaining to the trustees' meeting was unopened and untouched on the back seat. Shamefacedly, I hadn't admitted that I had these documents on board when the car was taken. There was much hilarity around my immediate circle as a result of this incident. Keys left in the car – ha, ha, ha. Engine running – what a wally. Valet parking – ha, ha, ha. Driving a Volvo – where are the wife and kids? – ha, ha, ha. And so on.

A year later, I was visiting Leeds Prison on a charity open morning. The idea was for prisoners to make coffee for a group of VIP visitors. I immediately felt the place was awe inspiring and threatening with its clanging and echoing, although when we entered the landing I was soon made to feel welcome. A voice boomed out, echoing around the galleries.

'Hey Whiteley, you fat bastard. Where's Carol?'

I looked up through all the mesh barriers to see a man standing three landings up. Everyone turned to him.

'Him, he's a hero in here,' said a prisoner who had been allocated as our guide.

'Why,' I asked. 'What's he done?' From my scant knowledge of prison life, I imagined you only became a hero in a tough world like that if you're worthy – some daring, cunning bounder of a criminal, who inspires the deep respect of his lesser achieving inmates. 'Why is he a hero?'

'He's the bloke what nicked your Jag.'

'He's in here just for nicking my Jag. Poor chap. I wouldn't have wanted that for him.'

'Na. He's nicked hundreds. He's in for 'em all. But yours was the most famous. We all love him for nicking your wheels.'

Well, it's nice to be famous in prison, and, of course you do have a captive audience. A couple of prison officers drew me aside once at a Labour Party conference and insisted on buying me a drink.

'We're so grateful to you,' they said. 'You deserve a large one.' Apparently, under the regime in their prison, the inmates have TV time in the afternoon, and their half hour with *Countdown* kept them all sufficiently quiet and out of trouble that the officers could have a quiet half hour themselves.

But famous? Well known I can accept. After all, I have probably made more single TV appearances than anybody else in the country. Twenty-eight years of daily *Calendar* programmes on Yorkshire Television, and then all the spin off shows we did – *Calendar Commentary, Calendar People, Calendar Sunday, Calendar Tuesday, Calendar Forum, Country Calendar, Calendar Calling* – are you still with me? I could go on and on.

Probably over ten thousand appearances on Yorkshire TV. And then with three thousand editions of *Countdown* since 1982, the ferret clip which has gone round the world, the Noel Edmonds 'Gotcha' which everyone thought was hilarious, Mrs Merton, *Have I got News for You* and so on and so on. Yes, well known surely, just for sheer persistence, for just being there and going on and on and on. Like the weather forecast I'm always there, but famous, well, of course, as Professor Joad used to say on the radio's *Brain Trust,* 'It all depends on what you mean by famous'.

A letter appeared in the *Grimsby Evening Telegraph* recently noting my record number of television appearances. 'You'd think he'd be able to do it by now' bleated the correspondent – one A. Mitchell. Another A. Mitchell, the member for Great Grimsby, wrote to me, enclosing the letter, and assuring me it was another 'A. Mitchell'. A likely story!

Famous enough to walk into a restaurant in Brighton on the personal recommendation of Keith Waterhouse. 'Tell Marion on the door that I sent you,' he had said. I duly did and Marion obliged with a very nice table for two and the flattering fussing around. The restaurant was, in fact, surprisingly deserted, this being 10.00 at night during the Labour party conference, so tables weren't exactly at a premium. I could hear the chef, clashing around with pans in the kitchen which was down a short corridor. Marion took our order as impressed with me as Keith Waterhouse said she would be.

I heard her going into the kitchen where I heard her say, 'We've got that quiz master, glasses, you know, wig hair – what's his name. You know, it's that Richard Whiteley. Yes he's out front.'

My companion and I, having plumped for the leek and potato soup and the sole meunière, then heard the following soundtrack, 'Richard Whiteley. That four-eyed git.' Clank crash clank. 'Richard Bloomin Whiteley... Speccy four-eyed, pompous twit. Can't stand him. I'll put pepper in his soup.'

Marion returned with all the aplomb and old school charm of Sybil Fawlty, and handed out the melba toast as though nothing had happened, although she must have known what we had heard in this empty restaurant. I was, shall we say, outwardly amused but deeply inwardly upset. Everybody likes to be loved. Meanwhile, Marion opened the door to another party, this time of six and they, I noticed, did not repeat the password 'Keith Waterhouse sent us'. That must have been the reason they were ushered speedily and discreetly into a private room upstairs.

Meanwhile, the clanking went on. The peppered soup duly arrived. Delicious in my view, so bad luck Mr Chef.

As the general clanking continued, we heard the following exchange. 'Neil Kinnock upstairs. Blooming Neil Kinnock. Four-eyed freckly git.' Clink clank clunk. 'Wind Bag, Welsh red head. Give me some more pepper, I'll put some in his soup as well. That'll give him a really hot head.'

I felt slightly better about the whole thing after that and found myself getting highly excited at the prospect of Keith Waterhouse himself walking in, wondering what the truculent chief would have to say about him.

So, being well known has its drawbacks as well as its advantages, it has to be said. But events like the Brighton restaurant do tend to make you oversensitive at times. I was asked to open an extension to a community centre on the outskirts of York. What was involved I was told was a tour of the old and the new, and the unveiling of a plaque in front of various civic dignitaries. Now I was pleased, and not a little honoured by this. It's very nice to have your name immortalised on a plaque for future generations to admire. My name in brass – very nice too.

'You will spell my name correctly, two e's,' I chortled merrily over the phone when we were discussing this matter. 'If I'm to be remembered they might as well get my name right.'

'Don't worry about that,' said a rather charmless voice at the end.

The day before, a check call to make the last minute arrangements. 'Don't forget to spell my name correctly, two e's,' I said merrily.

'Don't worry about that,' said the charmless voice.

Come the day, I duly arrived and set off on the grand tour. I was shown the plaque to mark the original opening, 'To commemorate the opening of this hall by the Rt Hon Victor Throgmorton, Lord Mayor of York 1927'. Who now will ever forget Victor Throgmorton I thought.

'That'll do for me,' I enthused. 'Hope you've spelt my name correctly.'

'Don't worry about that,' said Mr Charmless.

The tour over, the opening ceremony was about to begin. I had never seen my name in brass before, and was getting genuinely excited. My speech referred to the great honour being bestowed on me, in following the pioneering work of the Rt Hon Victor Throgmorton, whose name lived on in perpetuity, and would do so as long as this hall was standing, which it surely would do now for many a year, thanks to the extension which I was about to open. I prepared to pull the chord and did some infantile horseplay which only served to draw impatient and embarrassed titters from the assembled crowd. Here goes. I pulled the cord. The velvet curtains parted and there on wood painted in black, was the legend, 'This extension was opened on 15th March 1994'. No name in brass. No brass, even. More noticeably, no name at all. No wonder Mr 'I'm so lacking in any charm whatsoever' had told me not to worry about how my name was spelt. They hadn't even tried.

Sometimes I hear of some community centre or other sadly being burned down. I often wonder if that one is still standing. To be honest with you, I have mixed feelings.

Early this century, that is in February of the year 2000, I was invited to open the new stand at Wetherby Racecourse. John Sanderson, the managing director, made a phone call about three weeks before the event, inviting me to perform this ceremony.

'What's that sound I can hear in the background, John?' I asked.

'What sound, what do you mean. I can't hear anything.'

'I can. It's the sound of barrels being scraped.'

Anyway, I am not too proud to stand in for John McCririck at the last minute and happily went along for a very good day.

Come the opening I embarked on the above story and it seemed to me that everybody was really enjoying it judging by their faces, which were turning redder and redder with mirth, or was it perhaps the chilly February noonday temperature. However, I span the tale out. I caught John Sanderson laughing nervously in all the right places, but also as the audience turned redder, he became paler and paler. I knew what he was thinking.

'Hell, have I spelt his bloody name correctly on the plaque?' John later freely admitted that this was exactly what he was thinking. 'Whitley, Whitely, Whitly, Whiteley ... please God make it so that I've got it right.' He needn't have worried. It was all bright on the night and the plaque is there for all to see.

Naturally all famous people want to be loved. I have long consoled myself with the view that everybody watching me must like me. The thinking is that people who watch *Countdown* know I'm going to be on it. They have fair warning. After all, I have introduced every edition so far so I'm not going to spring onto the screen like a jack in the box saying, 'Cooee, look who's here'. Similarly, I introduced *Calendar* for most nights over twenty years. Therefore, I thought, those people who didn't like me, really couldn't stand me, people up whose noses I really got, wouldn't be watching, would they? Therefore, everybody watching *Calendar* and *Countdown* really quite likes me. QED. This theory gives you the confidence to go on the screen and Maggie Thatcher like, go on and on. So when someone turns round and says they don't like you, it's unwelcome in the extreme. It does occasionally happen, I freely admit, and one classic tale remains to haunt me.

In the YTV bar one night, I chanced upon a young lady I hadn't seen for ages. She was an actress and had been doing some presenting for a local radio station. I had always found her lively and attractive and a candle lit dinner in the then only bistro in Leeds followed naturally. As did the chat in which she told me about her boyfriend. Apparently he was some big cheese in property development in the Mediterranean and she was out of the country a lot of the time with him.

'He's out there right now,' she confided.

'Ah,' I thought to myself. She knew what I was thinking and the tank traps went up immediately.

'Anyway,' she said, 'Brian doesn't like you.'

'He'd like me even less if he knew what I had in mind,' I thought. 'Oh,' I said, feeling somewhat disappointed and unjustly too.

'In fact, he can't stand you. If your name ever comes up he badmouths you. If there's a piece about you in the paper, he screws it up and if you're ever on the screen when he walks in the room, the TV is zapped double quick. I'd say he absolutely loathes you.'

I determined that night I would give Brian a real reason for hating me. You bet. I thought quickly. Why doesn't he like me? Is it my personal hygiene? Is it my easy way with women? Is it my corner table in the Flying Pizza? Surely he can't envy my three year old BMW Three Series. He, a property wallah. He'd have something sporty in red. How could he possibly not like me?

'Um, why doesn't he like me?' I pathetically asked. I was on the floor with loss of self esteem.

'Remember that celebrity night at the Hilton when you drew the star raffle?'

'Yes,' I said vaguely, pretending, and quickly running through what I could have done or said. But I did remember the event, there were five prizes that night. First prize, holiday for two in the Maldives. On through a colour TV, a case of champagne, a weekend in London and a ten pound shopping voucher for Morrisons. I remembered that wanting to make a big thing of it, I decided completely off my own bat and not consulting the organisers, to make the draw in reverse order, Eric Morley style. No one seemed to object and it did generate some tension and fun around a hushed ballroom. So first out of the barrel, ticket number whatever, and up from the audience came a suntanned, bleach haired, finely coiffured, good looking chap with regulation medallion. 'Well done,' I said as I handed over the ten pound voucher with a big beam. He did look, I recall now, a bit sour. Perhaps he'd have preferred Asda, I assumed. On we went and fifth out of the hat, great excitement, a holiday for two in the Maldives. Up came the lucky winner, hugs and kisses all round, whoops and screams. What a happy night.

Brian, of course, should have been the winner. Not Morrisons but the Maldives. By my own action I had condemned him and unilaterally denied him the clear blue waters and sun and sand of the Maldives, to the charm of the late night shop at Morrisons in Morley. That's why, she said, Brian hated me. And do you know, I don't blame him. I would have hated me and if I had ever seen him again, I'd tell him how much I hated me. What a prat. I felt really awful and guilty, not only for what I did, but what I might have tried to do that night. I gave her ten pounds for a taxi and slunk off home.

Only one thing consoled me as I tossed and turned that night, ridden with angst. What about the couple who should have been shopping at Morrisons but swanned off to the sunshine? They should love me, absolutely adore me, be my loyal fans for ever. Surely. But, of course, they would never know the favour I did them. And in fact a worse scenario swam into my insomniac state. Consider this. She to her best friend or indeed anyone she chats to, 'We're just off to the Maldives. Simon won a holiday for two in a raffle at the Hilton. Richard Whiteley drew it. Never could stand him though. Still can't. I zap channels whenever he's on.'

Mind you, nice things do happen if you're nearly famous. I have met the Royals, you know, including the very top rank, and I now have a bit of an inkling of how they cope with all that excruciating meeting and greeting. If stuck for something to say, the Royals just repeat the introduction and then phrase it as a question, thus passing the onus of conversation onto you, given that you aren't allowed to initiate the conversation in the first place. For example, I met the Queen at a televised youth talent spectacular organised by YTV in Harrogate. Paul Fox had gallantly included me in the line up of YTV big cheeses. I was standing, yes I admit it, nervously, next to one such executive, waiting for my big moment. Why be nervous when all you are doing is shaking hands? I can't explain it, but indeed that's how it is. The Queen was standing next to me and Paul Fox was doing the introductions.

'This is Ted Harris, Head of International Business and Network Planning and Acquisitions,' he beamed. What on earth was her Majesty to reply to that? 'I've always thought that's just the sort of job my Edward should have. Have you got any tips?'

No, no, that's what she doesn't say. She's got it down to a fine art. 'Head of International Business and Network Planning and Acquisitions?' Leaving Mr Harris the pleasure of informing her exactly what he did.

For the record, her face was equally blank when I was introduced as presenter of *Countdown*. 'This is Richard Whiteley, presenter of *Countdown*,' said Paul Fox.

'Presenter of *Countdown*,' she repeated parrot like, although I could see a dozen question marks in a bubble coming out of her mouth.

'Yes, Malm (to rhyme with palm). It's an afternoon word game on Channel Four.'

'Oh, they have television in the afternoon, how interesting.' And she moved swiftly on to Graham Bairstow, Head of Digital Development and Analogue Design where she had an animated conversation about pixels.

Things did get better in the self esteem department a few years later when I was similarly introduced to Princess Margaret. 'This is Richard Whiteley who presents *Countdown.*'

'*Countdown,*' she intoned with, I thought, more of an accusatory manner than a questioning. I see the family tradition lives on.

'Yes, Malm, it's an afternoon word game on Channel Four.' Already I had this sense of déjà vu.

'Oh, one finds one is just too busy to look at the television in the afternoon.'

'Of course, Malm, but luckily three million or so people do find the time.'

'Actually,' she replied, after a pause for thought and a refreshing sip, 'I do believe my sister watches it after the racing.'

'That's great,' I said. But then I found myself thinking, 'who's her sister?' Then I suddenly realised. So her sister has now discovered afternoon television and watches *Countdown,* eh. This was subsequently confirmed for me by a palace mole I met who knew the footman who took up her tea, and guess what she was watching? Pity the sound was off.

And then there was Princess Alexandra. I was in the line up at the Flower Lunch at the Savoy where I was the guest speaker. Knowing my place, I expected little recog-

341

nition, certainly based on past experience of the family. But no, in this case, quite the reverse.

'This is Richard Whiteley who presents *Countdown*.' I had my reply well rehearsed by now knowing the viewing habits of several of her relations.

'Richard, I'm so sorry, I will have to go before your speech.' Charming I thought. Princess Blooming Charming! 'But I shall make sure I am back home at the palace in time for *Countdown*.' Just like I said. Charming, Princess Blooming Charming!

After royalty they don't come much grander than retired Archbishops of Canterbury. The late Lord Coggan was one such of a rare breed. As Donald Coggan, Bishop of Bradford, he had confirmed me at Giggleswick. He then progressed via York to Canterbury, to become the most senior and influential Christian leader in the world. Now that, in my opinion, is quite an achievement.

And so it came to pass that Lord Coggan was back in Bradford to speak at a literary lunch on the subject of his latest book, a treatise on some eclectic aspect of theology. Afterwards I was to interview him for that night's *Calendar*. We arranged for the interview to be done walking in the Norfolk Gardens, a grassy oasis of calm between the City Hall and the hotel. My Lord looked every inch a Lord, but also terribly ecclesiastic. The leggings, the purple vest, the dog collar, of course, and the impressive solid gold cross hanging from a superbly crafted gold chain round the episcopal neck. This man was truly a sort of god. As we walked and talked strolling through the gardens as naturally as we could with the cameraman walking backwards avoiding the lunchtime shoppers, we were both aware of a middle aged lady with a Morrisons carrier bag waving and making signs. With great professionalism, his Grace averted his eyes and kept on talking in his rich, deep and thoroughly convincing way. From the corner of my eye, I saw the bag woman still gesticulating and shooting knowing looks. We ended the interview, and his Grace duly strode off towards the woman to greet her.

'Now my dear ... I saw you waving ... what can I do for you?'

Her reply was immortal. I wished I was invisible because it caused me deep embarrassment. 'No Vicar. I wasn't waving at you, I were waving at our Richard.' All I can say is it shouldn't happen to a retired Archbishop.

He, I should record, was relaxed about the incident. So what if regional newsreaders are regarded before him in the suburban pecking order. Blessed are the meek. Didn't our Lord say that? I was impressed with his cool. In my view the Archbishop displayed the piece of cog which passeth all misunderstandings. And of course, out of the mouths of babes and sucklings, comes the truth, often the awful unpalatable truth. Anyone at all who is tempted to feel famous just needs a brief encounter with a member of our gilded youth to bring them thoroughly back to earth. It happened to me once in my own home. Sitting on the patio, reading the papers one Sunday afternoon, I heard two lads walking along the public footpath which runs by my fence.

'That David Whitehouse lives here,' said one.

'Who's David Whitehouse?'

'You know that chap on *Countdown* your mother can't stand.'

I really must get a more secluded house. Or if anyone knows of a fifteen foot fence going cheap.

On a walk in nearby woodland once, I encountered a crocodile of kids on a nature ramble. I was obliged to give way at a stile while thirty-three of them scrambled over. They in their turn looked at me, and took me in with some amusement, attired as I was for early morning walking, not for my usual teatime working. After a couple of surreptitious glances, kid number three gently hummed the famous *Countdown* theme tune, giving way to louder and louder versions from each child as they hopped over, so it became a ritual involved in getting over the stile. There was a chorus of giggling from those over the stile. I averted my eyes. Avoid eye contact is the classic way of not getting involved in situations. Eventually, the last boy, number thirty-three, arrived at the stile with two teachers at his rear. He obviously thought better of the chorus, aware of the proximity of the teachers, but he felt he had to say something.

'You're him off *Countdown* aren't you?'

'Yes,' I muttered, gaze averted.

'Thought you were ... you see, Sir, he is ... my mum watches you everyday.'

'Does she?' I said, eyes still contemplating the dandelions.

'She thinks you're really great.'

'Really?'

'Yes, and so do all her friends.' By now I was beginning to warm to this lad. 'And do you know what we all think?'

'No,' I said, by this time looking him firmly in the eye. 'What do you all think?'

'We all think you're dead boring.'

'Get over that stile.' said an apologetic teacher. 'Only a joke, ha, ha, ha.'

Which brings me to the subject of autographs. Anyone who has ever done anything will have an autograph tale to bore you with. Here's mine.

I was approached by a Scottish person during my stint on the Edinburgh Fringe.

'I know you,' he jabbed at me ... 'BBC.'

'Well no actually. I'm on Channel Four.'

'No, I know you ... BBC – Fourteen to One.'

'Well, actually I do *Countdown* ... and anyway it's *Fifteen to One*.'

'No, I know you ... BBC ... Fourteen to One. Here give me your autograph Bob.'

Later I walked into a bar just off Princes Street. It was a Saturday and therefore heaving. I was recognised and that started a cascade of autograph hunters which, frankly, slightly embarrassed me. 'That Lord Melvyn Bragg's just left,' said a Scotsman. 'But nobody asked for his autograph.' Well, we were a long way from the South Bank.

I have one piece of advice for anyone asked to give an autograph. Give it. You'll do yourself a lot of good by giving the autograph, but also a lot of harm if you don't, people being what they are. And I know. I have been people and I know what they are. In the Fifties I was mad about Yorkshire County Cricket and they were very good. For years they battled it out with Surrey for the County Championship, and for years they provided the backbone of the England side, including the captain, Len Hutton. I managed to get the autographs of every member of that famous side in the Fifties, with the exception of Vic Wilson. You got the autographs by turning up at Sunday charity matches, or hanging round the dressing room at Bradford Park Avenue. One day, there I was hanging round, but frankly unprepared for the arrival on the scene of Vic Wilson. Other kids spotted him and ran up and he duly obliged. I had no ready autograph book or other paper, so I picked up a discarded and shabby packet of cigarettes and joined the queue and shoved it in front of him.

'No,' he said. 'I'm not signing that,' and brushed it away and me with it, and retreated into the dressing room.

Well, since then, slightly demoralised and frankly a bit humiliated, I always had a thing about Vic Wilson. Johnny Wardle and Willie Watson ... OK ... Vic Wilson, well not my favourite. So now fast forward twenty years. In 1975 for a programme in my chat show series *Calendar People,* the subject was my great hero Sir Len Hutton. We had also managed to assemble in the audience, the entire Yorkshire team from those glory days. They were all there, the Wardles, the Watsons, the Truemans, the Yardleys and indeed Vic Wilson, now a cheery, rubicund, healthy looking farmer from East Yorkshire. And I remembered the incident twenty years earlier, and well, you know, sort of held it against him. The man, who out of all these greats, had not given me, eleven year old, soon to be famous, Richard Whiteley, an autograph. Nothing was said on the night, of course, and I forgot all about it for another twenty years, until I happened to tell this tale to a friend of mine whose father Bob Appleyard was in that Yorkshire side, and was still a friend of Vic Wilson. Shortly after this, completely out of the blue, the morning post brought a card with a simple inscription, 'To Richard, sorry it's taken so long – Vic Wilson'. Good on you Vic, you'll do for me lad.

To those whose autographs I have so cruelly refused, my apologies are heartfelt and deep. I only wish I could say, hang on, they're in the post.

DOES MY TUM LOOK BIG IN THIS?

'And now, Richard Whiteley will present a bouquet to our oldest resident.' The matron passed me the flowers.

'Here you are Audrey. Congratulations. These are from everybody.'

'Thank you,' she spoke in a clear firm voice. 'I watch you every day ... I'm eighty-nine you know ... and every time I see you,

I think you are just like my husband.'

I think I know what she meant. I think she thought that when her husband was in his mid fifties, he looked like me. Or did she really think that I looked like her husband would be looking now? I don't know. She has, of course, her memories, and I should imagine, everything, including her poor husband, unfortunate enough to look like me, seemed better in retrospect than at the time.

As I have written this, it's natural to remember the good bits, the highs rather than dwell on the lows. I have been lucky and certainly had more highs than lows. All along, I've had mini triumphs, some as a result of my own making, some by force of circumstance – by just being around.

Looking back, there were a few triumphs at school, though certainly none on the sports field. When cries of 'Authors, authors' went up at Heather Bank School, and Peter Siggs and I shuffled on to the stage following the performance of *Whose Pools*, that was a triumph for two eleven year olds. When I hosted a star studded dinner at Cambridge following the publication of the biggest ever edition of a student newspaper, that was a triumph.

When I was celebrating thirty years at YTV, an early day motion was signed in the Commons by every single one of our region's MPs, congratulating me on my services. Dennis Skinner even signed, and he hardly signs anything. It was a triumph, too, of a kind when, in my one man show at the Edinburgh Fringe in 1998, I got Steven Berkoff to raise his arm high in the air, and do the *Countdown* clock movement in front of a three hundred strong cheering audience, who were doing the same, ticking down in time to the theme music. Mr Berkoff had arrived after the show had started – on seeing what was going on on stage, that is, conversation of a dubious nature between me, Hattie Hayridge, Jenny Eclair and Mark Lamarr, he was distinctly unimpressed.

'I don't do this sort of thing,' he said to the backstage crew. 'I'm off.'

They persuaded him that I would treat him in a respectful way as befitted such a great man, and with this backstage spat unknown to me, the actor who had told the crew he didn't do 'turns', proceeded to wow the audience with his versions of Shakespeare's villains. So it was that, at the end of the show, we finished as usual with a song and the ritual *Countdown* arm dance, and he, black shirt and all, joined in with unimagined gusto.

It was a triumph too, certainly my greatest high, at the end of the first telethon in 1988. Twenty-seven hours, non stop. I'd appeared twice every hour, and in an effort to boost Yorkshire's textile and tailoring trade, I wore different clothes every time. As ten o'clock approached, Yorkshire viewers were pledging the cash in bucketloads. As we went off the air, I was carried shoulder high out of the studio and straight into the club bar, for a terrific party. I shall always remember that broadcast as the highlight of my time at Yorkshire. Strangely, the high gave way to a feeling of anti-climax and depression which took two weeks to get over. The following telethon, two years later, mindful of the end game, I flew off to Portugal within hours of the finish. The tangible result was that I was as depressed and miserable in the Algarve as I would have been at home in Yorkshire.

Michael Aspel jumped out at me with the red book when I was supposedly meeting *Countdown's* biggest fan at, for some reason, the *Emmerdale* studios. I am always the last to smell a rat. Believe me, I would have trouble spotting the Pied Piper if he came to town. Michael picked me up at 4.30 on a Friday. My accomplices, who had brilliantly kept the whole affair totally secret, felt they'd be unable to cancel, on my behalf, a ceremony in memory of Bob Cryer, the Labour MP sadly killed in a car crash. So I went over to Keighley that night, accompanied by two minders, with my heart in my mouth, wondering what was to befall me later on. The recording started at 10.30 and the subsequent party, thrown at vast expense by Bruce Gyngell, then the MD of Yorkshire Television, was the best in the thirty years. It's a funny feeling ... you look round at all the people, laughing and drinking, and you realise they are only there because of you, and the next time a similar crowd gather on your behalf and say nice things about you, it will probably be your funeral.

The programme itself starred the two Whiteley women. My mother was due to tell how I had always been fascinated by television, and had made a camera out of a cardboard box, with lavatory rolls as lenses. 'Subject's mother', as the production team charmingly calls such individuals, normally causes headaches, with her inability to remember lines, and general confusion as to why she is there. My own mother was no exception, and apparently staggered her way through rehearsals, getting everything wrong to the frustration of all concerned. 'Subject's mother' was fully living up to expectations. With the programme in full flow, and with me not knowing what was coming next, I had unwittingly volunteered the information to Michael about the cardboard camera, but Michael ploughed on, as per script.

'How did he become interested in TV, Margaret?'

'Well, Michael,' said subject's mother, 'I only had two lines in this show, and Richard has just spoken them.' Cheers and trebles all round in the production gallery. Subject's mother had been hilarious.

Equally funny was the contribution by my sister Helen. Speaking in the posh voice that I recognised she used to reserve for dinner parties in Ilkley with her QC husband's legal big wigs, she proceeded to tell a tale about Kimi my hamster. Helen and my mother had discovered Kimi cold and stiff in his cage one morning, and presuming him to be dead, my father had buried him by a tree trunk in the garden. In the weekly letter to school, I was duly informed of this sad demise. On receipt of the letter, I had, apparently, against all school rules, rushed into the sewing room where we knew there was an unattended phone, and rung home in panic. It was not dead, but hibernating. Dig it up at once ... there was no time to lose. Helen told this tale, saying that Kimi was dug up, and put in the Aga (good old Nellie – she always talked us up, we had an Esse). Sure enough, Kimi came to life, and lived to an even riper old age ... poor thing. I didn't even have a wheel for him.

Helen told this tale so wittily, and looked so pretty, she was the star of the show. For weeks everybody asked how an ugly old bugger like me could have a sister like that.

Well, I agree. She'd have been far better at my job than I am. She had everyone summed up pretty quickly, everyone had a telling nickname, and she would forever dissolve into infectious laughter. Everybody would seek her out at parties, and want to sit next to her at dinner. She gave me hell, I have to say. Hair too long, drank too much, who on earth was I seen with the other night (she missed nothing) and, above all, when would I lose two stone in weight?

She died, at the age of forty-nine of liver cancer, almost a year to the day since the *This is Your Life* broadcast. Although I can see the cassette tape from where I am sitting as I write this, I can't bear to watch it.

In my capacity as the rat's best friend, I suppose I was prime fodder for Noel Edmond's Gotcha team. Looking back, it may be that history judges the last couple of years of his *House Party* harshly, but in my view, the early days were compulsive viewing. The camera in the house, especially, was a terrific innovation, and the gunging, at least when the viewers voted for who was to be gunged, was great fun. My Gotcha had been worked out to the smallest detail by the team, and turned out to be a little gem. Always precarious, it could have been cocked up the night before. Two team members sat anonymously in the audience for the two evening recordings, sampling the atmosphere and assimilating final details. As they chatted away, about their big secret, they were not to know they were sitting right next to my niece Georgina, who'd come in on a break from Cambridge with one of her pals. Careless talk can cost Gotchas. The next morning, there was a lot of studio rehearsing to do, and there was extreme anxiety that I may poke my head into the studio and find them out. Luckily for them, I was only a mile away – but quite safe. I was locked up in Armley jail on the charity coffee morning I described earlier.

On the night, we had only one more show to do. We had done thirty-five so far that week, and as I changed for the thirty-sixth time into yet another perfectly matched outfit, Mark Nyman, producer, came in. There was a problem. Chap who'd just won, and would therefore be the champion in the next game, had had a phone call from home. Big family trouble ... he was on his way home.

'But he lives in Orpington,' I said. This was 8.30 on a Friday night.

'He's gone nevertheless,' said Mark.

'OK, so we're all off to the bar,' I said. I knew we had used that day's standby contestant.

'No, we've another standby,' he said. Wow ... that's what I call taking precautions.

So began the Gotcha with everyone, apart

from the audience and me, in the know. The standby, an actor, was in place. Looking at his card, it said he came from Ilkley. My town. In the prerecording small talk, we discussed Ilkley. I remember he said, shiftily, it wasn't really Ilkley, it was more the Dales.

'Oh where?' I said.

'Near Ripon – Masham,' he said.

'Well, I've a weekend cottage there, where's yours?' He was getting quite edgy by now. His cover was nearly blown. He had never been anywhere near Ilkley or Masham, he'd once had a girlfriend from there. But we were saved by the clock – away we went, and the recording started.

Suffice it to say that Noel, standing behind the scenery, thought that after three or perhaps four rounds, I would have cottoned on, and he'd be out with the Oscar. It was beyond his wildest expectations that I would lurch on through each round, each containing a gag. In round two, the contestant's mobile rang – it was his mother asking when he was going to be home for his tea. When I told her he was on *Countdown*, and it was me speaking, she asked me if I could open the Christmas fête at the church. Then the lady contestant asked to go to the lavatory. Unheard of. I would have thought it should have happened, but it never had. 'Don't let her go,' were my instructions in the earpiece. But I just had to. When she came back, she offered a nine letter word 'diarrhoea' to huge hilarity. The clock ticked forty seconds instead of thirty. There was a huge fart from somewhere and a word selection which came out as OME-THINGS. No one, including Richard Stilgoe in Dictionary Corner, got more than a six letter word. The man didn't know the rules of the numbers game, the woman burst into tears, and asked if I could tell her the conundrum, so she wouldn't lose by as much.

Now all this time, what was I thinking? Well, at first, I was amused. After the forty second clock I did actually say, 'Am I being set up here?'

In the earpiece, stern commands, 'Get on – we're losing time.'

My mind raced. I half expected Michael Aspel to arrive, but then I'd already been done. What could it be? Only at the end, when I'd done the nine rounds, did I realise. The conundrum, ridiculously, was 'Hogcat' which was interpreted 'Gotcha'. Noel emerged, helpless with laughter. I was well and truly taken in. The edited transmission was cut down to seven or eight minutes. The actual real time tape, uncut, runs to fifty minutes, and is still in huge demand round the black-market network of hot tapes.

Carol Vorderman, was, of course, privy to

all this intrigue and did a class act worthy of a best actress performance. But then, she is a class act. I often refer to her as my screen wife. Certainly, there are times when she spends more time in my company than with her real husband. A postcard received at the office recently was addressed to Richard and Carol Whiteley. I must say, it amused me greatly, but scared the wits out of Carol. Carol Whiteley ... no, it doesn't work, does it. However, our on screen partnership must be one of the longest running around.

Who else can you think of? Nick and Anne, Wilfred and Mabel, Terry and June, Hilda and Stan, Hughie Greene and Monica. Where are they now? All long gone. Only Richard and Carol survive. Why? Is it about sexual chemistry? Difficult. Her place in the studio is a cricket pitch away from where I sit, so tactile and affectionate though I am, any great tangible display of mutual attraction has limited potential. My dominant personality, and her servility? Well, hardly. Carol did receive the much coveted Game Show Assistant of the Year award from Challenge TV in 1997, but doesn't really see herself as an assistant. Certainly not to me. After all, look at the way we behave with each other. To me, and in my remarks to the viewers, she is beautiful, brilliant, witty, rich, successful, generous, sparkling, young (although crisis year is rapidly approaching). She is all these things, and I unreservedly hail her as such. And what she says of me? I am a wig wearing, numerical incompetent, incapable of matching a tie with a jacket, certainly incapable of pronouncing contestants' names correctly, and not altogether sure what planet I am on. That's her view of me. No wonder the prospect of Carol Whiteley filled her with dread. She has, of course, tremendous presence. Many's the time I notice on the warm up I get a huge welcome from the studio audience when I'm introduced. I see all their faces, all eyes and teeth – eyes sometimes a bit watery, and teeth sometimes a bit loose – but kind and gentle faces full of expectation. As I begin my words of welcome, and point out various aspects of the programme they are about to watch, I notice their attention wandering. Their eyes pick out the soundman wiring up a contestant, a make-up girl dabbing a face with a puff, a light being lowered from the roof, a studio hand pouring my glass of water. Their eyes even rest on the water glass when he's finished, anything but staying with me as I drone on. Then, on she comes, and suddenly, like Sleeping Beauty, they are all awake, alert and fresh, all roaring with laughter as Carol jokes, and shows them pictures of her children. They pay rapt attention to her every word, laughing at the joke she tells every time – the punchline being, 'I think we've been to the same doctor'.

Now, this joke has always left me cold. I just don't get it. But for some reason, the audience love it. Mind you, they are the same audience who cheer wildly when our warm up man, Greg Scott, introduces me as the man who puts the Down into *Countdown*. Carol, of course, is immensely successful, being recognised now as one of the leading female personalities in the business. This she has achieved by hard and consistent work. Success hasn't come overnight for her, and likewise, neither will it drift away overnight. From those early *Countdowns*, and we laugh now to see how slow she was in those days, she decided that she was going to be successful. She admits to being driven and ambitious, but her success comes from the simple fact that she is very good indeed at what she does.

In the early days, when we were very shaky, I used to close my eyes and pray that she could get the numbers game. Hurrah when she did. With *Countdown* as her base station, Carol has launched herself into the very stratosphere of stardom. She is, to us at least, unaffected by her great success, and just 'Our Carol'. Don't however, sit next to her at any pop music show, where she goes mad. She is, in my view, too thin, although I admit with her make up on, and a nice frock, she does look glamorous. I'm always telling her she's getting too thin. She, in return, is too nice to tell me I am getting too fat, although she does subtly suggest from time to time that I should start using some sort of high tech margarine she does educational broadcasts about. 'She brings the sex appeal to *Countdown*,' some say. Charming. I suppose it all depends what sex you are in the first place. Believe it or not Carol, I do get some fan mail, and even a few Valentines.

And so the *Countdown* clock ticks on ... and as we come to the end of these ramblings ... we hear the cheerful Boo Boo Boo Boo de Boo of the final notes. The clock spins quickly through the other thirty seconds, and we are back where we started all those pages ago.

Like J.B. Priestley, the hand that starts the *Countdown* clock has done no real work ... not what I'd call a day's work, as the great man said. I have, I hope, helped to give a little pleasure to as many people as possible. And that reminds me, you are probably saying to yourselves that you've ploughed all the way through this book, and there's been no sex. Where are the juicy bits? What can I say ... that there hasn't been any? Well, I was going to call this book 'Richard Whiteley's

Guide to Clean Weekends', but clearly there have been moments in my life. Why no sex in this book? Well, don't tell me you really expected it, did you? I'm a teatime idle. Sex starts after the watershed. And me and Carol? Well, the closest it got was when I discovered there was a hole in the wall between her dressing room and mine. I was tempted to report it to studio security, but I thought, 'To hell with it, let her look.'

So, there it is. If it's the naughty bits you're after, well, there may be a second volume, and I promise I'll try to remember a few interesting experiences. Although, of course, people who have been close to me know who they are and I thank them for all the many happy times. In fact, I thank everyone I know because, as you can see from the foregoing, I have had a marvellous time, and I am deeply grateful to everyone who has played any sort of part in the Whiteley life.

As middle age approaches, that is assuming I am going to live until I am one hundred and twelve, one asks, as we all surely have done, are doing or will do ... where will it all end, was it all worth it, and what's it all for? Shall I apologise for the jackets and ties? No. Some people take bets on what I'll be wearing.

As usual, the young cut us down to size with deadly perception. My thirteen-year-old son deserves the last word. 'What do you tell people I do?' I wondered.

'I say you just sit at a desk and press a button.'

A true manual worker in fact. J.B. Priestley would have been proud. And I reckon, young James, you got it just about spot on. He could have said I was Mayor of Wetwang. But that's another story.

The publishers hope that this book has given you enjoyable reading. Large Print Books are especially designed to be as easy to see and hold as possible. If you wish a complete list of our books please ask at your local library or write directly to:

Magna Large Print Books
Magna House, Long Preston,
Skipton, North Yorkshire.
BD23 4ND

This Large Print Book for the partially sighted, who cannot read normal print, is published under the auspices of

THE ULVERSCROFT FOUNDATION